Out of the Midst of the Fire
Divine Presence in Deuteronomy

SOCIETY
OF BIBLICAL
LITERATURE

DISSERTATION SERIES
Michael Fox, Old Testament Editor
Pheme Perkins, New Testament Editor

Number 151

OUT OF THE MIDST OF THE FIRE
Divine Presence in Deuteronomy

by
Ian Wilson

Ian Wilson

Out of the Midst of the Fire
Divine Presence in Deuteronomy

Scholars Press
Atlanta, Georgia

OUT OF THE MIDST OF THE FIRE
Divine Presence in Deuteronomy

Ian Wilson

Library of Congress Cataloging in Publication Data
Wilson, Ian.
    Out of the midst of the fire : divine presence in Deuteronomy /
Ian Wilson.
        p.   cm. —(Dissertation series / Society of Biblical Literature ; no. 151)
    Revision of the author's thesis (doctoral)—Cambridge University, 1992.
    Includes bibliographical references and indexes.
    ISBN 0-7885-0160-7 (cloth : alk. paper). — ISBN 0-7885-0161-5
(paper : alk. paper)
    1. Presence of God—Biblical teaching. 2. Bible. O.T. Deuteronomy—
Criticism, interpretation, etc. I. Title. II. Series: Dissertation series
(Society of Biblical Literature) ; no. 151.
BS1275.6.P695W55   1995
222'.1506—dc20   95-37970
                                                                         CIP

Printed in the United States of America
on acid-free paper
∞

CONTENTS

ACKNOWLEDGEMENTS

This monograph represents, with only minor changes, a doctoral thesis submitted to Cambridge University in March 1992.

Although final responsibility for the present work must remain my own, there are a number of people to whom I owe a debt of gratitude for their guidance and help along the way. In particular, my supervisor, Dr. Robert Gordon, was exemplary in his availability, patience and support throughout the duration of the research. I very much appreciated his breadth of knowledge, academic rigour, and concern for clarity of expression, as well as his many attempts to keep my sights firmly on the Book of Deuteronomy.

I would also like to thank Professor John Emerton for his encouragement during a term when Dr. Gordon was on sabbatical leave, Dr. Walter Moberly for his written observations on a draft discussion relating to Chapter 4, and a number of other scholars who commented on a lecture presentation of some of the material contained in Chapters 2 and 4. I am particularly grateful to those colleagues and friends who kindly translated articles written in languages not accessible to me, in particular, Dr. Chris Caragounis for rendering R. Sollamo's Swedish into English and Dr. Philip Jenson for translating N. Rabban's modern Hebrew. Last but not least, special thanks are due to Jenny Smith whose linguistic expertise saved me much precious time during the closing stages of the research, Dr. Philip Johnston and our son Alex for checking the bibliography, and Linda Leggett and Jonathan Wilson for help with the indexes.

For the financial assistance which made this work possible I would like to thank the Tyndale House Council, the Governing Body of Clare Hall and a number of personal friends who have so generously supported my family and me and have expressed a continuing interest in my work. More recently I have appreciated receiving from the Theological Studies Fund of the Faculty of Divinity a grant which has facilitated conversion of the original manuscript into camera-ready copy for publication. In that connection thanks are also due to the editor of the SBL Dissertation Series, Professor Michael J. Fox, for accepting the manuscript for publication.

Finally, I would like to thank my wife Margaret for her support over the years, both in encouraging me in what I have been doing and in shouldering the burden of much of the everyday running of our domestic affairs. Without her able help and encouragement the work would not have been possible.

ABBREVIATIONS

AARSR	American Academy of Religion, Studies in Religion
AB	Anchor Bible
AnBib	Analecta biblica
ARW	*Archiv für Religionswissenschaft*
ASV	American Standard Version
AT	Altes Testament
ATANT	Abhandlungen zur Theologie des Alten und Neuen Testaments
ATD	Das Alte Testament Deutsch
AV	Authorized Version
BA	*Biblical Archaeologist*
BBB	Bonner biblische Beiträge
BDB	F. Brown, S.R. Driver, and C.A. Briggs, *Hebrew and English Lexicon of the Old Testament*
Bib	*Biblica*
BKAT	Biblischer Kommentar: Altes Testament
BTAVO	Beihefte zum Tübinger Atlas des Vorderen Orients
BWANT	Beiträge zur Wissenschaft vom Alten und Neuen Testament
BWAT	Beiträge zur Wissenschaft vom Alten Testament
BZ	*Biblische Zeitschrift*
BZAW	Beihefte zur *ZAW*
CAT	Commentaire de l'Ancien Testament
CBC	Cambridge Bible Commentary
ConBOT	Coniectanea biblica, Old Testament
CBQ	*Catholic Biblical Quarterly*
CBSC	Cambridge Bible for schools and colleges
CeB	Century Bible
ch.	chapter
chs.	chapters
CRB	Cahiers de la Revue biblique
CV	*Communio viatorum*
Diss.	Dissertation

Ebib	Etudes bibliques
ed.	edited, editor
eds.	editors
EHAT	Exegetisches Handbuch zum Alten Testament
EHS.T	Europäische Hochschulschriften. Reihe 23: Theologie
EncJud	*Encyclopaedia judaica* (1972)
ErFor	Erträge der Forschung
esp.	especially
ETB	Evangelisch-theologische Bibliothek
ETS	Erfurter theologische Studien
EVV	English versions
FB	Forschung zur Bibel
FRLANT	Forschungen zur Religion und Literatur des Alten und Neuen Testaments
Fs	Festschrift
GKC	Gesenius' Hebrew Grammar, ed. E. Kautzsch, tr. A.E. Cowley
GTA	Göttinger theologische Arbeiten
GThW	Grundriß der theologischen Wissenschaft
HAR	Hebrew Annual Review
HAT	Handbuch zum Alten Testament
HBK	Herders Bibelkommentar
HKAT	Handkommentar zum Alten Testament
HSAT	Die Heilige Schrift des Alten Testaments
HSM	Harvard Semitic Monographs
HTR	*Harvard Theological Review*
HUCA	*Hebrew Union College Annual*
IB	*Interpreter's Bible*
IDB	G.A. Buttrick (ed.), *Interpreter's Dictionary of the Bible*
IDBSup	Supplementary volume to *IDB*
ICC	International Critical Commentary
IEUS	International Encyclopedia of Unified Science
Int	*Interpretation*
ITC	International Theological Commentary
ITL	International Theological Library
JAOS	*Journal of the American Oriental Society*
JB	A. Jones (ed.), *Jerusalem Bible*
JBL	*Journal of Biblical Literature*
JBTh	*Jahrbuch für Biblische Theologie*
JETS	*Journal of the Evangelical Theological Society*
JHNES	The Johns Hopkins Near Eastern Studies
JNSL	*Journal of Northwest Semitic Languages*
JPSA	*A new translation of The Holy Scriptures according to the Masoretic text,* The Jewish Publication Society of America, Philadelphia, 1962.
JSOT	*Journal for the Study of the Old Testament*
JSOTSup	Journal for the Study of the Old Testament-Supplement Series
JSS	*Journal of Semitic Studies*
JTS	*Journal of Theological Studies*
KD	*Kerygma und Dogma*
KEH	Kurzgefaßtes exegetisches Handbuch

KHC	Kurzer Hand-Commentar zum Alten Testament
LWC	Living word commentary
LXX	Septuagint
MT	Masoretic Text
MThSt	Marburger Theologische Studien
n.	note
NAB	New American Bible
NASB	New American Standard Bible
NCB	New Century Bible
n.d.	not dated
NEB	New English Bible
NICOT	New International Commentary on the Old Testament
NIV	New International Version
NJB	H. Wansbrough (ed.), *New Jerusalem Bible*
NKZ	*Neue kirchliche Zeitschrift*
nn.	notes
NRSV	New Revised Standard Version
NTG	Neue theologische Grundrisse
OBO	Orbis biblicus et orientalis
OBT	Overtures to Biblical Theology
OT	Old Testament
OTL	Old Testament Library
OTM	Old Testament Message
p.	page
PCB	M. Black and H.H. Rowley (eds.), *Peake's Commentary on the Bible*
PIBA	*Proceedings of the Irish Biblical Association*
pp.	pages
RB	*Revue biblique*
RSV	Revised Standard Version
RTR	*Reformed theological review*
RV	Revised Version
SANT	Studien zum Alten und Neuen Testament
SB	Sources bibliques
SBBS	Soncino books of the bible (series)
SB(J)	Sainte bible traduite en français sous la direction de l'école biblique de Jérusalem
SB(PC)	*Sainte bible*. Publ. sous la direction générale de Louis Pirot et continuée par A. Clamer
SBT	Studies in Biblical Theology
SchL	Schweich lectures of the British academy
Schol	*Scholastik*. Freiburg
SEÅ	*Svensk exegetisk årsbok*
Ser.	Series
SHR	Studies in the history of religions
SJLA	Studies in Judaism in Late Antiquity
SJT	*Scottish Journal of Theology*
ST	*Studia theologica*
STAT	Suomalaisen tiedeakatemian toimituksia. Annales academiae scientiarum Fennicae

Syr.	Syriac
TBC	Torch bible commentaries
TEV	Today's English Version
TGl	*Theologie und Glaube*
TICP	Travaux de l'institut catholique de Paris
TOTC	Tyndale Old Testament commentaries
THAT	E. Jenni and C. Westermann (eds.), *Theologisches Handwörterbuch zum Alten Testament*
ThJb	*Theologisches Jahrbuch*, Gütersloh
ThPh	*Theologie und Philosophie*
Th Wiss	Theologische Wissenschaft
tr.	translated
TTh	*Tijdschrift voor theologie*
TWAT	G.J. Botterweck and H. Ringgren (eds.), *Theologisches Wörterbuch zum Alten Testament*
TWNT	G. Kittel and G. Friedrich (eds.), *Theologisches Wörterbuch zum Neuen Testament*
TynBul	*Tyndale Bulletin*
UF	*Ugarit-Forschungen*
v.	verse
Vol.	Volume
VS	Verbum salutis
VT	*Vetus Testamentum*
VTSup	*Vetus Testamentum*, Supplements
Vulg.	Vulgate
vv.	verses
WB	Welt der Bibel
WBC	Word Biblical Commentary
WC	Westminster commentaries
WMANT	Wissenschaftliche Monographien zum Alten und Neuen Testament
ZA	*Zeitschrift für Assyriologie*
ZAW	*Zeitschrift für die alttestamentliche Wissenschaft*
ZBK	Zürcher Bibelkommentar

1

INTRODUCTION

This study is concerned with the Book of Deuteronomy and its view of the Presence of God. In particular it focuses on the portrayal of that Presence found in the deuteronomic and deuteronomistic material usually thought to constitute the major part of the book.[1]

Occasionally, appeal will also be made to related texts from Joshua to 2 Kings, since it has long been recognized that deuteronomic influence extends into the historical books which make up the so-called "Former Prophets".[2] Earlier this century the general consensus among scholars was that the Pentateuchal sources J, E, D and P were also present in the book of Joshua, that it was therefore correct to refer to a "Hexateuch", and that the remaining books from Judges to 2 Kings exhibited deuteronomic editorial activity to a greater or lesser extent.[3] In 1943, however,

---

[1] The terms "deuteronomic" and "deuteronomistic" are used of material deriving from the original Book of Deuteronomy ("Ur-Deuteronomy") and the Deuteronomist(s) respectively, while "deuteronom(ist)ic" refers to anything which has been variously allocated to both sources.

[2] E.g. by Oesterley and Robinson 48 n. 1, Gray (1913) 52, Driver (1902) xci-xcii, Robinson (n.d.) 47-48.

[3] See, for example, Robinson (1937) 44-64, Eißfeldt (1934) 278-340, Oesterley and Robinson 68-108, Driver (1913) 103-116, 160-203, Sellin 51-68, Cornill 92-138. In addition, Provan 1-3 provides a more detailed summary of the views held about the composition of Josh.-2 Kings prior to the publication of Noth's *Studien* (see n. 4).

Martin Noth proposed[4] that the entire corpus of material from Deuteronomy to 2 Kings had been put together as a history of Israel from the
Conquest to the end of the monarchical period by a single deuteronomistic author writing during the Exile.[5] This same author had composed
Deut. 1-3(4)[6] and parts of 31-34 as the introduction to his History, using
these sections to frame the already-existing Deut. 4:44-30:20. The latter
contained the deuteronomic law,[7] and to this the historian assigned a crucial role, regarding it both as setting forth the norm for the relationship
between God and Israel and as the yardstick by which to judge the conduct of those featuring in his History.[8] Since 1943 the broad outlines of
Noth's thesis have come to be widely accepted, but the so-called Deuteronomistic History is now commonly believed to have been composed in
at least two stages, while the date of its initial composition (prior to the
redaction[s] believed to have occurred during the Exile) is a matter of
dispute.[9]

Nevertheless, it remains the case that, whether Joshua to 2 Kings has
been viewed (pre-Noth) as a collection of individual books or (post-
Noth) as a composite unit, there has been broad agreement as to the reality of deuteronomic influence upon these books, both in terms of lan-
guage[10] and of theology.[11] It is for this reason that deuteronomistic texts
from within the larger corpus will occasionally be introduced into the
discussion that follows.

---

[4] In *Überlieferungsgeschichtliche Studien*. Halle an-der-Saale: Niemeyer; 3rd edition: Tübingen: Niemeyer, 1967 (English translation: *The Deuteronomistic History*,
JSOTSup 15. Sheffield: JSOT, 1981).
[5] (1967) 12, 91.
[6] The parentheses (used by Noth [1967], e.g. on pp. 14, 16, 28 n. 1, 97) appear to reflect his uncertainty as to whether Deut. 4:1-40 should be attributed to the Deuteronomist or should be seen as a later addition (pp. 38-39). See, however, Christensen 71.
[7] (1967) 16.
[8] (1967) 92.
[9] Scholars supporting a Josianic date include O'Brien 288-292, Provan 172, Friedman
171, Nelson 120, Levenson (1975) 218-221 and Cross 274-289, while those advocat-
ing an exilic one include Smend (1978) 123, Veijola (cited by O'Brien 7-10, Provan
15-20) and Dietrich 143, 144. For recent discussions of the two positions, together
with references to further scholars holding or influenced by the two views, see the
monographs by O'Brien (pp. 6-12) and Provan (pp. 8-20).
[10] See especially: Weinfeld (1972a) 320-365 and Driver (1902) lxxviii-lxxxiv. For
additional lists of deuteronomic idioms see also Thompson (1974) 31-34, Steuernagel
(1900) XXXIII-XLI, Holzinger (1893) 283-291.
[11] Clements (1989) 98, Fretheim (1983) 40, Noth (1967) 3-4, Cunliffe-Jones 29.

DIVINE PRESENCE IN DEUTERONOMY

Several OT traditions held to be earlier than the Book of Deuteronomy portray the Deity as being in some sense present on the earth or, in certain contexts, present with the people of Israel. The Yahwistic and Elohistic sources, for example, in their accounts of the law-giving at Sinai in the Book of Exodus, are considered by many scholars to represent God as either descending to (J) or dwelling on (E) the mountain,[12] while the Zion tradition, as found in some of the Psalms and in the pre-exilic prophets, portrays him as inhabiting the city of Jerusalem.[13]

In Deuteronomy and related writings, however, there is thought to be a *different* concept of divine Presence. Scholars represent this by the term "Name Theology", and derive it from two sets of texts, namely references to YHWH's *Name* dwelling, or being in some other sense present, at the sanctuary (e.g. in Deut. 12-26[14] and throughout the Deuteronomistic History[15]) and those to YHWH *himself* dwelling or being in heaven (e.g. Deut. 4:36; 26:15 and 1 Kings 8, in Solomon's prayer of dedication of the temple). Gerhard von Rad's oft-quoted remarks[16] are the classic formulation of Name Theology, and well illustrate the typical deduction which is made from the data:

> Das dt. Theologumenon vom Namen Jahwes enthält deutlich ein polemisches Element, oder besser gesagt: ein theologisches Korrektiv. Nicht Jahwe selbst ist am Kultort gegenwärtig, sondern nur sein Name als der Garant seines Heilswillens...Das Dt. ersetzt die alte massive Vorstellung von Jahwes Gegenwart und Wohnen am Kultort durch eine theologisch sublimierte.[17,18]

---

[12] Jeremias (1976) 897, Hyatt (1971) 23, 196, 202, Kuntz 98, Newman 47-48, 61, Beyerlin 14, Noth (1959) 128, 141, Eißfeldt (1922) 46-47, Driver (1911) 168, Morgenstern (1911) 186 *et passim*, Westphal 14.

[13] Mettinger 19-37, esp. 24-28, 36-37, Terrien (1978) 189, 196, Roberts 985, Metzger 139-141, Clements (1965) 40-78, de Vaux (1960) 166-168, von Rad (1958) 54-56, Westphal 118-214.

[14] 12:5, 11, 21; 14:23, 24; 16:2, 6, 11; 26:2.

[15] See Mettinger 39-40 for a complete list.

[16] E.g. by Janowski (1987) 175 n. 40, Kaiser 137, Mettinger 42, Maly 28, McBride 29, Nicholson (1967) 55-56, 71, Dumermuth 69. Cf. Braulik (1983) 19.

[17] (1947) 26.

[18] "The Deuteronomic theologumenon of the name of Jahweh clearly holds a polemic element, or, to put it better, is a theological corrective. It is not Jahweh himself who is present at the shrine, but only his name as the guarantee of his will to save...

This distinction between YHWH and his Name is fundamental to Name Theology. In contrast to those traditions in which the Deity is represented as being localized on the earth, here it is his *Name* which is conceived as being thus present, in this case at the sanctuary. YHWH himself is in heaven.

Such an understanding of the significance of the cult-place in Deuteronomy was already in print by the end of the nineteenth century.[19] However, it was von Rad who popularized it, in the short essay published in 1947 from which the above quotation is taken.[20] It now commands a wide acceptance.[21]

Deuteronomy is replacing the old crude idea of Jahweh's presence and dwelling at the shrine by a theologically sublimated idea." (Von Rad [1953b] 38-39).

[19] Cf. Stade (1888) 247: "Die Schriftsteller, welche das Deuteronomium bearbeitet... haben, stoßen sich an der Vorstellung, daß Jahwe Jerusalem erwählt hat, um dort zu wohnen, und ersetzen dieselbe durch die Vorstellung, daß Jahwe es erwählt habe, 'um dorthin seinen Namen zu setzen', oder ihn 'dort wohnen zu lassen'. Sie meinen also, daß Gott nicht selbst im Tempel wohnt."

[20] "Die deuteronomische Schem-Theologie und die priesterschriftliche Kabod-Theologie", *Deuteronomium-Studien*, 25-30.

[21] Clements (1989) 52: "[By the concept of the name of God] the Deuteronomic authors have sought to avoid too crude a notion of the idea that God's presence... could...be located at the sanctuary. They have sought to emphasise the fact that God's true place of habitation could only be in heaven", Preuß (1982) 17: "Jahwe nicht selbst in Jerusalem 'wohnt', sondern dort nur seinen 'Namen' wohnen läßt... Jahwe wohnt...für das (dtr) Dtn im Himmel", Gese 87: "[E]s ist der Name, den Gott [auf dem Zion] wohnen läßt (Dtn 12,5.11.21 etc), eigentlich aber ist Gott im Transzendenzbereich des Himmels", McCurley 308: "[The] concept in Deuteronomy... seems to be that *only* Yahweh's name dwells in the chosen place. Yahweh himself lives in heaven", Weinfeld (1972a) 197: "[T]he very book which elevates the chosen place to the highest rank of importance in the Israelite cultus...emphasize[s] that it is God's name and not himself who dwells within the sanctuary", Seitz 222: "[D]as Dt [will]...eine Korrektur an der bisherigen Wohnvorstellung vornehmen; nicht mehr Jahwe selbst, sondern nur sein Name wohnt am erwählten Ort", Metzger 149: "[D]as *Deuteronomium* [vermeidet] die Aussage, daß Jahwe im Tempel wohne. Im Deuteronomium findet sich stattdessen die charakteristische Formel vom 'Ort, den Jahwe erwählt hat, um daselbst seinen *Namen* wohnen zu lassen'...Das Deuteronomium reflektiert nicht darüber, wie sich das Wohnen des Namens Jahwes im Heiligtum zum Wohnen Jahwes im Himmel verhält", Nicholson (1967) 55-56: "[I]n Deuteronomy... not Yahweh himself but his name is present in the sanctuary", Dumermuth 69: "Nicht mehr ist...Jahwe selbst am Kultort gegenwärtig gedacht, sondern nur sein Name... Jahwe selber wohnt im Himmel", Bietenhard 256: "[Deuteronomium läßt] den Schem und nicht Jahve selbst im Tempel wohnen...Jahve ist nicht an den Tempel gebunden, er thront im Himmel", Procksch 452: "Das hat...im Deuteronomium zu einer eigentümlichen Trennung des Namens von Jahve geführt. Während Jahve selbst im Him-

The Name placed at the sanctuary is commonly viewed as distinct from, yet related to YHWH himself, and a variety of terms has been used to describe the relationship between the two.[22] Moreover, deuterono-m(ist)ic affirmations of the presence of the Name at the cult-place are generally regarded (with von Rad) as *correcting* the view that YHWH

---

mel wohnt...läßt er seinen Namen am Heiligtum wohnen". Cf. also the following earlier expressions of the same idea: Phythian-Adams (1942) 56-58, Grether 32-34, Westphal 194, Steuernagel (1900) 44.

[22] Most commonly the Name "*represents*" YHWH at the sanctuary (Clements [1989] 52: "[T]he name...serv[es] as the representation of God's presence", cf. *idem* [1968] 78: "Yahweh's name is...the representative of Yahweh himself", Vriezen [1970] 208: "[T]he *name of God* can occur as something independent representing God", Jacob [1968] 66: "Le Deutéronome entend affirmer...que ce n'est pas Yahweh en personne qui habite le Temple, mais qu'il s'y fait représenter par son nom", Kuntz 37: "[W]e have in these vehicles, which are technically known as *theologoumena*, the 'represen-tations' or 'presentations' of the deity as he draws near to man in his real yet never fully revealed nature", Lindblom 92: "Yahweh...was represented by...His name [Deut. 12:5, 11; 14:23...]", Procksch 453: "Der Name [repräsentierte] Jahves Gegen-wart", Eichrodt [1935] 16: "[Im Deuteronomium] bekommt...der Name eine selb-ständigere Funktion als Vertreter des überweltlichen Gottes", Grether 34: "Jahwe... ist...durch den schem am Kultort vertreten", Westphal 194: "[D]er Name [ist] ein Repräsentant der Gottheit im Tempel"), or is the "*form*" of his manifestation there (Nicholson [1967] 55: "[T]he 'name' [is] the form of Yahweh's manifestation", Dumermuth 69: "[D]er 'šem' Jahwes [ist] die eigentliche Offenbarungsform Jahwes" [cf. von Rad (1947) 26], Eichrodt [1935] 16: "Damit ist...eine Erscheinungs- und Offenbarungsform Jahves erreicht", Grether 35: "Der an der Zentralkultstätte lokali-sierte schem wird...zu einer Hypostase...welchen S. MOWINCKEL als eine halb selbständige, halb als Offenbarungsform einer höheren Gottheit betrachtete göttliche Wesenheit definiert", Gulin 25: "[D]ieser Name [auftritt] gleichsam als Jahwes Er-scheinungsform"). Other suggestions are that it fulfils a "*mediating*" role (Von Rad [1964] 90: "[Der] Name [ist] de[r] Mittler zwischen Jahwe und seinem Volk"; cf. McBride 141, Clements [1968] 79), is an "*extension*" of the Deity (Cairns 127: "God places the 'name' as an extension of the divine self in the earthly shrine", McBride 3: "[T]he divine 'name' acted as an extension of God", Johnson [1961] 17: "[T]he 'Name' is an...'Extension' of Yahweh's Personality" [cf. p. 19]), or denotes his "*cultic presence*" (cf. Terrien [1978] 200, McBride 140-141, 193, 209). It has also been pro-posed that the Name formulae express YHWH's "*ownership*" of the temple (Braulik [1977] 75-76: "Das 'Wohnen-Lassen' und 'Deponieren' des Namens...meint die Be-sitzergreifung des Heiligtums durch Jahwe", Schreiner 163: "In dem erwähnten tran-sitiven Sinn weist die Wendung auf das Besitzrecht Jahwes hin. Der Ort, auf den er seinen Namen...gelegt hat, ist sein Eigentum", Stade [1888] 247: "Wenn...die Deuteronomisten...die Redensart setzen, daß [Jahwe] seinen 'Namen' [im Tempel] wohnen läßt oder dorthin setzt, so wollen sie sagen, daß er ihn als sein Eigenthum sich erwählt hat". Cf. Weinfeld's [1972a] discussion of de Vaux' view [pp. 194-195]).

himself resided there.[23] Various suggestions have been offered in explanation of such a change of belief. Some scholars consider that the assertion of a personal dwelling of YHWH at the sanctuary could be construed as implying the limiting of his Presence to that place[24] and thus a

[23] Preuß (1982) 16: "[D]as Dtn [versucht] mit seiner Theologie des 'Namens' Jahwes...eine bewußte Korrektur [der Jerusalemer] Theologie", Weinfeld (1972a) 193: "[T]he repeated employment of [the expression 'to cause his name to dwell'] is intended to combat the ancient popular belief that the Deity actually dwelled within the sanctuary", Seitz 222: "[D]as Dt [will] mit der Wendung 'um seinen Namen dort wohnen zu lassen (oder niederzulegen)' eine' Korrektur an der bisherigen Wohnvorstellung vornehmen", Metzger 150: "Durch dieses Tempelweihgebet interpretiert und korrigiert der Deuteronomist die im Tempelweihspruch sich aussprechende Wohn und Thronvorstellung", McBride 186: "According to Stade and most commentators since, Name Theology was promulgated as a substitute for the view that Yahweh himself dwelt in an earthly abode. Whether this was the sole or even primary motive informing its earliest usage remains to be seen, but a corrective intent is decisive in the way the tradition has been employed by the Deuteronomic historians", Nicholson (1967) 56: "Deuteronomy...is attempting to replace...the old crude idea of Yahweh's presence and dwelling at the shrine", Clements (1965) 94: "[I]n place of the older mythology, by which Yahweh's abode on earth was thought to be united to his abode in heaven, the Deuteronomists offered a theological concept...that of Yahweh's name...set in the place which he had chosen", Dumermuth 69: "Die Vorstellung vom 'šem'...enthält deutlich ein theologisches Korrektiv. Nicht mehr ist wie früher Jahwe selbst am Kultort gegenwärtig gedacht, sondern nur sein Name", Grether 33: "[A]m Theologumenon des schem läßt sich die Absicht des Deuteronomiums erkennen...im Gegensatz zur Volksmeinung...[wonach] ist Jahwe...Bewohner des Tempels", Westphal 266: "Wir sahen...daß durch die Bildung der Kompromißformel: 'Jahwes Name wohnt im Tempel'...mit der Vorstellung, daß Jahwe leibhaftig im Hinterraume des Tempels wohne, endgültig gebrochen werden sollte", Giesebrecht 126: "Man nahm Anstoss an der Vorstellung, dass Jahve selbst im Heiligthum Wohnung genommen habe, und suchte nach einem Ersatz [dem Namen]". See also above, p. 4 n. 19.
[24] Cairns 127: "Almighty God cannot be limited to any earthly sanctuary, because God is enthroned in heaven and fills all things (Deut. 26:15)", Janowski (1987) 174: "Um das Mißverständnis einer zu engen Bindung Jahwes an das Heiligtum auszuschließen, vermeidet das Deuteronomium...die Aussage, daß *Jahwe* im Tempel wohnt", Maly 27: "Almost all...scholars see in D's use of this phrase ['the place he has chosen to make his name dwell there'] a reaction to a gross conception of God's presence being limited, or at least bound, to the material temple", Braulik (1977) 181: "Um das Mißverständnis einer Begrenzung der Wirksamkeit oder einengenden Bindung Jahwes an das Heiligtum auszuschalten, vermeidet das Dtn die Aussage, daß Jahwe im Tempel wohne", Metzger 149: "Die mit dem Heiligtum verbundene Vorstellung von der Wohnung Jahwes konnte zu dem Mißverständnis führen, daß Jahwe an das Heiligtum gebunden, durch das Gebäude begrenzt oder eingeengt sei", Clements (1965) 104: "Yahweh...cannot be said to be located and confined to this or that place", Wright (1960) 72: "In...the Deuteronomic school...the cosmic and omnipotent God [cannot] be confined to an earthly sanctuary", Bietenhard 256: "[E]s

restriction upon his freedom of action.[25] Others relate the introduction of
the "Name formulae", as they are often called, to particular historical
events, for example, the centralization of the cult,[26] the loss of the ark
from the northern kingdom,[27] or the destruction of the temple.[28] However, despite the resulting deuteronom(ist)ic emphasis on the transcendence of YHWH according to this view,[29] the sanctuary retains its importance for the Israelite worshipper, since the presence there of the
Name is seen as providing indirect access to that of the Deity himself.[30]

[läßt] den Schem...im Tempel wohnen...Jahve ist nicht an den Tempel gebunden",
Grether 33: "[Der Kultort] ist nicht mehr Wohnhaus Jahwes sondern Wohnstätte
seines Namens...Eine falsche Bindung Jahwes an den Kultort...ist unmöglich ge-
macht".
[25] Brueggemann (1976) 681: "Aware that such presence [in the shrine] tends crudely
to deny Yahweh his freedom...Deuteronomy...articulated a 'theology of name'",
Rose 86: "Die Lösung des Dilemmas zwischen dem traditionsbedingten Anspruch
eines מקום und dem Bewußtsein der Freiheit Jahwes geschieht also 'durch die theologische Differenzierung zwischen Jahwe einerseits und seinem Namen andererseits'",
Terrien (1970) 334: "The theology of the sojourning name...was compatible with the
freedom of God", Clements (1965) 100: "[The Deuteronomic writers'] real concern
had been to avoid a one-sided doctrine of immanence which reduced Yahweh to the
level of a nature-spirit, and which obscured the reality of his freedom to act towards
his people in judgment as well as mercy." Cf. Schmidt 93.
[26] Grether 35.
[27] Kaiser 137, Nicholson (1967) 72-73, Dumermuth 70-76.
[28] Kaiser 137, Mettinger 50, 59-62, 78-79, 133, McCurley 310-311. Cf. Preuß (1982)
17, Braulik (1977) 182, Clements (1965) 92.
[29] Kaiser 137: "Die...Glaubensprobleme wurden durch die šem (Namens-)-*Theologie*
gelöst, nach der...unter Wahrung der Distanz zwischen Gott und Welt allein 'sein
Name als Garant seines Heilswillens' am Kultort gegenwärtig ist", Cross 30: "The
'name'...of Yahweh act[s] for him, in effect protecting his transcendence", Vriezen
(1970) 208: "[The Deuteronomist] emphasizes this doctrine that the name of Jahweh
dwells in the temple...in order to create a distance between God Himself and the
temple", McBride 1: "In the Deuteronomic literature...in an effort to protect the transcendence of God, the fullness of his being is removed from the terrestrial realm and
enthroned in the heights of heaven", Nicholson (1967) 56: "Deuteronomy is concerned with emphasizing the distance between God and the sanctuary", Clements
(1965) 90: "The Deuteronomists...in accordance with their desire to emphasize the
transcendence of Yahweh, lay great stress upon Yahweh as the God of heaven",
Eichrodt (1933) 218: "Noch stärker scheint die göttliche Transzendenz unterstrichen,
wenn Gottes Selbstmitteilung wesentlich in die Offenbarung seines Namens und die
dauernde Gegenwart desselben verlegt wird".
[30] Cairns 127: "[B]elievers may worship and enter into true meeting with the transcendent God, through the name extension located at the place of worship", Terrien
(1978) 200: "[T]he Deuteronomic law...demanded that the nation gather at...'the
place which Yahweh chooses to set his name there for its sojourn' (Deut. 12:5). It

Finally, the presence of the Name at the cult-place is not regarded as an isolated phenomenon, but is linked to a whole complex of new ideas involving changes in the conception of the ark (from being YHWH's footstool or throne to being a mere container for the law)[31] and of the temple (from being YHWH's dwelling-place and therefore a place of sacrifice to being a place of prayer).[32]

The theory of a Name Theology in Deuteronomy and the Deuteronomistic writings has not, however, gone unchallenged, and those objecting to it have proposed three main interpretations of the Name formulae: that they express the actual Presence of YHWH,[33] or his taking possession of the sanctuary,[34] or the proclamation of his Name in the cult.[35] It is impor-

---

thus appears that, in the North…religionists developed a notion of cultic presence that was…spatially limited", McCurley 308: "Thus…for Deuteronomy, the name is Yahweh's *means* of making himself available to his people", McBride 3: "First, there is no mistaking the fact that *šēm* in the various formulations of Name Theology connoted a mode of divine immanence at least in part distinct from God himself" (cf. pp. 140-141, 193, 209), Nicholson (1967) 73: "Yahweh's name [was] the manifestation of his presence in the sanctuary", Clements (1965) 94: "[T]he name of Yahweh was made the vehicle of his presence. It was his *alter ego*, by means of which he made himself present to men" (cf. pp. 95, 104, 113, 137), Dumermuth 70: "Jahwes 'šem' am Kultort verbürgt Jahwes Heilsgegenwart unter seinem Volk" (cf. p. 73), Bietenhard 255-256: "Die Anwesenheit des Schem im Tempel bezeichnet…Jahwes heilsgeschichtliche Nähe; der Schem verbürgt Jahwes Gegenwart im Tempel", Procksch 453: "So wohnte der Name im Tempel als die geistige Gegenwart Jahwes", Grether 34: "[Am Kultort] läßt [Jahwe] sich in seinem schem vom Menschen finden", Giesebrecht 124: "[D]er Name [ist] Bedingung und Träger der Anwesenheit Jahves im Heiligthume" (cf. p. 126), Steuernagel (1900) 44: "[D]er 'Name'…ausdrückt, dass Jahve dem ihn Verehrenden [im Tempel] besonders nahe ist".

[31] Cairns 107, Braulik (1986) 98, Kaiser 137, Mettinger 50-51, Preuß (1982) 17, Terrien (1978) 201, Weinfeld (1972a) 208-209, McBride 2, Fretheim (1968a) 6, Nicholson (1967) 31, 56, 71, 112, Clements (1965) 35, 96, Dumermuth 71-74, Schmidt 250 n. 241, von Rad (1947) 27.

[32] Mettinger 48, Clements (1978) 68-69, Braulik (1977) 182, Weinfeld (1972a) 36-37, 209, Metzger 150, 154, Wright (1960) 71.

[33] Mayes (1979) 225: "[T]he basic idea is an affirmation of the real and actual presence of Yahweh at the sanctuary" (cf. pp. 59-60), McConville (1979) 162: "The presence of the name of Yahweh at the cult-place of Israel means that it is Yahweh who dwells there", Rennes 68: "Dans la perspective du Deut., il s'agit…d'affirmer la présence de Yahweh au sanctuaire", Myers (1961) 27: "[Yahweh] had placed his name in their midst…which meant that he had taken up residence among them", Clamer 590: "'Mettre son nom' au lieu choisi par Yahweh signifie, d'après l'identité établie entre le nom et la personne, mettre Yahweh lui-même".

[34] McConville (1979) 152: "The phrase 'the place which the Lord shall choose to put his name there' indicates that the chosen sanctuary will be Yahweh's possession for

tant to note, however, that not all such scholars object to Name Theology *per se*. Some deny it to Deuteronomy while at the same time affirming it to be present in the Deuteronomistic History.[36]

INTRODUCTION TO THE PRESENT WORK

As indicated earlier, Name Theology is based primarily on two sets of data: references to the divine Name at the sanctuary and references to heaven as YHWH's abode.[37] It is largely against this background that the discussion as to the interpretation of the various Name formulae has been carried out. However, while much of that discussion has involved an appeal to other Ancient Near Eastern data,[38] and in particular to the Amarna letters,[39] little of substance has appeared querying whether the above two sets of data exhaust the *biblical* material in Deuteronomy or the Deuteronomistic History in relation to the subject of divine Presence.

But, although nothing substantial has been done, some scholars *have* appealed to biblical data (usually in Deuteronomy) to support their rejection of Name Theology, though mainly in throw-away lines and foot-

ever", Braulik (1971) 24 n. 3: "[Die] Formulierungen...drücken nur Jahwes Besitz des Tempels aus", Wenham (1971) 114: "The phrases in Deuteronomy...specify that the sanctuary in question belongs to Yahweh", de Vaux (1967) 225: "Les formules du Deutéronome sont...une affirmation que Yahvé est possesseur du temple". Cf. above, p. 5 n. 22.
[35] Braulik (1986) 99: "Doch geht es auch bei dem im Dtn irrtümlich mit 'wohnen lassen' übersetzten Ausdruck nur um die Proklamation des Jahwenamens an der auserwählten Stätte", Weippert 78: "Die Bezugnahme auf den Namen drückt vielmehr etwas über die Funktion aus, die Jahwe an diesem Ort für sein Volk erfüllt, nämlich eine kultische...an der von Jahwe gewählten Stätte sein Name vollmächtig proklamiert wird...", van der Woude (1977) 207: "All diese Erwägungen führen zum Ergebnis...dass *šēm* den (im Kultgeschehen) *ausgesprochenen*...Namen bedeutet d.h. dass Jahwe sich einen Ort wählt, wo er in Zukunft seinen Namen...etabliert, bzw. proklamiert", Zimmerli (1956) 159: "Es wird...ernsthaft erwogen werden müssen, ob nicht auch die Rede vom 'Namen' Jahwes im Deut...richtiger...der Selbstkundgabe Jahwes in seinem Namen...verstanden wird"; cf. Weiser (1950) 521, Jacob (1903) 14.
[36] Janowski (1987) 178, Mettinger 60-61, 78, Weippert 84-85, de Vaux (1967) 225-228.
[37] See above, p 3.
[38] Notably by McBride 66-141.
[39] Knudtzon, *Die El-Amarna-Tafeln* I, 287:60-63, 288:5-7. Both refer to the king having "established his name" (šakan šumšu). Cf. Braulik (1986) 98, McConville (1979) 152, van der Woude (1977) 205-206, McBride 114-117, de Vaux (1967) 221, Schreiner 163, Jacob (1903) 45-46.

notes. Deut. 4:7;[40] 12:5[41] and 23:15 (EVV 14)[42] are occasionally cited, but the point most frequently made concerns the use of the expression "before YHWH" (לפני יהוה). The preposition is given the meaning "in the presence of",[43] and so the phrase as a whole is taken to indicate YHWH's spatial proximity to whatever is taking place "before" him. Mettinger, for example, remarks:

> To this we should add the fact that cultic activities take place...'before the Lord'...Admittedly, this usage may well be a sort of linguistic fossil, bearing no semantic cargo of importance, but taken at face value this expression makes it difficult to speak of a Name theology in Deuteronomy.[44]

However, neither he, nor any of the other scholars who refer to such usage of לפני יהוה, makes any attempt to justify his understanding of the expression.

These data constitute the principal ground on which the existence of Deuteronomic Name Theology has sometimes been challenged,[45] but few *advocates* of the theory have felt the need to respond. Those who have, do so in one of two ways. Clements detects "older ideas of Yahweh's accompanying presence" in Deut. 2:7; 4:7, 37; 7:21; 9:3; 23:15 (EVV 14) and 31:3, but is convinced that "it is with the doctrine of Yahweh's name set in Israel's sanctuary that the Deuteronomic interpretation of this belief is given."[46] Nicholson, on the other hand, refers to

---

[40] Maly 26, Mayes (1979) 60, Myers (1961) 27.

[41] Braulik (1986) 95, Lohfink (1984) 303-304.

[42] Mayes (1979) 59, Gordon (1974) 118, Wenham (1971) 112, Myers (1961) 28.

[43] Mettinger 53, Weippert 77-78, esp. n. 4, Mayes (1979) 59, McConville (1979) 159 n. 41, van der Woude (1977) 208, 210 n. 34, Wenham (1971) 112-113, de Vaux (1967) 227-228, Myers (1961) 27, esp. n. 19.

[44] P. 53.

[45] In addition, Maly claims that Deuteronomy's picture of God "is a strongly immanent one, in the sense...of intimate association with the world and mankind" and that the striking hortatory character of Moses' address shows that God is not aloof from his people. He also cites God's love, choice and blessing of Israel as "indications of divine immanence" (pp. 25-26). Mayes (1979) argues that the descriptions of YHWH as "jealous" (4:24; 5:9 and 6:15), "great and terrible" (7:21), "faithful" (7:9) and "merciful" (4:31) "point to an involvement with Israel which may be described only in terms of his active presence in her life and history" (p. 59). None of this evidence, however, refers to the Presence of God in the kind of *localized* sense which Name Theology is held to oppose.

[46] (1965) 94 n. 4.

passages such as Deut. 7:21 "where Yahweh is conceived of as being in the 'midst' of Israel in battle", but considers that "in actual cultic practice the authors of Deuteronomy have dispensed with [such a] notion."[47] The former presupposes (in Deuteronomy) a universally consistent presentation of YHWH and his relationship to the world,[48] whereas the latter distinguishes between God's involvement in war and his involvement in the cult. Neither scholar devotes more than a footnote to his disclaimer.

No advocate of Name Theology has been found to discuss the possibility that לפני יהוה refers to the divine Presence.

From the foregoing remarks, and from a closer inspection of the book, it becomes clear that, in Deuteronomy at least, a substantial body of *biblical* material has been overlooked or disregarded by most writers on the subject.[49] In addition, the evidence most widely cited against Name Theology (i.e. the cultic instances of לפני יהוה) has been ignored by advocates of the theory and inadequately expounded by its opponents. Moreover, the relative importance accorded what *has* been written can be gauged from the fact that much of it appears in footnotes.

The existence, therefore, both of largely unconsidered evidence and of a major difference in perception as to the significance or even relevance to the debate of certain data would appear to provide adequate grounds for a more detailed discussion than has hitherto been carried out.

THE AIM OF THE PRESENT WORK

The aim of the present work is neither to propose a new interpretation of the Name formulae in Deuteronomy (or elsewhere), nor to evaluate any of the already-existing proposals. Rather, it is to query the adequacy of the twofold biblical foundation (the presence of the Name at the sanctuary and of YHWH in heaven) upon which many such proposals have

---

[47] (1967) 73 n. 1; cf. Fretheim (1968a) 7, Dumermuth 71 n. 66.

[48] A similar expectation of consistency is implied by von Rad's perplexity over the presence of Deut. 23:15 (EVV 14): "Merkwürdig ist...dass der Deuteronomiker, der so konsequent Jahwes Wohnen im Himmel betont, so dass er nicht einmal von einer persönlichen Gegenwart Jahwes am Kultort zu reden wagt, - hier von einem Einherziehen Jahwes im Lager spricht" ([1952] 70).

[49] Cf. Kuhn's observations in the field of natural science: "[N]ormal science...seems an attempt to force nature into the preformed and relatively inflexible box that the paradigm supplies. No part of the aim of normal science is to call forth new sorts of phenomena; indeed *those that will not fit the box are often not seen at all* [our italics]" (p. 24).

so far been predicated. In particular, our aim is to see whether there are sufficient grounds for proposing that the basis of future discussions of the significance of the Name formulae in Deut. 12-26 should include the recognition that the *earthly* Presence of YHWH is also represented in those chapters.[50] The discussion will therefore concentrate on examining a number of possible references to divine Presence in Deuteronomy, rather than the Name formulae themselves.

THE DATA TO BE EXAMINED

Within Deuteronomy, those expressions which may refer to YHWH's earthly Presence fall, broadly speaking, into two groups. Some occur in the *historical* sections of the book and consist of a variety of terminology used in relation to the Wilderness wanderings, Holy War, or events at Horeb. Others are found in the *legal* section. Here one expression predominates (לפני יהוה), but it is used to qualify a variety of activities carried out, in the main, at the "chosen place". Both these groups of expressions are relevant to the question of Name Theology, but those in the legal section are especially important, since they are found in connection with the very place from which YHWH is believed *ex hypothesi* to be absent. The references to divine Presence in the historical material should be taken into account for two reasons. First, much of the material is considered to derive from the Deuteronomists, who are also held to have espoused Name Theology.[51] Deut. 1-3[52] and 4:1-40,[53] for example,

---

[50] It is this which tends to lead scholars to deny Name Theology to Deuteronomy, whilst allowing it elsewhere in the OT. See above, p. 9 n. 36.

[51] Janowski (1987) 178: "[D]er deuteronomistische Tempelweihbericht 1 Kön 8,14-66 [schließt] 'Jahwes Anwesenheit im Tempel selbst aus; die Präsenz seines Namens impliziert nicht die Jahwes'", Mettinger 46-50, esp. 50: "[W]e find it meaningful to speak of a Deuteronomistic Name theology", Clements (1978) 68-69: "Deuteronomic theology...asserted that it was God's name which was present at his sanctuary... and...re-interpret[ed] the temple as essentially a house of prayer to the God who dwelt in heaven (1 Kgs. 8.22-53)"; cf. *idem* (1965) ch. 6, Terrien (1978) 198: "By using the theology of the name...the theologians who formulated [1 Kings 8:22-53] reflect the thinking of the Deuteronomists", McCurley 310: "[The Deuteronomist] spoke of the Temple as the place where *only* Yahweh's name dwelt", Weinfeld (1972b) 1017-1020, esp. 1020: "[T]he abstract notion of the Divine Presence associated with the so-called 'Name' theology found its full expression in Deuteronomy and in the Deuteronomic school", Seitz 222: "Diese Korrektur wird besonders deutlich in der Fortsetzung, die ein dtr Verfasser dem Tempelweihspruch in 1 Kg 8,14ff. gibt: Jahwe wohnt im Himmel, der Tempel ist die Wohnstätte seines Namens", Metzger

are usually attributed to their hand, while other historical sections (e.g. 9:7-10:11) are increasingly assigned to the same source.[54] Assuming, therefore, that at least in their own writings such authors would display a measure of consistency, we would expect that their views on divine Presence would be reflected not only in their references to the cult, in terms of a commitment to Name Theology, but also in their version of

---

149-151, esp. 150: "[Der Deuteronomist] übernimmt...vom Deuteronomium das Theologumenon von 'Namen Jahwes'...der Name Jahwes [ist] im Tempel anwesend, während Jahwe selbst im Himmel thront", McBride 2: "[In the Deuteronomic literature] the presence of Yahweh's 'name'...rather than Yahweh himself...constitutes the sanctuary as an efficacious place of worship", Nicholson (1967) 96: "[The Deuteronomic circle] accorded no room to the belief that Yahweh himself dwelt in the sanctuary; only his name dwelt on earth", Schreiner 159: "[Die Schem-Theologie auftritt]...im Dt und beim Dtn", Dumermuth 75: "Daß der Deuteronomist die šem-Theologie vertritt, geschieht...nicht bloß aus ideeller Anlehnung an das Deuteronomium, sondern...", Bietenhard 256: "[D]ie deuteronomistische Fortführung des Gebetes [Salomos] läßt nur den Schem Jahves im Tempel wohnen und verneint geradezu die Frage, ob Jahve auf Erden wohnen könne", Procksch 453: "In der deuteronomischen Literatur...hat sich diese Vorstellung vom Wohnen des Namens im Tempel weithin eingebürgert", Wright (1944) 75: "[In the writings of the Deuteronomic school]...the clearest example...[being] Solomon's prayer of dedication at the Temple's completion...there is a clear rejection of the whole attempt to localize God or to consider the Temple as his dwelling...the Temple's significance...is [as] the place where God's name is", Grether 32: "[D]ie deuteronomistische Fassung [des Tempelweihegebetes Salomos] (1 Reg. 8,14ff.)...[preist] den Tempel als den Ort des schem jahwe", Stade (1905) 319: "Das theologische Denken der deuteronomistischen Schriftsteller...wird dadurch charakterisiert, dass sie Jahve nicht auf Zion wohnen lassen, sondern dorthin seinen Namen versetzen", Giesebrecht 36: "[D]ie Vorstellung, im Heiligthume wohne oder weile der Name Jahves, [ist] ein Lieblingsgedanke der deuteronomistischen Schule". Cf. Westphal 194.

[52] Clements (1989) 10, 99, Clifford (1982) 1-2, Preuß (1982) 77 (cf. p. 46), Nelson 91-92, 97, Mayes (1979) 42, Levenson (1975) 210-211, Rose 146-149, Cross 249, Phillips (1973) 3, 12, Seitz 311, Watts (1970) 182, Brueggemann (1968) 387 n. 2, Nicholson (1967) 31-32, 36, 108, Noth (1967) 47, von Rad (1964) 7, Buis and Leclercq 17, Lohfink (1960b) 403 n. 6, Wright (1953) 316-317. See above, p. 2.

[53] Clifford (1982) 2, Mayes (1979) 44-45, Levenson (1975) 221, Rose 146-149, Phillips (1973) 3, 12, Seitz 311, Watts (1970) 182, Brueggemann (1968) 387 n. 2, Nicholson (1967) 31-32, Lohfink (1965) 18, von Rad (1964) 7, Wright (1953) 316-317.

[54] G.M. de Tillesse has argued that within Deuteronomy itself the deuteronomistic influence be extended to include all sections in which the Israelites are addressed in the second person plural, i.e. as opposed to in the singular (*re* 9:7b-10:11 see pp. 45-46). In this he has been followed by Kaiser 126, Phillips (1973) 3, 12, 69, Cazelles (1967), 208, 219, Nicholson (1967) 23-36, Buis and Leclercq 10. Cf. Preuß (1982) 102, Mayes (1979) 195.

Israel's history. Secondly, there is a precedent for introducing such non-cultic material into the discussion. Several advocates of Name Theology have pointed to parts of these same historical sections to show that the perceived emphasis on divine transcendence is reflected in Deuteronomy's account of Israel's past.[55] In particular, appeal is sometimes made to Deuteronomy's version of the giving of the law at Horeb[56] and the deuteronomic view of the ark,[57] usually by way of contrast with earlier traditions.

Both groups of expressions will therefore be examined in some detail, in order to discover whether or not they include references to YHWH's earthly Presence.

OUTLINE OF THESIS

The main body of the study divides into two parts. Chapters 2-4 consist of an investigation of some of the historical material in Deuteronomy by means of a series of "synoptic" comparisons with parallel narratives occurring elsewhere in the Pentateuch. The purpose of each comparison is to determine relative emphases on divine Presence; at least one of the accounts in each pair contains some (possible) reference to the phenomenon. Chapter 2 deals with Deut. 1-3 (principally the Wilderness wanderings), comparing these chapters with Exod. 18 and Num. 11, 13-14 and 32. Chapter 3 examines Deut. 4-5 (the first giving of the law on Horeb/Sinai) in the light of Exod. 19-20, while chapter 4 compares Deut. 9-10 (the Golden Calf incident) with Exod. 32-34.

By contrast, chapters 5 and 6 comprise an investigation of the significance of the expression לפני יהוה as it occurs in the legal section of the book (principally), the aim being to discover whether its proper status is higher than that of a "linguistic fossil".[58] Chapter 5 considers the general

---

[55] Mettinger 46, 48, 124-125, Terrien (1978) 201-202, Rose 148, Weinfeld (1972a) 198, 206-208, McBride 2, Clements (1965) 90.

[56] For example, in Exodus YHWH descends on to Sinai, but in Deuteronomy there is *no* descent (Mettinger 48, 125, Weinfeld [1972a] 206-207, Clements [1965] 90, Westphal 266); again, in Exodus and Numbers the conception of God is anthropomorphic in that Moses beholds YHWH's back and gazes on his form, whereas in Deuteronomy it is more abstract, since Israel perceives *no* form (Weinfeld [1972a] 198; cf. Mettinger 46, 124).

[57] See above, p. 8 n. 31.

[58] See the quotation from Mettinger on p. 10.

characteristics of its usage in the legal section as a whole, while chapter 6 deals in turn with each of the various activities which it qualifies (eating, rejoicing, standing, etc.).

In the final chapter the results are summarized and some conclusions drawn.

2

DEUTERONOMY 1-3

Deut. 1-3, following the original publication of Noth's *Studien* in 1943,[1] is widely accepted as forming the introduction to the Deuteronomistic History and thus as being largely[2] attributable to a[3] deuteronomistic hand.[4] Four of its sections are paralleled, in either Exodus or Numbers, by accounts in which the Deity is portrayed as being present on the earth.

METHODOLOGY

The existence of parallel material offers the possibility of ascertaining the deuteronomistic view of divine Presence by carrying out a "synoptic" comparison of each Deuteronomy account with the corresponding one from Exodus or Numbers. The procedure, which will also be applied to Deut. 4-5 and 9-10,[5] has several features. First, each of the passages being compared is treated as a unit in accordance with the source-critical consensus on the passage, to the extent that this may exist.[6] Secondly, no

---

[1] See above, pp. 1-2.

[2] More detailed source analyses will be referred to (where relevant) in each of the four sections.

[3] The question of *multiple* redactions will not be considered. It is enough that the chapters are regarded as deuteronomistic.

[4] See above, p. 13 n. 52.

[5] See below, chs. 3 and 4 respectively.

[6] Note the similar procedure adopted by Balentine (1985): "I do not propose to offer a fresh source analysis of [the wilderness tradition] narratives or even a critique of the traditional views. Rather I have endeavored to determine, where possible, what is simply the consensus opinion and to begin from that point" (p. 56). Cf. Kuntz 75.

assumptions are made as to relative priority. This means that the deuter-
onom(ist)ic accounts are compared with J, E *and* P material, those from
the Tetrateuch being viewed purely as controls.[7] Thirdly, each pair of
passages contains at least one expression believed to refer to God's
earthly Presence. Justification for this interpretation (frequently on the
supposition of a uniform OT usage) is generally offered for such expressions in Deuteronomy, but not for those in Exodus or Numbers. Fourthly,
the examination and, in some cases, exegesis of the passages is intended
to determine whether, consistent with Name Theology, the earthly Presence of the Deity has been edited out of the deuteronom(ist)ic material.
Finally, in those cases where such reference is absent from Deuteronomy, an attempt is made to see whether this absence can be understood either on the basis of context (deuteronom[ist]ic and/or tetrateuchal) or in terms of any difference of emphasis within the respective
pericopes, i.e. without having to appeal, in the case of Deuteronomy, to
the operation of a conscious theology of transcendence.

The four sections will be examined in turn.

THE APPOINTMENT OF MEN TO SHARE MOSES' RESPONSIBILITY FOR THE PEOPLE

The appointing of the heads of the tribes in Deut. 1:9-18 is generally
regarded as representing the same development as that recorded in Exod.
18:13-27,[8] though with some literary influence from Num. 11. It is also
implied by those scholars who, in treating the relationship only in
source-critical terms, regard Exod. 18 as the main source of Deut. 1:9-
18.[9]

---

[7] Compare Peckham's analysis of Deut. 9:1-10:11, in which Exod. 32 is used "only as
a 'model text', for comparison and for appreciation of the DTR narrative" (p. 10
n. 13).

[8] This is indicated either explicitly by direct statement to that effect (Ridderbos 56-
57, Clifford [1982] 11, 14, Clamer 515, Reider 8, Junker 24, Driver (1902) xviii,
Bertholet [1899] 4, Robinson [n.d.] 59) or implicitly by comparison of some feature
of the deuteronomistic account with that in Exod. 18, e.g. the timing of the incident
relative to the Israelites' sojourn at Horeb/Sinai (Wright [1953] 335-336) or the identity of the initiator of the burden-sharing idea (Buis and Leclercq 35).

[9] Mayes (1979) 118, Phillips (1973) 15, Steuernagel (1900) 3.

DEUT. 1:9-18 // EXOD. 18:13-27

Exod. 18:13-27 contains three possible references to divine Presence:

Deut.	Exod.
————	"God be *with you* ! You shall represent the people *before God*, and bring their cases *to God*..." (18:19)[10]

Few scholars,[11] however, view them this way.[12] Nevertheless, although the first is too vague[13] and the second without parallel,[14] the reference to Moses bringing the people's cases "to (אל) God" is reminiscent of two situations envisaged in the so-called "Book of the Covenant" (Exod. 20:22-23:33), namely the bringing "to (אל) God" of a slave by his master (Exod. 21:6) and the coming near "to (אל) God" of a house owner (Exod. 22:7 [EVV 8]). Many writers see one[15] or both[16] of these actions as tak-

---

[10] Biblical quotations are from the RSV, unless otherwise stated.

[11] Though see Cole 141.

[12] The occasional commentator (e.g. Hyatt [1971], 193) relates Moses' inquiring of God (Exod. 18:15) to his use of the tent of meeting (33:7-11). Westermann (1960), however, has made a study of the expression "to inquire of (דרש) YHWH". He makes no mention of the divine Presence in this connection, but focuses rather on the role of the human intermediary (a man of God or prophet) who deals with the "inquiry". Westermann regards "inquiring of YHWH" as an institution prevalent during the monarchical period, and considers that Exod. 18:15 is probably "eine Rückprojektion dieser Institution" (p. 21 n. 17).

[13] Instances of God being "with" (עם/את) someone are unlikely to designate his *localized* Presence unless accompanied either by an appropriate locative adverb[ial phrase], as in "he was *there* (שם) with the LORD" (Exod. 34:28a), or by a locative verb, as in "he *stood* (ויתיצב) with him there (שם)" (Exod. 34:5). Note Davies' (1962b) observation that "Such sentences as 'God is with you in all that you do' [or] the frequent 'The LORD was with him'...are simply the recognition of good fortune interpreted as the evidence of divine blessing" (p. 874). Cf. Mann 111-112.

[14] Although מול generally has a locative sense in the OT (Deut. 3:29; 4:46; 11:30, etc.), Exod. 18:19 is its only occurrence in relation to the Deity (i.e. as opposed to places, or in one case [Deut. 2:19] humans). Thus while such locative usage is suggestive, there is no clear precedent for understanding Moses' representation of the people "before God" in terms of divine Presence, a lack which may well account for its generally being understood metaphorically, e.g. "representing God to [the people]" (BDB 557); cf. Driver (1911) 166, McNeile (1908) 107.

[15] *Re* Exod. 21:6, cf. Gispen 207; *re* Exod. 22:7 (EVV 8), cf. Michaeli (1974) 205, Clements (1972) 142-143, Hyatt (1971) 238, Noth (1959) 149, Holzinger (1900) 89.

[16] Durham 321, 326, Childs (1974) 469, 475, Cole 166, 171-172, Weinfeld (1972a) 233-234, Davies (1967) 175, 181, Fensham (1959) 160-161, Heinisch (1934) 164-165, 177, Driver (1911) 211, 226, McNeile (1908) 127, 133.

ing place at a sanctuary, and since the Book of the Covenant is generally regarded as being the oldest OT law code,[17] and thus as pre-dating the laws of Deuteronomy,[18] it is likely that Exod. 21:6 and 22:7 (EVV 8) presuppose what the deuteronomic Name Theology is thought to have replaced, i.e. "die alte massive Vorstellung von Jahwes Gegenwart und Wohnen am Kultort".[19] It may well be, then, that the bringing of the people's cases "to God" in Exod. 18:19 is also a bringing to the *divine Presence* at a sanctuary.

With the exception of Zenger,[20] the majority of scholars attribute virtually the whole of Exod. 18:13-27 to a single author,[21] usually the Elohist.[22] Similarly, apart from Phillips[23] and Mittmann,[24] most commentators consider that nearly all of Deut. 1:9-18 comes from one (deuteronomistic) hand.[25,26]

In their initial presentations of Moses' problem, i.e. before any alleviation is proposed, the two accounts betray differing concerns. Exod. 18:13-27 indicates not only the number of people with whom Moses has

---

[17] Patrick 63, 255, Hyatt (1971) 218, Paul 1 *et passim*, Davies (1967) 171-172, Alt 281, Jepsen 22, Driver (1911) 202.

[18] Childs (1974) 458, Clements (1972) 128, Noth (1959) 141, McNeile (1908) xxvii-xxviii.

[19] Von Rad (1947) 26. Cf. above, p. 6 n. 23.

[20] He identifies a number of almost certain (vv. 16b, 20, 21b, 25b, 27) and possible (vv. 15b, 19b) later additions ([1978] p. 283 n. 102).

[21] Scharbert 75, 77-78, Burns 136, 138-139, Knight 125, 126-127, Childs (1974) 321, 329-332, Michaeli (1974) 156, 159-160, Clements (1972) 107, 109-110, Hyatt (1971) 186, 192-194, Fritz 14, Davies (1967) 147, 149-150, Noth (1959) 117, 120-121, Beer 93-96, Driver (1911) 161, 165-167, McNeile (1908) xxiii-xxiv, 106-108. See, however, Eißfeldt (1922) 144*-145*), Smend (1912) 154.

[22] Although a number of half-verses (vv. 16b, 20a, 21b, 25b) are sometimes regarded as being secondary in context (see Scharbert, Hyatt [1971], Fritz, Davies [1967]), the comparison with Deut. 1:9-18 would not be materially affected by their removal from the pericope.

[23] Phillips (1973) describes vv. 16ff. as a "hortatory addition" (p. 15).

[24] According to Mittmann's rather complex analysis, the first part of the section to be inserted into ch. 1 consisted of only vv. 9-10, 12 and 15abα without "the heads of your tribes" (p. 183).

[25] Clifford [1982] 1-2, Preuß (1982) 46, Mayes (1979) 118, 121-125, Rose 149, Watts (1970) 182, 192-193, von Rad (1964) 27-29, Buis and Leclercq 17, 35-37, Wright (1953) 316-317, 335-336.

[26] A number of short phrases (in vv. 11, 13, 15, 17) are occasionally regarded as secondary (see Preuß [1982], Mayes [1979], Clamer, Driver [1902], Bertholet [1899]), but none are of any consequence for the comparison.

to deal ("all the/this people" [vv. 14, 23]), but also the nature of his dealings with them (the people's coming to him to inquire of God, his decid-
ing between a man and his neighbour and telling them "the statutes of
God and his decisions" [vv. 15-16], as well as the descriptions of his activity in vv. 13-14). By contrast, Deut. 1:9-18 is primarily concerned
with the number of people. This is shown first by Moses' reference to the
great increase in the Israelite population (v. 10), and secondly by the
sandwiching of that observation between the two statements about his
inability to bear the people alone (vv. 9 and 12). Such a juxtaposition
points to the sheer number as the reason for that inability. Only inciden-
tally is there any hint of what Moses' responsibility entails (v. 12). The
proposed solutions in the texts are appropriate to the problems as described. Both accounts address the question of the number of people by
mentioning the delegation of Moses' authority and the instruction of the
newly appointed judges. However, apart from the references to his taking
responsibility for the "hard" cases (Exod. 18:26 [cf. v. 22]; Deut. 1:17), it
is only in the account which has included the nature of his dealings with
the Israelites, i.e. in Exod. 18:13-27, that there is any information regarding what Moses *himself* will do in the new situation (vv. 19-20). The
absence from Deut. 1:9-18 of the possible allusion to divine Presence
(referred to in Exod. 18:19) is thus consistent with that passage's initial
lack of interest in the details of Moses' task.

DEUT. 1:9-18 // NUM. 11

Num. 11:4-35 is considered by most scholars as comprising two originally independent stories, one concerning the divine provision of quails
in response to the Israelites' craving for meat, and the other dealing with
the divine provision of elders in alleviation of the burden experienced by
Moses in carrying the people (v. 17b). Within the elders' story (regardless of which group of verses is considered)[27] there are two references to
divine descent (vv. 17, 25).[28] Neither occurs in Deut. 1:9-18:

---

[27] See below, p. 22.
[28] The quail story refers to YHWH being *among* the people (בקרבכם), and to the Israelites weeping *before him* (ויבכו לפניו): v. 20, which Davies (1942) regards as referring to the divine Presence (p. 16). Both expressions occur elsewhere in deuterono-
m(ist)ic contexts: Deut. 1:42; 6:15; 7:21 (cf. 23:15 [EVV 14]); Josh. 3:10 (בקרב);
Deut. 1:45; 2 Kings 22:19 (בכה לפני יהוה).

	Deut.	Num.

Deut.

Num.

     "I will *come down* and talk
with you there..." (11:17)

     [T]he LORD *came down in
the cloud* and spoke to him...
(11:25)

If we exclude the view of this section as a unity,[29] the following three groups of verses have been variously proposed as constituting the Num. 11 account of the appointment of the elders:

> Vv.   16-17, 24b-30[30]
> Vv.   14-17, 24b-30[31]
> Vv. 11-12, 14-17, 24b-30[32]

No substantial agreement has been reached regarding the existence of possible additions within these groups.[33]

It has already been observed that, despite the fact that the Deut. 1 and Num. 11 accounts concern the appointment of men to share the burden of the people with Moses, most scholars consider that it is *Exod. 18* which deals with the same development as Deut. 1:9-18.[34,35] Moreover, this consensus is supported by a number of features which the Deuteronomy and Exodus accounts have in common, and which further militate against a meaningful comparison of any part of Num. 11 with Deut. 1. The most significant of these features is the fact that Deut. 1 and Exod. 18 involve only *human* actors. The broaching of the subject of Moses' burden, the suggestion that it be shared, and the choosing and accreditation of those appointed are all carried out by human beings. YHWH is not involved.[36]

---

[29] Wenham (1981) 108 n. 2, Heinisch (1936) 52.

[30] De Vaulx 150, Coats 97-98, Binns xxix, 69-73, McNeile (1911) 58-59, 61-64, Morgenstern (1911) 157 n. 1, 163-164, Gray (1903) 97.

[31] Mettinger 81, Noth (1966) 75, Rudolph 276.

[32] Budd 124, Mann 145, Sturdy 83-84, Fritz 16, Holzinger (1903) 41-42.

[33] Gray (1903) regards v. 17b as editorial (cf. McNeile [1911] 62), and in consequence considers that Exod. 18 and Num. 11:16, 17a, 24b-30 "are not parallel accounts of the same incident" (p. 116).

[34] See above, p. 18.

[35] For scholars who view the Deut. 1 and Num. 11 accounts as in some sense parallel, cf. Braulik (1986) 24, Smith (1918) 9 (though see his comment: "this deuteronomic review is based on Exod. xviii. 13ff." [p. 12]).

[36] Except in so far as he is referred to by Moses (Deut. 1:10-11, 17; Exod. 18:15-16) or his father-in-law (Exod. 18:19, 21, 23).

In addition, the two accounts either imply that Moses is matter-of-fact about his inability to cope unaided (Deut.),[37] or betray no hint that he feels dissatisfied with his lot (Exod.). Since, therefore, his situation is not portrayed as in any way hopeless, there is no need for him to appeal for divine aid and thus no call for YHWH to intervene. Instead, Moses resorts to the simple expedient of delegating his responsibility. In Num. 11:16-17, 24b-30,[38] however, both human *and* divine actors appear on the stage, with YHWH himself playing a key role. He addresses Moses, initiates the burden-sharing and is personally involved in the setting aside of the elders that Moses has chosen.[39] His descent makes sense in terms of his general involvement in the story, and is consistent with other OT instances of descent which occur in similar contexts.[40] Thus, despite dealing with the appointment of men to share Moses' responsibility for bearing the burden of the people, the variously proposed Num. 11 accounts are insufficiently similar to Deut. 1 (or Exod. 18) to warrant comparison.

---

[37] Cf. Cairns: "Moses exudes calm capability…it is a sense of inherent appropriateness rather than an urgent need for assistance which inspires Moses' sharing of 'clerical' responsibility with the 'laity'!" (p. 33), Craigie (1976): "Moses' request for further increase and further blessing makes it clear that his need to delegate responsibility, stated already (1:9) and to be repeated more emphatically (1:12), was in no sense a complaint" (p. 97).

[38] These are the verses common to all three analyses.

[39] Note that if vv. 14-15 (with or [following Mettinger, Noth, Rudolph] without vv. 11-12) are included in the Num. 11 account, they reveal YHWH's involvement in the narrative to be consistent with Moses' extremely negative response to his burden. In particular his desire to die, in the event of no alleviation of the *status quo* (v. 15), implies that he perceives no *human* way out of his predicament (or at least none that he is prepared to countenance). That his complaint is directed towards *YHWH*, who in consequence enters the narrative, is clearly understandable in the circumstances.

[40] In the context of accreditation, YHWH only descends when *he himself* takes the initiative for the procedure. He does so in Num. 12:5 to endorse Moses' authority (vv. 6-8), and in Deut. 31:15 (implied by the reference to his appearing in the pillar of cloud: Cairns 273, Mayes [1979] 377, Jeremias (1976) 897, Phillips [1973] 208, Weinfeld [1972a] 201-202, von Rad [1964] 135, Newman 66, 69, Morgenstern [1911] 160-162; cf. Cunliffe-Jones 170) for the commissioning of Joshua (v. 23). In both cases it is *YHWH* who initiates the proceedings (Num. 12:4; Deut. 31:14); cf. his coming in a thick cloud "that the people may…believe you [Moses] for ever" (Exod. 19:9).

THE SPIES' RECONNAISSANCE OF CANAAN

Deut. 1:19-40 and Num. 13:1-14:38 deal with the initial reconnaissance of the Promised Land by the twelve spies, their reporting back, and the various reactions to their account. Both passages contain several references to divine Presence. They will be dealt with in turn.

DEUT. 1:29-30 // NUM. 14:9

The statements in Deut. 1:30 about YHWH going ahead of and fighting for the Israelites are generally categorized as Holy War terminology[41] and thus as implying the divine Presence on the battlefield.[42] They occur as part of Moses' response (vv. 29-31) to the people's murmuring against having to go up into the Promised Land, and so, strictly speaking, have no parallel in Num. 13:1-14:38, where Moses' only reaction is to fall on his face before the people (14:5). Nevertheless, there is in Num.

---

[41] Von Rad (1952) 9; cf. Lohfink (1960a) 112, de Vaux (1960) 82. On the almost identical terminology in 20:4 see Jones (1975) 654, Thompson (1974) 219-220, Phillips (1973) 135-136, Buis and Leclercq 23.

[42] Von Rad (1959) refers to "the tradition of the holy wars of Yahweh, in which Yahweh appeared personally, to annihilate his enemies...In these wars Israel experienced something like a theophany, a personal entry of Yahweh. Yahweh himself went to war" (p. 104). Cf. Lind, referring to Num. 14:42ff. as an example of an Israelite defeat: "As Yahweh's presence was the important factor in victory, so his absence resulted in defeat...[this]...represent[s] a reversal of the usual concept of holy war" (pp. 109-110), Miller (1973): "The emphasis [in Israel's Holy Warfare]...lay on the activity of the divine, the involvement of Yahweh as warrior and commander of the heavenly armies. The theophany of Yahweh and his coterie was the foundation stone. Yahweh fought for Israel...[and] was general of both the earthly and the heavenly hosts" (p. 156), Craigie (1969): "War was for [the early Israelites] a natural - if unpleasant - part of the world in which they lived. The reality of God to them was the reality of His presence and help in a crisis" (p. 185), Preuß (1968): "Jahwes Mitsein in Kämpfen [ist] nur ein besonderer Aspekt seines mitgehenden Geleitens" (p. 154), de Tillesse: "L'idéologie de la guerre sainte inclut les points suivants: 1) Yahwèh est avec toi, au milieu de toi" (p. 75), Myers (1961): "Yahweh...is present...and fights on behalf of his people" (p. 26), de Vaux (1960): "[Yahvé] marche lui-même en tête de l'armée...Dans la bataille, c'est Yahvé qui combat pour Israël" (pp. 74-75), Eichrodt (1933): "Jahves mächtige Gegenwart als Herrscher und Helfer [wurde] nie intensiver erlebt als am Tage der Schlacht" (pp. 247-248), Schwally: "Die Anteilnahme Jahve's [*sic*] am Kriege wird nicht als Wirkung aus geisterhafter Ferne gedacht. Vielmehr zieht der Gott mit dem Heerbanne aus" (p. 6). See also Mann's remarks on "the divine vanguard motif" (pp. 27, 234, 236) and Fredriksson, pp. 9-14, in the light of his comment: "Als Himmelsgott war er der weit entfernte, nicht mitkämpfende oder persönlich anwesende Gott. Er war im Himmel" (p. 108).

14 a verbal response similar in kind to that in Deuteronomy, though attributed to Joshua and Caleb:

Deut.	Num.
"Do not be in dread or afraid of them. The LORD your God *who goes before you will himself fight for you...* " (1:29-30)	"[D]o not fear the people of the land...the LORD is *with us*; do not fear them." (14:9)

This also attempts to counter the people's objections to going up into the land, and so the comparison would appear to be valid. It is important to note, however, that while the reference in Num. 14:9 to YHWH "[being] with us" fulfils a function within the narrative similar to that of YHWH's "fight[ing] for you" (Deut. 1:30),[43] it is unaccompanied by any locative verb or adverb[ial phrase],[44] and so represents a much less localized form of divine Presence, if it connotes such at all.

The discussion will entail an examination of the two responses (from Joshua and Caleb in Num. 14, and Moses in Deut. 1) in the light of the previously offered objections:

	Deut.	Num.
Objections offered:	1:27-28	13:28-29, 31-33; 14:2-3
Objections answered:	1:29-31	14:6-9

It is generally considered that Num. 13-14 contains two distinct accounts of the spies' reconnaissance of the land, usually attributed to J/JE and P respectively.[45] Of the verses listed above, 13:28-31 are usually regarded as coming from J/JE, while those remaining are distributed, by *older* commentators, equally between the two sources:[46]

13:32[47]	13:33	14:2	14:3	14:6	14:7	14:8	14:9
P	JE	P	JE	P	P	JE	JE

---

43 See the discussion below, pp. 26-28.

44 Surprisingly, the possible significance of such contextual features has not been noted by either Görg (1980) or Preuß (1968). See above, p. 19 n. 13.

45 Budd, Sturdy, de Vaulx, Fritz, Coats, Snaith, Noth (1966), Rudolph, Binns, Driver (1913), McNeile (1911), Gray (1903), Holzinger (1903), Dillmann, Kennedy.

46 Rudolph 277, Binns xxxi, Driver (1913) 62, McNeile (1911) 68, Gray (1903) 130-131, Holzinger (1903) xv.

47 Up to and including "inhabitants."

More recently, however, there has been a tendency to attribute to P a greater proportion of 13:28-14:9, in particular 13:33; 14:3[48] and, in the case of Budd, Coats and Noth, 14:8-9.[49] For the comparison we shall follow Noth and the others, and consider Num. 13:32-33; 14:2-3, 6-9 as the priestly counterpart of the exchange recounted in Deuteronomy.

Deut. 1:27-31 is generally regarded as coming from a single hand,[50] though a number of scholars have queried whether v. 31a, which uses the singular mode of address (in a predominantly plural context), is a later addition.[51] Its removal, however, would not substantially alter the discussion presented below.

Num. 13:32-33; 14:2-3, 6-9

Objections offered. Examination of Num. 13:32-33; 14:2-3, 6-9 reveals two reasons for not beginning the conquest. First, the land itself is presented as undesirable.[52] This is spelled out in 13:32 by both the narrator ("they brought...an evil report of the land") and the spies ("[it] devours its inhabitants"). It is also implied in 14:2-3 by the people's reaction to the spies' report. Their fear that they themselves will die ("fall by the sword") and their families be hunted down ("become a prey") is expressed in the context of several clear territorial references. They would rather have died "in the land of Egypt" or "in this wilderness", they question YHWH's bringing them "into this land, to fall by the sword" and they think of returning to Egypt.[53] Secondly, the inhabitants of the land are presented as superior to the Israelites.[54] This is indicated in 13:32-33

---

[48] Sturdy 94, Fritz 20.

[49] Budd 143, 151-152, Coats 138, Noth (1966) 90.

[50] See above, p. 13 n. 52.

[51] Preuß (1982) 46, 83, Mayes (1979) 131, Noth (1967) 31 n. 2, Smith (1918) 21, Steuernagel (1900) 6, Bertholet (1899) 3, 6; cf. Watts (1970) 195.

[52] Budd sees "a despising of land as 'evil'" as characteristic of the book as a whole (p. xxvi).

[53] Contrast Deut. 1:27-28, in which there is only *one* territorial reference, i.e. to YHWH bringing them "out of the land of Egypt", and the accusation that he has brought them forth "to give [them] into the hand of the Amorites, to destroy [them]" makes no mention of Canaan.

[54] It appears, however, that it is *the land itself* which constitutes the main objection to the Israelites entering, since its inhabitants are presented not just as enemies, who might be encountered anywhere, but as features of the landscape. The description "men of great stature" refers to "all the people that [the spies] saw *in it* (בתוכה)" (13:32), and the Nephilim, relative to whom they seemed like grasshoppers, were seen "*there* (ושם)" (13:33).

by the reference to their "great stature" and by the comparison with grasshoppers, and in 14:3 by the people's fears regarding their own fate.

Objections answered. Joshua and Caleb address both objections, though without answering every individual point raised. First, in response to the "evil report of the land" they affirm, on the basis of their own experience,[55] that it is "exceedingly good", "flow[ing] with milk and honey", and that entering it will be a consequence of YHWH's "delight" in the Israelites (14:7-8). Secondly, in response to the concern about the indigenous population, they inform the people that "the LORD is with us". While no indication is given as to how such assurance might allay the Israelites' fears, they clearly intend it to do so, since it is sandwiched between two injunctions against fearing the inhabitants of the land (v. 9).

Deut. 1:27-31

Objection offered. In Deut. 1:27-31 only *one* main reason is given for not entering the land, namely the perceived superiority of its inhabitants. The Israelites refer to their greatness and height, their fortified cities, the "sons of the Anakim", and to the likelihood of being destroyed by the Amorites (vv. 27-28). However, no mention is made of any undesirable features of the land as a reason for not beginning the conquest.[56]

Objection answered. As in the Numbers account, the leader (Moses) addresses the objection raised by the people. He also exhorts them not to fear the inhabitants (v. 29), but in this case because "The LORD your God...will himself fight for you" (v. 30). In contrast to Num. 14, however, he does not merely assert that God will be present, i.e. on the battlefield, but reminds the Israelites of a number of well-known instances of YHWH's acting on their behalf, in order to reassure them as to the certainty of his future assistance. First, Moses qualifies his initial reference to YHWH in such a way as to indicate that he is appealing to an aspect of the divine activity which is familiar to all. He describes the one who will fight for them as the God "who goes before [them]" (v. 30). In other words, they can be assured that YHWH will fight for them in the future because, as they themselves are aware, he is already acting on their be-

---

[55] Being "among those who had spied out the land" (v. 6), they refer to "[t]he land, which *we passed through*" (v. 7).

[56] Note the comments by Miller (1969) about the way in which the land is presented (in Deuteronomy) as "good" (pp. 456-457). Cf. Weinfeld (1991) 145, Brueggemann (1968) 394-396, Rennes 182.

half in the present by reconnoitring the territory ahead of them on their journeyings. Secondly, he cites from the past two, equally familiar, instances of YHWH's activity on their behalf which together cover the entire period from the Exodus to the present, and provide impressive grounds for believing that such activity will continue into the future. In v. 30 he reminds the Israelites that, as ("before [their] eyes") YHWH fought for them in Egypt, so he would be present and fighting for them in Canaan. And finally in v. 31, he recalls for them how (as "[they] have seen") "the LORD...bore [them]...in all the way that [they] went until [they] came to this place".[57]

It can thus be seen that the references to YHWH being with the people (Num. 14:9) and going ahead of and fighting for them (Deut. 1:30) play similar roles within their respective narratives. Both occur within the leaders' response to the people's murmuring, and both serve as part of an attempt to allay the Israelites' fear regarding the perceived prowess of the Canaanites. However, in view of the absence from Num. 14:9 of any locative verb or adverbial phrase qualifying YHWH's being "with" the people, it is likely that the Holy War terminology in Deut. 1:30 expresses a more localized form of divine Presence.

DEUT. 1:32-33 // ---

Both Num. 13:1-14:38 and Deut. 1:19-40 record the Israelites' response to their leaders' attempt at persuading them to begin the conquest. Num. 14:10 refers to the people's talk of stoning them, while Deut. 1:32 records merely their lack of belief in YHWH. In the latter case, however, the reference to the Deity is qualified in v. 33[58] by a reminder of his localized Presence with them in the wilderness:

Deut.	Num.
"Yet in spite of this word you did not believe the LORD your God, who *went before you* in the way to seek out a	

---

[57] The reference to YHWH bearing the Israelites "as a man bears his son" (v. 31) also serves, by the intimacy of its imagery, to counter the people's accusation that YHWH had brought them out of the land of Egypt because of his alleged hatred of them (v. 27).
[58] Generally thought to come from the same deuteronomistic hand as the rest of vv. 19-40, though see Preuß (1982) 46.

> place to pitch your tents, *in fire* by night, to show you by what way you should go, and *in the cloud* by day." (1:32-33)

Two points can be made about the role of this qualification within the narrative. First, since Moses is not representing it as a feature of the original incident, but as his subsequent reflection on their unbelief on the verge of the Promised Land,[59] one would not *expect* it to have any parallel in the Numbers account. Secondly, in contrast to v. 31, which by its use of the verb "bear" contains a figurative reference to YHWH's activity on the people's behalf in the wilderness,[60] v. 33 refers to the fire and the cloud veiling his guiding[61] Presence[62] during that period. In this way, Moses appeals yet again to the people's experience of phenomena which they themselves have observed, and indicates the absurdity of their unbelief. Deut. 1:33 thus constitutes a clear example of a heightened emphasis on divine Presence.

--- // NUM. 14:14

Following the report (14:10a) of the failure of Caleb and Joshua to persuade the Israelites to begin the conquest, Num. 14 records the appearing of the divine glory at the tent of meeting, and the subsequent conversation between YHWH and Moses. YHWH threatens to destroy the people (v. 12, cf. vv. 15-16) in response to their unbelief, but Moses successfully intercedes on their behalf (vv. 13-20). In Deut. 1, however,

---

[59] Lohfink (1960a) 116: "Nun schaltet sich Moses der Erzähler ein"; cf. Buis and Leclercq, who see the *narrator* as resuming speaking in v. 32 (p. 39).

[60] Smith (1918) regards the reference to YHWH bearing the Israelites as a "figure for the Divine Providence" (p. 21); cf. Watts (1970) 195.

[61] There may also be a touch of irony in the reference to YHWH looking for a site for them to pitch their tents, since according to v. 27 it is in these very tents that the people's rebellion is expressed.

[62] Many scholars relate Deut. 1:33 to (among others) Exod. 13:21(-22), which refers to YHWH's leading the Israelites in a *pillar* of cloud and fire: Ridderbos 61-62, Mayes (1979) 131, Cazelles (1966) 27, Davies (1962b) 874, Reider 16-17, Smith (1918) 21, Driver (1902) 25. In addition, Mann regards both הלך לפני and ענן as part of the OT terminology of divine Presence, and cites Deut. 1:33 in connection with both (pp. 253, 257).

there is no reference either to the glory of YHWH,[63] or to the ensuing dialogue. The failure of Moses' attempt at persuasion is indicated in vv. 32-33, but is followed immediately by a statement of YHWH's intention to prevent "this evil generation" from ever seeing the Promised Land (v. 35, cf. Num. 14:22-23). Consequently, the references to divine Presence[64] occurring in Moses' intercession in Num. 14:13-19 have no real[65] parallel in Deut. 1:

Deut.	Num.
————	"They have heard that thou, O LORD, art *in the midst of this people*; for thou, O LORD, art *seen face to face*, and thy cloud stands over them and thou *goest before them, in a pillar of cloud* by day and *in a pillar of fire* by night." (14:14aβb)

Broadly speaking, commentators fall into two groups in their source analyses of this section: those who regard it either as JE[66] or as a late/secondary expansion of J/JE,[67] and those who view it as being to a greater or lesser extent deuteronom(ist)ic.[68]

---

[63] If, as many scholars affirm, the "glory of YHWH" here is associated with the divine Presence, then Num. 14 reveals a heightened interest in the subject (i.e. relative to Deut. 1) at this point; cf. Budd 156-157, Wenham (1981) 122, Mann 258 with 261 n. 37, Jeremias (1976) 897, Snaith 243, Greenstone 140, Davies (1942) 28, McNeile (1911) 73, Gray (1903) 154, Holzinger (1903) 57.

[64] Cf. Levine 77, Eichrodt (1935) 2.

[65] The closely similar expressions occurring in Deut. 1:33 do not constitute a *real* parallel, since they are part of Moses' reflection on the people's lack of faith rather than of his intercession for them.

[66] Snaith 237, McNeile (1911) 68, 74-75, Gray (1903) 129, though see xxxii.

[67] Sturdy 102, Rudolph 77-78, 277, Binns xxxi, 93-94, Holzinger (1903) XV.

[68] Cf. Balentine (1985): "This framework [i.e. of Num.14] is supplemented by material from…the Deuteronomistic editors (vv. 11b-23)" (p. 66), Budd: "[V]v 11b-23a…are an expansion of the Yahwist's text…In view of the prominent deuteronomistic elements it would not be inappropriate to call it a deuteronomistic gloss" (pp. 152-153), Coats: "[The] intercession shows strong signs of late elements…it has strong reminiscences of the deuteronomistic theology of Yahweh's name" (p. 147), Noth (1966): "[D]er mit V. 11b einsetzende 'deuteronomistische' Einschub [wird] als mit V. 23a abschließend anzunehmen sein" (p. 97, cf. p. 96), von Rad (1964): "[D]ie grosse interzessorische Rede des Mose in 4. Mose 14, 13-19…[wird] meist als späterer und dem dt. Geist nahestehender Einsatz beurteilt" (p. 30).

Num. 14:13-19: deuteronom(ist)ic

While neither Coats nor von Rad presents a detailed analysis of the intercession, both Budd and Noth regard the greater part of v. 14aβb as deuteronomistic,[69] as presumably so does Balentine. If this ascription is correct, then Num. 14:14 constitutes a further instance of references to divine Presence coming from the hand of a deuteronom(ist)ic author.

Num. 14:13-19: JE, or a late/secondary expansion of J/JE

If, however, Moses' intercession is denied to a deuteronom(ist)ic hand, then its absence from Deut. 1 is unlikely to be due to deuteronom(ist)ic aversion to its notion of divine Presence, since all three expressions can be paralleled elsewhere in deuteronom(ist)ic contexts, two of them in Deut. 1 itself.[70] In any case, if Buis and Leclercq are correct in suggesting that a dominant theme in the historical retrospective (1:6-3:29) is the efficacy of the divine word in determining the course of Israelite history,[71] then the omission from Deut. 1 of all reference to Num. 14:11-20 is understandable,[72] since the latter concerns a divine word (v. 12) which, as a result of Moses' intercession (vv. 13-19), was *not* carried out (v. 20).

THE ISRAELITES' ABORTIVE ATTEMPT TO BEGIN THE CONQUEST

Following YHWH's instruction to head back towards the wilderness,[73] the people confess that they have sinned, and decide to enter the

---

[69] Apart from the references to YHWH's cloud "stand[ing] over [Israel]", his being "seen face to face" (Budd 152) and his being "in the midst of this people" (Noth [1966] 96).

[70] For references to YHWH being in the midst of the people see above, p. 21 n. 28, and to his going before them, in cloud and fire, cf. Deut. 1:33. There are no identical deuteronom(ist)ic instances of his being seen face to face (עִין בְּעַיִן), but cf. Deut. 5:4.

[71] "[L]es thèmes dominants…rôle de la parole de Dieu (ordres, promesses) qui dirige les événements et finit toujours par se réaliser" (p. 33); cf. Wolff: "[D]ie theologischen Leitmotive [des DtrG] sind weithin überzeugend geklärt. Die Geschichte wird als Eintreffen prophetisch verkündeten Gotteswortes verstanden" (p. 172), Lohfink (1960a): "[D]as eigentliche theologische Grundanliegen von Dtr ist das Funktionieren des göttlichen Wortes in der Geschichte" (p. 128 n. 7), and von Rad's observations on the interrelationship between YHWH's words and history ([1947] 52-64).

[72] Cf. Lohfink (1960a) for an alternative explanation for the non-occurrence of Moses' intercession in Deut. 1 (pp. 117-118).

[73] Deut. 1:40 // Num. 14:25.

land as originally commanded. Moses warns them against doing so, but
they refuse to listen. They are defeated (as predicted), and pursued by the
local inhabitants as far as Hormah (Deut. 1:41-44 // Num. 14:39-45).
Finally, they return to Kadesh (Deut. 1:45-46 // ---). Each account contains two references to divine Presence, that in Deut. 1:42 being paralleled in Num. 14:42, 43, while the one in Deut. 1:45 has no parallel.
These two references in Deut. 1 will be dealt with separately.

DEUT. 1:42 // NUM. 14:41-43

Deut.	Num.
"[T]he LORD said to me, 'Say to them, Do not go up or fight, for I am not *among you*;[74] lest you be defeated before your enemies.'" (1:42)	Moses said, "…Do not go up lest you be struck down be- fore your enemies, for the LORD is not *among you*… you shall fall by the sword… the LORD will not be *with you*." (14:41-43)

With the exception of the occasional scholar who tries to separate J
and E,[75] the majority allocate Num. 14:39-45 to J/JE.[76] Some regard
v. 39a as coming from P or consider the qualification ark "of the covenant" to be a deuteronom(ist)ic gloss. Neither of these suggested modi-
fications affects the discussion presented below.[77] Deut. 1:41-46 is generally regarded as coming from a single deuteronomistic hand.[78]

Num. 14:39-45

Before considering Num. 14:39-45 in detail, it will be necessary to
offer an interpretation of the apparently conflicting time references
which it contains. In v. 42 Moses tells the people not to go up into the
heights of the hill country, although, according to v. 40, they appear to

---

[74] The English of the RSV has been altered slightly in order to indicate the identity of
the Hebrew expression with that in Num. 14:42.
[75] De Vaulx 14-17, 177-179.
[76] Budd 154, Sturdy 106, Stolz 71, Fritz 20, 23, Coats 139, Snaith 237, Noth (1966)
98, Rudolph 277, Binns xxxi, 98-99, Eißfeldt (1922) 172*-173*, McNeile (1911) 68,
78, Gray (1903) 164, Holzinger (1903) XV, 54, 60.
[77] While Fritz (p. 23) and Maier (p. 4) eliminate *all* mention of the ark, most commentators regard v. 44b as an integral part of the narrative.
[78] See above, p. 17. Note, however, that v. 46 is sometimes viewed as an addition:
Mayes (1979) 133, Phillips (1973) 19, Smith (1918) 28.

have already done so.[79] These verses could be taken chronologically, in which case the positioning of Moses' injunction would seem to necessitate the reconstruction of a number of significant details.[80] Such scenarios are not without objection,[81] however, and it is preferable to take the v. 40 statement that they "went up" as a proleptic summary anticipating the slightly more detailed reference in v. 44 to their doing so, following on from the failure of Moses' attempts at dissuasion. On this view, all the direct speech recorded in these verses takes place *within the camp*, and the observation in v. 44, "[b]ut they presumed to go up", shows that Moses' warnings were of no avail, and that, as indicated earlier in the narrative, they did indeed go up. This interpretation puts the pericope in the category of "dischronologized" narrative as described by W.J. Martin,[82] and has the advantage of making sense of all the references to "going up" and, consistently with v. 44b, of confining Moses to the camp throughout the duration of the events described.

In Num. 14:39-45 a number of features stand out as being important regarding the question of divine Presence. First, despite the fact that both affirmations of YHWH's absence are made within the camp, the divine Presence is denied only to the *raiding party*. The warning in v. 43 makes this clear by its use of the imperfect: "the LORD will not be (ולא־יהיה)

---

[79] Gray (1903) wonders why the people should ascend to the summit (v. 40a) before announcing their intention of doing so (v. 40b). He resolves this and other difficulties by regarding the v. 40a reference to their going up as "an accidental intrusion" from v. 44 (p. 165).

[80] Such as the people's *descent*, i.e. assuming v. 40a to represent an initial sortie, in which case Moses is warning them against going up again (v. 42), or Moses' *accompanying or overtaking the people part way towards the hill country*, in which case he is telling them not to go up any further. Having failed to deter them he would then need to *return to the camp*.

[81] The use of the perfect with the conjunction in v. 40 ("we will go up" [ועלינו]) implies that the people's statement of intent was expressed prior to (or even during) their departure, i.e. while they were still in the camp, and the placing of Moses' dissuasion speech (vv. 41-43) immediately afterwards that it was made forthwith. Vv. 40-43 thus allow no room for the Israelites to have set out for, and possibly returned from, the hill country.

[82] The v. 40 reference to the people's "[going] up to the heights of the hill country" before Moses exhorts them "Do not go up lest you be struck down before your enemies, for the LORD is not among you" is an example of what Martin (1969) calls "[t]he later [being] mentioned before the earlier" (p. 182).

with you", while the presence of the ark within the camp (v. 44)[83] allows that the warning in v. 42, "the LORD is not among you", applies only to those about to set out, and does not necessarily preclude the possibility of YHWH being present elsewhere in the camp. Secondly, although both references to divine Presence are expressed negatively, YHWH's absence from the raiding party is presented as a merely *temporary* aberration resulting from the people's apostatizing behaviour: "because (כי־על־כן) you have turned back from following the LORD, the LORD will not be with you" (v. 43). This clearly implies that normally he is present on such raids, "among" or "with" the people. Thirdly, the forthcoming absence of YHWH from the battlefield is given by Moses as the reason why the Israelites will be defeated: "for (כי) the LORD is not among you" (v. 42). This absence is also implied in his further warning: "For there the Amalekites and the Canaanites are before you, and you shall fall by the sword; because you have turned back from following the LORD, the LORD will not be with you" (v. 43). Fourthly, the placing of the comment about the ark not leaving the camp (v. 44b) between the statement about the Israelites going up into the hill country (v. 44a) and the account of their rout (v. 45) strongly implies that the defeat is in some way connected with the ark's remaining behind. Thus in Num. 14:39-45, the Israelite defeat is ascribed *explicitly* to the absence of YHWH, and *implicitly* to that of the ark.

The section can therefore be understood in the following way: the presence (or otherwise) of YHWH in battle is the key factor determining whether (or not) the Israelites will win. The presence of the ark is significant only in so far as it functions as a focus for that Presence.[84] Thus, throughout the events described in the narrative YHWH remains in the camp, localized (in some sense) at the ark, and refusing to accompany the people into battle. Prior to the Israelites' setting out, Moses forecasts their defeat on the grounds that YHWH neither is, nor will be, among them, and that is substantiated by the narrator who indicates the absence from the battlefield of the ark. The defeat is clearly attributed to the absence from the skirmish of *YHWH himself.*

---

[83] Cf. Budd: "[The ark] remains in the camp, as a witness to Yahweh's absence from the expedition" (p. 160).
[84] Contra van Unnik 284 with 301 n. 51.

Deut. 1:41-44

First, as in Num. 14, it is from the *raiding party* that the divine Presence is withheld. YHWH's instruction to Moses in v. 42: "Say to them, Do not go up or fight, for I am not in the midst of you", is to be passed on to every man who has "girded on his weapons of war" (v. 41). Secondly, here also the reference to divine Presence (i.e. in v. 42) is expressed negatively, and here also YHWH's absence is represented as an anomalous state of affairs. Earlier in the chapter, when the people were originally commanded to go up into the land (v. 26),[85] Moses' words (vv. 26-33) indicate that, had they then obeyed, YHWH *would* have accompanied them on the battlefield (v. 30).[86] Their rebellion, however, has given rise to a new command, namely that they head back towards the wilderness, and it is in *this* situation that the divine Presence is denied to the expedition. Here also YHWH's absence is a *temporary* one, and his Presence "in the midst of" the people is regarded as the normal mode of his relationship with them.[87] Thirdly, as in Num. 14, YHWH's absence from the ranks is given as the reason why the Israelites will be defeated in battle:[88] "Do not go up or fight, for (כי) I am not in the midst of you; lest you be defeated before your enemies" (v. 42). In contrast to Num. 14, however, there is only one reference to divine Presence, though this is consistent with the relative amount of text devoted to the dissuasion attempt in the two accounts: vv. 41-43 in Num. 14, but only v. 42 in Deut. 1. It is also of interest to note that apart from minor differences resulting from a change in speaker, the reference to divine Presence in Deut. 1:42 (אינני בקרבכם) is identical to that in Num. 14:42 (אין יהוה בקרבכם). Fourthly, but in contrast with Num. 14, there is no mention of the ark. This however, has no significance for the current discussion,[89]

---

[85] The more obvious reference to the command to enter the land (v. 21) has not been cited, since it is sometimes considered (on the basis of its singular mode of address) to be an addition, cf. Preuß (1982) 46, Mayes (1979) 128, Smith (1918) 15, Steuernagel (1900) 4-5, Bertholet (1899) 5.

[86] See the discussion of Deut. 1:27-31 above, pp. 27-28.

[87] For positive deuteronom(ist)ic affirmations of YHWH's Presence "among" the people, see above, p. 21 n. 28.

[88] In this case, by YHWH himself, who is instructing Moses what he is to tell the people.

[89] Weinfeld (1972a), in a chapter arguing that the deuteronomic school "regarded *heaven* [our italics] as the exclusive place of God's abode" (p. 197 n. 3), i.e. in opposition to the belief that "the Deity sat enthroned [over the ark] between the cherubim in the temple" (p. 195), sees great significance in the omission of the ark from Deut.

since our concern is with the Presence of *YHWH* in the two accounts. As we have seen in the Numbers passage, the ark is significant only as a localization point for that Presence.

It thus appears that both Num. 14:39-45 and Deut. 1:41-44 refer directly to YHWH's localized Presence. They do so by affirming his absence, but in such a way as to imply that this was only temporary, and that normally he would be "among" his people. In Deut. 1:42 and Num. 14:42 the divine Presence references are virtually identical, and the occurrence of only *one* such expression in the Deuteronomy passage is in keeping with the very much shorter treatment accorded to its dissuasion section. It is clear that the narrator has made no attempt to remove the allusion to divine Presence at this point.

DEUT. 1:45 // ---

Both Deut. 1:41-46 and Num. 14:39-45 refer to the Israelites being chased by the inhabitants of the land as far as Hormah.[90] However, while Num. 14 finishes there, Deut. 1 concludes with a brief account of their return to Kadesh (vv. 45-46), and in this context there is a further possible reference to the divine Presence:

Deut.	Num.
"[Y]ou returned and wept *before the LORD*; but the LORD did not hearken to your voice or give ear to you." (1:45)	———

1:42-43. He points out that the change in its conception from being "God's seat upon which he journeys forth to disperse his enemies (Num. 10:33-6)" to being "only...the vessel in which the tables of the covenant are deposited" becomes quite clear when one compares Deut. 1:42-43 with Num. 14:42-44. He asserts that while Num. 14:44 gives the *ark's* remaining in the camp as the reason why the Israelites were defeated in their subsequent battle with the Amalekites and Canaanites, the deuteronomic account "omits the detail of the ark and ascribes the Israelite defeat to the fact that God was not in their midst without referring to the whereabouts of the ark" (p. 208); cf. Mayes (1979) 133. It would appear, however, that he has proved too much, since, in his concern to show that the ark is divested of any significance as a focus for the divine Presence, he has had, at the same time, to affirm the existence within Deut. 1 of the very notion which he claims to be absent, i.e. YHWH's being "in the midst of" the people (v. 42); cf. Gordon (1974) 118.

[90] *Re* the source allocations of these passages see above, p. 32.

The people weep after *returning*, i.e. at the place from which they originally set out. That their doing so "before" YHWH[91] *could* be a weeping
in the divine Presence can be seen from Num. 11:20,[92] in which the one
"before" whom they display such emotion is described as being "among"
them. The resulting portrayal, in Deut. 1:41-46,[93] of the divine whereabouts, would then be the same as that in Num. 14. YHWH is absent
from the raid (v. 42) but remains behind in the camp (v. 45).

Thus, to the extent that the people's weeping "before" YHWH can be
understood literally, it is clear that Deut. 1:41-46 contains a greater emphasis on divine Presence than Num. 14:39-45.

MOSES' INSTRUCTIONS TO THE TRANSJORDANIAN TRIBES

DEUT. 3:18 // NUM. 32:20-21

In Deut. 3:18-20 Moses reminds the Reubenites, the Gadites and the
half-tribe of Manasseh that, before they settle on the east bank of the
Jordan, they must first cross the river in order to assist the rest of the
people in their conquest of Cisjordan. In the passage from Numbers most
closely corresponding to this, i.e. 32:20-24, there are *four* occurrences of
the expression "before the LORD", the most significant being in v. 21.
The latter forms an interesting contrast to Deut. 3:18:

---

[91] Very few scholars comment on the significance of the phrase in Deut. 1:45, though
van der Woude (1976) refers to it (and other instances of לפני יהוה) as being "über den
Ort seiner Präsenz" (p. 458), and BDB includes it as an example of an act "done with
a solemn sense of [YHWH's] presence" (p. 817).

[92] The other OT instances of the expression are found in Judg. 20:23 (cf. v. 26; 21:2);
2 Kings 22:19; 2 Chron. 34:27.

[93] The additional verses (45-46) may have been included here in order to make a
point by linking v. 45 to v. 43 with the aid of the catch-word שמע ("to hearken"). Although YHWH tells the people not to go up or fight, they take no notice: "you *would
not hearken* (ולא שמעתם); but...rebelled...and went up into the hill country" (v. 43).
As a result they are defeated, return and weep before him. His response, however, is
the same as theirs was earlier: "the LORD *did not hearken* to your voice (ולא־שמע
יהוה בקלכם) or give ear to you" (v. 45). Cf. Mayes (1979): "Just as the people did not
listen to Yahweh...so Yahweh does not now listen to them" (p. 133). Note, however,
that such a link would not have been possible in the Numbers account since its dissuasion attempt is followed not by "you would not hearken" (as in Deut. 1:43), but by
"they presumed to go up to...the hill country" (14:44). In fact, the verb שמע does not
occur in Num. 14:39-45.

Deut.	Num.
"I commanded you at that time, saying, 'The LORD your God has given you this land to possess; all your men of valour shall pass over armed before your brethren the people of Israel.'" (3:18)	Moses said to them, "If...every armed man of you will pass over the Jordan *before the LORD*, until he has driven out his enemies from before him" (32:20-21)

The above juxtaposition raises the question as to whether the expression *"before your brethren"* represents a deliberate avoidance of the localized Presence of YHWH, i.e. in the service of a conscious theology of transcendence, or whether it can be explained in terms of the differing emphases of the two narratives concerned.

Apart from a few scholars whose analyses are rather complex,[94] most regard Num. 32:20-24 as coming from one source.[95] Some consider v. 24 to come from a different (usually later) hand,[96] but its omission would not affect the argument presented below. Deut. 3:18-20 is generally regarded as a unity.[97]

Num. 32:20-24

Between Num. 32:20-24 and Deut. 3:18-20 there are several clear differences, the interpretation of which would need to take into account any adjacent material from the same hands. In the case of Num. 32, however, while there is reasonable scholarly agreement as to the nature of its subdivisions, there is none as to the sources to which they should be allocated.[98,99] Thus, until such time as more of a consensus has developed, it will be necessary to propose a *provisional* interpretation of vv. 20-24.

Besides the four instances of לפני יהוה,[100] several features distinguish Num. 32:20-24 from Deut. 3:18-20. First, Moses envisages the possibility of the Reubenites and Gadites refusing to cross the Jordan: "if you

---

[94] Wüst 95, 99, 106, Holzinger (1903) XVII.
[95] Budd 342, de Vaulx 16, 367, Snaith 10, Noth (1966) 206, Heinisch (1936) 124, Binns XXXVIII, McNeile (1911) 170, Gray (1903) 426.
[96] Sturdy 221, Mittmann 104, Rudolph 278, Eißfeldt (1922) 193*-194*. Note that Mittmann and Eißfeldt also attribute v. 20α to the same source as v. 24.
[97] See above, p. 13 n. 52.
[98] See Budd 337-341 for a survey of scholarly views from Wellhausen onwards.
[99] Vv. 25-27, which are generally regarded as coming from the same hand as vv. 20-23/24, add little to our understanding of Moses' words in the latter.
[100] In vv. 20, 21, 22 (2x).

will not (ואם־לא) do so" (v. 23). Secondly, such a refusal is presented as
sin: "if you will not do so...you have sinned (חטאתם) against the LORD"
(v. 23). Thirdly, the giving of the land east of the Jordan to the two (and
a half) tribes is made conditional on their assisting the rest of the people
in their conquest of Cisjordan. This is stated explicitly in vv. 20-22:

> "*If* you will do this, *if* you will take up arms...and every armed
> man of you will pass over the Jordan before the LORD, *until*
> he has driven out his enemies from before him...then *after that*
> you shall return...and this land shall be your possession..."

It is also implied by the mention of their freedom from obligation to
YHWH and Israel (v. 22). Fourthly, these verses tend to refer to YHWH
as the one in relation to whom the actions of the Reubenites and Gadites
are carried out,[101] rather than as the subject of any action himself.[102]

These features can be understood as arising from Moses' stated antici-
pation of a Reubenite and Gadite refusal to assist in the conquest of Cisjordan. First, his specification of several of their activities as taking place
in relation to YHWH (i.e. as opposed to other humans) prepares the
ground for his evaluation of non-participation as sin against that same
YHWH, and serves to indicate to the Transjordanians both the true nature of the conquest and the way in which their refusal to assist in it
would be viewed. And secondly, the conditional nature of the gift of land
to them is clearly intended to discourage any such non-involvement.
Thus the reference to "every armed man...pass[ing] over the Jordan *before the LORD*" (v. 21) is to be seen as one aspect of Moses' attempt to
ensure that the Reubenites and Gadites do actually help in the conquest
of Canaan.

Deut. 3:18-20

For the following two reasons, the command to the men of valour to
"pass over armed" (v. 18) is unlikely to have entailed a deliberate rejection of "before the LORD" in favour of "before your brethren". First, and
despite Driver's (1902) contention that Deut. 3:18b is dependent on Num.

---

[101] Cf. their taking up arms (v. 20), crossing the Jordan (v. 21), obligation (v. 22),
possession of land (v. 22) and possible sinning (v. 23).
[102] Apart from: "until he has driven out his enemies from before him" (v. 21).

32:21,[103] the two verses exhibit a number of differences which would appear to militate against such a claim:

Num. 32:21a: ועבר לכם כל־חלוץ את־הירדן לפני יהוה

Deut. 3:18bβ: חלוצים תעברו לפני אחיכם בני־ישראל כל־בני־חיל

The differences can be illustrated by considering the part which חלץ plays in each of the two verses. In Num. 32:21 כל־חלוץ ("every armed man") is the third person singular subject of the verb עבר.[104] In Deut. 3:18, however, חלוצים serves as an adjective qualifying the second person plural subject of the verb תעברו, to which כל־בני־חיל ("all the men of valour" - roughly equivalent to "every armed man") stands in apposition. In view of such dissimilarities and the lack of any verbatim correspondence between the two verses, it would appear that evidence for the *literary* dependence of Deut. 3:18 upon Num. 32:21 is lacking. Secondly, even if such a relationship were to be demonstrated, it would be difficult to establish that the use of "before your brethren" constitutes a deliberate rejection of "before the LORD", since it is known that the Deuteronomist frequently incorporates within his œuvre traditions which include that very expression.[105] In any case, the notion of acting "before" human beings is already present in Num. 32, i.e. in v. 17,[106] and, provided that it is attributed to the same hand as vv. 20-23/24,[107] the most that could be asserted would be that the Deuteronomist has selected from his *Vorlage* one mode of crossing ("before [one's] brethren") rather than another ("before the LORD").

---

[103] See his Table on p. 51 in conjunction with the general remarks in his Introduction, pp. xiv-xv.

[104] Note, however, that the sentence also incorporates the *second* person form of address by using the preposition ל with the appropriate suffix.

[105] Within the Deuteronomistic History alone there are over ninety occurrences of לפני in combination with יהוה, אלהים or a suffix referring to the Deity. Few are regarded as post-deuteronomistic, and some are even thought to have come from the Deuteronomist himself.

[106] "[W]e will take up arms, ready to go *before the people of Israel*".

[107] Budd 342, Sturdy 221, de Vaulx 16, 367, Snaith 10, Rudolph 278, Heinisch (1936) 124, McNeile (1911) 170, Gray (1903) 426.

The meaning of "before your brethren". Few scholars comment on the expression, whether in this verse[108] or in the related Josh. 1:14 and 4:12.[109] Those who do, however, generally regard it as meaning "ahead of" the other tribes,[110] and thus that Moses is reminding the Transjordanians that they are to cross the river *first*. This interpretation is supported by those English versions which propose a rendering of the לפני other than the literal "before".[111]

The non-usage of "before the LORD". With respect to all four points[112] Deut. 3:18-20 contrasts noticeably with the Numbers account. There is no mention of the possibility of not crossing the Jordan, and so the designation of such as sin does not arise. The conditionality (which is merely implied [v. 20]) affects only the *return* to Transjordan (i.e. after the conquest), since its land has already been given (נתן [v. 18], נתתי [vv. 19, 20], cf. vv. 12-17). And finally, the emphasis on human action as taking place in relation to the Deity is lacking.[113] The key factor appears to be the absence of any anticipated Transjordanian reluctance to participate, and this would account for the absence of "before the LORD", as of any reference to sin or to the land as a gift conditional upon the Transjordanian

---

[108] Most tend to see Moses' instructions to the Transjordanians as indicating in a general way that they must participate in the conquest, i.e. as an expression of the "all-Israel" nature of the enterprise.

[109] Regarded as deuteronomistic by Gray (1986) 58, 72-73, Butler xxi, 19-21, Boling and Wright 126, 170, 175, Miller and Tucker 7, 21, 24, 42, Noth (1971) 9.

[110] Cf. Cairns: "The inheritors of Transjordan...are therefore urged to head the ongoing struggle" (p. 49), Ridderbos: "[T]hey were to cross the Jordan ahead of the other tribes" (p. 78), Rennes: "Moïse ordonne à celles...de passer en tête des autres tribus" (p. 26), and the translations by Weinfeld (1991): "You must go as shock troops, warriors all, at the head of your Israelite kinsmen" (p. 187), Clamer: "[I]l faut en faire la conquête à la tête de vos frères, les Israélites" (p. 533) and Steuernagel (1900): "[I]hr müsst...kampfgerüstet euren Brüdern, den Kindern Israel, voranziehen" (p. 13). Note also the comments on Josh. 1:14; 4:12 by Gray (1986) 58, 61, 72-73, Woudstra 66, 93, Mann 208 n. 9, Noth (1971) 29, Hertzberg (1959) 16, Bright 557, 570, Maclear 49, Roussel 37.

[111] In Deut. 3:18 לפני is variously rendered: "at the head of" (NEB, JB, JPSA), "ahead of" (NJB, NIV, TEV), "in front of" (Moffatt) and "in the vanguard of" (NAB). Others offer no interpretation of the preposition, preferring to translate it as "before" (NASB, RSV, ASV, RV, AV). The identical pattern emerges with Josh. 1:14; 4:12 (and Num. 32:17), though several of the versions are not particularly consistent in the way they express the idea of being "ahead of".

[112] See above, pp. 38-39.

[113] In Deut. 3:18-20 YHWH is the *subject*, being presented as the giver of both land (vv. 18, 20) and rest (v. 20).

tribes' co-operation. The whole mood of Deut. 3:18-20 is much lighter than that of Num. 32:20-24, and Moses' instruction to the Transjordanians to pass over "before [their] brethren" can be seen as a rather matter-of-fact reminder of what he had commanded them "at that time" (v. 18), i.e. to cross the river first.[114]

OVERALL COMPARISON OF THE DEUTERONOMY AND TETRATEUCHAL ACCOUNTS

Before an overall comparison of the Deut. 1-3 material with that in the Tetrateuch is attempted it will be useful to make a few observations about some obvious differences between them.[115] First, the Exodus and Numbers accounts consist of narrative about Moses and the people and, apart from the high proportion of dialogue which they contain, are written in the third person. In contrast, the deuteronom(ist)ic accounts, which also concern Moses and the people (or, in the case of 3:18-20, the Transjordanian tribes), do not consist of straightforward narrative, but are found within a speech addressed by Moses to the people and therefore have much material in the first and second persons. Secondly, the combined Exodus and Numbers accounts are much longer than those in Deuteronomy (42 verses, as opposed to 26).

THE FREQUENCY OF DIVINE PRESENCE REFERENCES

In sections common to Deuteronomy and the Tetrateuch

First, a comparison of those sections which Deuteronomy and Exodus/Numbers have in common[116] reveals that the deuteronom(ist)ic accounts have three-fifths the number of divine Presence expressions found in the tetrateuchal ones: while 14%[117] of the verses in Deuteronomy con-

---

[114] Cf. the comments on Josh. 4:12 by Roussel: "S'ils défilèrent devant les Israélistes, ils ont donc été mis en avant; est-ce parce qu'on voulait être sûr que, au dernier moment, ils ne resteraient pas, volontairement, en Transjordanie?" (p. 37), and Maclear: "Contrary to the usual order...as if to secure that they should fulfil their vow" (p. 49).
[115] The material compared concerns, in the Tetrateuch: Exod. 18:13-27; Num. 13:32-33; 14:2-3, 6-9, 13-19, 39-45; 32:20-24, while that in Deuteronomy incorporates 1:9-18, 27-31, 32-33, 41-46; 3:18-20.
[116] Deut. 1:9-18 // Exod. 18:13-27; Deut. 1:27-31 // Num. 13:32-33; 14:2-3, 6-9; Deut. 1:41-44 // Num. 14:39-45; Deut. 3:18-20 // Num. 32:20-24.
[117] The twenty-two verses concerned contain three references to divine Presence: 1:30 (2x) and 1:42.

tain such a reference, 23%[118] of those in Exodus/Numbers do so. Secondly, the two accounts twice employ parallel expressions in referring to the divine Presence. Both represent the people's leaders as answering their objection to beginning the conquest by assuring them of the divine Presence in order to allay their fears: in Deuteronomy Moses assures them, "The LORD your God *who goes before you will himself fight for you*" (1:30), while in Numbers Joshua and Caleb assure the Israelites, "the LORD is *with us*" (14:9). And both affirm the withdrawal of the divine Presence from the disobedient raiding party, while at the same time implying that such absence is only temporary: in Deuteronomy Moses is instructed by YHWH to tell them, "I am not *among you*" (1:42),[119] while in Numbers he warns them first, "the LORD is not *among you*" and subsequently, "the LORD will not be *with you*" (14:42-43). Thirdly, the tetrateuchal accounts have five references unique to themselves. In Exod. 18:19 Moses' father-in-law advises Moses to "bring [the people's] cases *to God*" (contrast Deut. 1, in which Jethro does not figure). And in Num. 32:20-24, which contains four instances of the expression "*before the LORD*", v. 21 refers to "every armed man of you [passing] over the Jordan *before the LORD*" (contrast Deut. 3:18, in which Moses instructs all the men of valour to pass over armed "before [their] brethren the people of Israel"). In both cases, however, an appeal to context adequately explains why the various (possible) references to divine Presence in Exod. 18 and Num. 32 have not been included in Deuteronomy: Deut. 1:9-18 shows little interest in the details of Moses' task and so contains no mention of his bringing the people's cases *to God*, while in Deut. 3:18-20 the absence of the four-fold occurrence of "*before the LORD*" (present in Num. 32:20-24) is primarily related to the absence of any anticipated Transjordanian reluctance to participate in the conquest of Canaan.

In sections occurring only in Deuteronomy

There are two groups of references to divine Presence occurring in Deuteronomy in passages without parallel in Exodus or Numbers: in 1:32-33 in Moses' subsequent reflection on the people's reluctance to enter the Promised Land he refers to YHWH's "[*going*] *before* [*them*]...*in fire* by night...and *in the cloud* by day" (v. 33). The reminder is *post-*

---

[118] The thirty-five verses concerned contain eight references to divine Presence: Exod. 18:19; Num. 14:9, 42, 43; 32:20, 21, 22 (2x).

[119] See above, p. 32 n. 74.

eventum, and so would not be expected to occur in Num. 13-14. Moreover, in 1:45-46, following the Israelites' ignominious rout at the hands
of the Amorites, he refers to their "[weeping] *before the LORD*" (v. 45).
No equivalent is found in Num. 14, since the latter makes no mention of
the return to Kadesh.

In sections occurring only in Numbers

Finally, there is one group of divine Presence references in Numbers
in a passage without parallel in Deuteronomy. Num. 14:14 is part of Moses' intercession in vv. 13-19 and refers to YHWH being "*in the midst of
this people*", "*seen face to face*" and "*[going] before [this people], in a
pillar of cloud* by day and *in a pillar of fire* by night". However, the portrayal in Deut. 1-3 of the efficacy of the divine word adequately explains
the absence from ch. 1 of the entire intercession, since Moses' prayer was
one which successfully *averted* the divine word (of judgement) promised
in Num. 14:12.

CONCLUSION

Within Deut. 1-3 references to divine Presence have been shown to
occur in two types of material. First, in passages where they parallel
similar (1:30 // Num. 14:9) or identical (1:42 // Num. 14:42) expressions
in the Tetrateuch and fulfil similar functions within their respective narratives. And secondly, in contexts which either could not or do not occur
in the corresponding accounts in Exodus/Numbers (1:32-33, 1:45).
Where, however, such expressions occur in the Tetrateuch (Exod. 18:19;
Num. 14:14; 32:20, 21, 22 [2x]) but not in Deuteronomy, their absence
from the latter can generally be attributed to the special emphases of one
or other of the accounts being compared. No necessity has been found
for positing a deuteronom(ist)ic antipathy to the notion of divine Presence.

3

DEUTERONOMY 4-5

Deut. 4-5 refers to the initial giving of the law on Horeb and thus deals with the same events as those described in Exod. 19-20. Both accounts contain a variety of possible references to divine Presence, and these will be considered in groups according as they occur in relation to the various phases of the law-giving.

PREPARATIONS FOR THE DECLARATION OF THE DECALOGUE

Deuteronomy devotes very little space to the time spent at Horeb immediately prior to the giving of the law. In marked contrast to Exod. 19, the whole of which is taken up with preparations for the declaration of the Decalogue, it allocates only two verses (4:10-11) to the same period. However, while the majority of references to divine Presence in Exod. 19 are conspicuous by their absence from Deut. 4,[1] both versions affirm that the Deity was present in the vicinity of the people just before his giving of the law. The evidence for this will be considered first, and then an attempt will be made to explain some of the more obvious omissions from the short account in Deuteronomy.

DEUT. 4:10-11 // EXOD. 19:17

Both Deut. 4 and Exod. 19 appear to indicate that the people's standing at the foot of the mountain was in close proximity to the Deity:

---

[1] See below, p. 50 nn. 22-24 for a complete list.

45

Deut.	Exod.
"[O]n the day that you stood *before the LORD your God* at Horeb, the LORD said to me, *'Gather the people to me...'* And you came near and stood at the foot of the mountain..." (4:10-11)	Moses brought the people out of the camp to *meet God*; and they took their stand at the foot of the mountain. (19:17)

In Exod. 19:17 the narrator refers to the people "meet[ing] God", whereas in Deut. 4:10 Moses reminds them of the occasion when they "stood before the LORD" and he was instructed to: "Gather [them] to [the LORD]". It will be necessary to consider each of these Deuteronomy expressions separately to determine whether or not they can be taken as indications of divine Presence.

Exod. 19:17 is usually attributed to the Elohist.[2] Deut. 4:9-14 is generally considered to come from a single deuteronomistic hand,[3] though the occasional scholar has queried whether vv. 9-10aα/10, which use the singular form of address (in contrast to the plural of the rest of the pericope), are a later addition.[4]

Exod. 19:17

According to Exod. 19:17 Moses brings the people out of their camp so that they can "meet God". This stated purpose implies that once they have taken their stand at the foot of the mountain, the Deity, if not already present, would approach sufficiently close to them so that they would then be in a position to "meet" him. That this denotes his localized

---

[2] Hyatt (1971) 199-200, Davies (1967) 153, Jeremias (1965) 103, 104, Beyerlin 16, Noth (1959) 123, 127, Beer 12, 96-97, Eißfeldt (1922) 147*, Driver (1911) 168, 173, McNeile (1908) xxvi, xxvii, 112, Holzinger (1900) XVIII.

[3] Knapp 112, Clifford (1982) 2, Preuß (1982) 47, Nelson 94, Mayes (1979) 44-45, 148-149, Levenson (1975) 221, Rose 149, Phillips (1973) 3, Watts (1970) 182, 200, Cazelles (1967) 219, Nicholson (1967) 31-32, Noth (1967) 39, Lohfink (1965) 18, 91-97, 100, von Rad (1964) 7, Buis and Leclerq 57 (see however, pp. 16-17, where 4:1-28 is allocated to the "première rédaction" before "L'École deutéronomique"), de Tillesse 32-33, Wright (1953) 317, 351. Note that Rose regards v. 9 as "sekundärer [dtr] Bestand" (pp. 149, 153).

[4] Preuß (1982) 47 (*re* vv. 9-10): "sing. Bearbeitung (bzw. Zusätze)", Mittmann 184 (*re* vv. 9-10aα): "eine singularische Ergänzungsshicht"; cf. Cazelles (1967), who regards vv. 9-10 as Deuteronomic, and therefore predating the Deuteronomistic Historian (pp. 215-219), Noth (1967), who refers to Dtr incorporating a short account (vv. 10-14) of the events at Horeb, but makes no comment on v. 9 (p. 39), de Tillesse 33 n. 3.

Presence in the immediate vicinity of the people is consistent with the earlier (Elohistic)[5] reference to Moses going up to God (v. 3a),[6] and is also stated explicitly by a number of scholars,[7] though the majority make no comment of any kind on it.

The act of "standing before"

Usage elsewhere. One way of discovering what is signified in Deut. 4:10 by the people's *"standing before* (עמדת לפני)*"* the Deity, is to examine instances of the same activity carried out in relation to human beings or objects. If this is done for its (for example) eighteen occurrences in the Deuteronomistic History, it is found that "to stand before" has at least three distinct meanings. First, there is the *literal* one. When A "stands before" B, A is presumed to be stationary, in an erect position on his/her feet, and in front of B.[8] The expression also occurs, with similar import, in a legal setting, where it is used of someone on a manslaughter charge appearing in front of the congregation for judgement.[9] Both usages clearly denote that B is in the immediate vicinity of A. Secondly, it is used in connection with *war*. When A "stands before" B, A is able to hold his own against B, or to "stand up to" B.[10] In this usage also, B *can* be in the immediate vicinity of A. There is, however, a non-literal aspect to the phrase, since although it may retain the aspect of A being in front of B, the *mode* of that being no longer refers primarily to A as stationary and erect, but rather involves the idea of A having sufficient skill in battle to avoid being put to flight. Thirdly, it can refer to *service*. When A

---

[5] Scharbert 80, Hyatt (1971) 200, Davies (1967) 153, Newman 40, 46, Beyerlin 13-16, Noth (1959) 123, 126, Eißfeldt (1922) 146*, Driver (1911) xxvii, 169, McNeile (1908) xxv, xxvii, 110, Holzinger (1900) XVII, 64.

[6] Frequently appealed to in support of the idea that in E God dwells on the mountain. Cf. Gispen 179, Knight 128, Michaeli (1974) 164, Hyatt (1971) 23, 196, Jeremias (1965) 104 n. 4. Newman 47, Beyerlin 12, Noth (1959) 128, Eißfeldt (1922) 46, Driver (1911) 169, Westphal 14.

[7] Durham 271, Gispen 183, Cassuto 232, Jeremias (1965) 104, Beyerlin 12, Noth (1959) 128.

[8] E.g. "Then King David answered, 'Call Bathsheba to me'. So she came into the king's presence, and stood before (ותעמד לפני) the king" (1 Kings 1:28); cf. 1 Kings 3:15, 16; 8:22; 2 Kings 4:12; 5:15; 8:9.

[9] Josh. 20:6, 9.

[10] E.g. "So the anger of the LORD was kindled against Israel, and he gave them over to plunderers, who plundered them; and he sold them into the power of their enemies round about, so that they could no longer withstand (לעמד לפני) their enemies" (Judg. 2:14); cf. 2 Kings 10:4.

"stands before" B, A is involved in serving B.[11] Here it is possible for B to be in the immediate vicinity of A, though not necessarily so. To "stand before" in this sense may include the literal meaning, but it is much broader. It has a clear metaphorical dimension, in that A's "standing before" may involve him not only in non-stationary duties, but also in fulfilling them out of B's presence, since his service to B may take him elsewhere.

To determine which usage of עמד לפני is intended in any given instance is clearly a matter of judgement, as there are no hard and fast rules. However, the presence or absence of certain features in the context tends to indicate whether the expression should be understood in a literal or more metaphorical sense. Any features of the narrative which show that the activity occurred on a specific occasion, e.g. references to time and place or to particular remarks made or actions carried out, point in the direction of a literal understanding, whereas their absence, coupled with indications that the activity occurred over an extended period of time or that service or aggression was involved, suggests a more metaphorical one.[12] Thus, in 1 Kings 1:28, when Bathsheba "stands before" David in his chamber on the day that she has told him about Adonijah becoming king, and hears him affirm his promise regarding the succession of Solomon, it is the very specificity of the occasion which leads one to deduce that she "stands before" him in a literal sense. On the other hand, in 1 Sam. 16:21, although David comes to Saul as a result of a particular request by the latter to David's father, when he "stands before him (i.e. Saul)"[13] there is nothing either said or done which indicates that his doing so takes place on a single specific occasion. We *are* told that "Saul loved him greatly" and that David "became his armour-bearer", but neither statement is restricted to a particular day. Thus the relative lack of specificity associated with David's "standing before" Saul, together with the clear intimations of a servant role (carrying Saul's armour and playing the lyre for him) lead one to deduce that the "standing before" is intended in a metaphorical way.

[11] E.g. "And David came to Saul, and entered his service (ויעמד לפניו). And Saul loved him greatly, and he became his armour-bearer" (1 Sam. 16:21); cf. Deut. 1:38; Judg. 20:28; 1 Sam. 16:22; 1 Kings 1:2; 10:8; 12:8.
[12] See below the similar point about interpreting לפני יהוה in general, pp. 156-157.
[13] Cf. "entered his service" (NRSV, NJB, JPSA, NIV, NEB, TEV, NAB, JB, RSV), "attended him" (NASB).

Significance in Deut. 4:10. Returning now to Deut. 4:10, with its reference to the people's "standing before *the LORD*", we discover several features of the narrative which indicate that Moses is referring to one particular occasion: both the time ("the day that...") and the place ("at Horeb") are specified, as are the instructions which YHWH gave to Moses ("Gather the people to me..."). It thus seems likely that in this instance the expression is intended to be understood literally, with the people conceived of as standing in front of YHWH.[14] This being the case, the corollary is that YHWH himself is regarded as being in *their* immediate vicinity, and thus present at Horeb.

The act of "gathering to"

Usage elsewhere. Deut. 4:10 also records YHWH's instruction to Moses: "*Gather the people to me...* (הקהל־לי את־העם)", which is the only OT instance of קהל (Hiph.) occurring with ל and followed by a person, object or place.[15] Elsewhere the Niphal is used with ל (once),[16] and the Hiphil and Niphal with אל (seven[17] and five[18] times respectively). Since, however, there is a straightforward relationship between the Niphal ("to assemble") and the Hiphil ("to gather", i.e. "to cause to assemble"), and ל and אל are often interchangeable, it would seem reasonable to presume that these other occurrences of קהל can be invoked in order to throw light on its usage in Deut. 4:10. In all thirteen instances the preposition is applied to a person, object or place, and in three of them it is clear from the context that when קהל (Hiph. or Niph.) is followed by either ל or אל the conclusion to be drawn is the same as that from their English equivalents, i.e. when A gathers B to C or when B assembles to C, then B ends up in the immediate vicinity of C. In Deut. 31:28 Moses requests that the elders etc. be gathered to him that he might speak these words "*in their ears*", in 1 Kings 8:2 the Israelites who assemble to Solomon are subsequently described as "*with him*" (v. 5), and in Jer. 26:9 the people

---

14 Reindl gives Deut. 4:10 as an example of "der wörtliche, lokale Sinn der Präposition [לפני]" (pp. 32, 245 n. 50). Cf. Nötscher 87: "Wo ihr buchstäblicher Sinn erhalten ist, bezieht sie sich auf den durch die Theophanie lebendig gegenwärtig gedachten Jahwe (vgl....etwa noch Dt. 4,10)", BDB 763.
15 In the other OT occurrences it is followed by an infinitive: 1 Kings 8:1; 12:21; Ezek. 38:13; 1 Chron. 13:5; 15:3; 2 Chron. 5:2; 11:1.
16 2 Chron. 20:26.
17 Lev. 8:3; Num. 16:19; Deut. 31:28; 1 Kings 8:1; 1 Chron. 15:3; 28:1; 2 Chron. 5:2.
18 Lev. 8:4; Judg. 20:1; 1 Kings 8:2; Jer. 26:9; 2 Chron. 5:3.

gather about Jeremiah, who subsequently *speaks to them* (vv. 12-15). The other ten instances are most naturally understood in the same way.

Significance in Deut. 4:10. Thus, when in Deut. 4:10 YHWH tells Moses, "Gather the people *to me*", it is strongly implied that as a result of doing so they would find themselves in close proximity to him. The injunction therefore provides further evidence of the divine Presence at Horeb.

This interpretation of YHWH's instruction to Moses is consistent with the purpose for which he wishes the people to be "gathered to him", namely, "that I may let them hear my words". The latter implies that if the people remain where they are they will not hear what he has to say, but that if they are "gathered to him" then they will. That their hearing of his words to them is dependent on where they themselves are located is consistent with YHWH himself being localized at a particular place,[19] i.e. in the fire with which the mountain was burning (v. 11).[20]

OMISSIONS FROM DEUT. 4:10-11

Exod. 19

It was indicated above that in Exod. 19 there are a number of other expressions which refer to the divine Presence in the vicinity of Horeb.[21] They can be classified into three groups: references to the Deity on the mountain following the Israelites' encampment before Sinai,[22] those to his approaching the mountain (mainly by descending on to it),[23] and those to the danger of the people and priests coming too near to him.[24] None of these has any parallels in Deut. 4:10-11. Before, however, their

---

[19] Hardly any scholars have been found to comment on either of the two allusions to divine Presence in v. 10. See, however, Braulik (1986) 41: "Die gemeinsame Gottesbegegnung lehrt 'Furcht'".
[20] See below for a detailed justification of this assertion (pp. 60-66).
[21] P. 45.
[22] "Moses went up *to God*, and the LORD called to him *out of the mountain*" (v. 3).
[23] "And the LORD said to Moses, 'Lo, I *am coming to you in a thick cloud*'" (v. 9), "[O]n the third day the LORD *will come down upon Mount Sinai*" (v. 11), "Mount Sinai was wrapped in smoke, because the LORD *descended upon it in fire*" (v. 18), "[T]he LORD *came down upon Mount Sinai*, to the top of the mountain" (v. 20a).
[24] "[W]arn the people, lest they break through *to the LORD to gaze* and many of them perish. And also let the priests who *come near to the LORD* consecrate themselves, lest the LORD break out upon them" (vv. 21-22), "[D]o not let the priests and the people break through *to come up to the LORD*, lest he break out against them" (v. 24).

absence from the latter can be explained, it will be necessary to ascertain the central concern of the pericope in which it is found.

Deut. 4:9-14

The focus of Deut. 4:9-14. In referring to the first giving of the law the writer is primarily interested in emphasizing those aspects of the event which the *Israelites* personally experienced. The positioning of vv. 10-14 immediately after v. 9, which is generally regarded as coming from the same hand,[25] and which exhorts Israel not to forget the things "which [*their*] eyes have seen", leads one to anticipate that the account will concentrate on what the people themselves had experienced on that occasion. Such an expectation is in fact borne out:

> "[O]n the day that *you* stood...the LORD said to me, 'Gather *the people* to me, that I may let *them* hear...so that *they* may learn...and...that *they* may teach *their* children so'. And *you* came near and [*you*] stood...Then the LORD spoke to *you*... *you* heard the sound of words, but [*you*] saw no form...And he declared to *you* his covenant, which he commanded *you* to perform...And the LORD commanded me...to teach *you* statutes and ordinances, that *you* might do them..." (vv. 12-14)

Moreover, in line with this emphasis on the people's experience the account betrays a marked lack of interest in what *Moses* did or said at Horeb.[26] This is clear from the fact that he is mentioned specifically only twice (in vv. 10 and 14), and in neither case as the subject of the sentence.

As to which aspect of their experience is highlighted, in v. 9 the people are exhorted not to forget what they themselves have seen. In vv. 10-14, there is a stress on YHWH's declaration of his words to them.[27] This is the aspect of the Horeb event to which attention is first drawn (v. 10) when the narrator reminds the people that the purpose for which YHWH wanted them gathered to himself was "that I may let them hear my words". It is also what appears to be emphasized once the people have assembled at the foot of the mountain:

---

[25] See above, p. 46 n. 3.

[26] Note Clifford's (1972) observation that in the Horeb traditions "the people generally play a large role, not Moses" (p. 109).

[27] Cf. "[W]e have this day *seen* (ראינו) God speak with man" (Deut. 5:24).

> "Then the LORD spoke to you...you heard the sound of
> words...And he declared to you his covenant, which he com-
> manded you to perform..." (vv. 12-13)

It is therefore difficult to avoid the conclusion that the writer is mentioning Horeb primarily to remind the Israelites that on that occasion they
themselves personally heard YHWH's declaration of his covenant to
them. The whole focus is on the *people's* experience, with that of Moses
occupying very much of a secondary role.

Explicable omissions from Deut. 4:10-11. It has already been noted that
the account of events at Sinai/Horeb prior to the first giving of the law
occupies an entire chapter of Exodus, but only two verses in Deuteronomy.[28] This fact alone should serve to explain why some of the references to divine Presence present in the former are absent from the latter.
More specifically, however, the concern of Deut. 4:9-14 to concentrate in
general on the experience of the people and in particular on the divine
speech addressed to and heard by them is sufficient to explain why all
reference to the events of Exod. 19:3-8, 10-15 and 20b-25 has been omitted. In all three sections *Moses* is the principal (human) actor,[29] YHWH's
words are addressed to *him* and not to the people, and the latter can reasonably be presumed to be out of earshot. None of the sections contains
divine speech either spoken to, and in the direct hearing of, the Israelites,
or taken up with the actual giving of the law (though all involve preparations for it). They therefore fall outside the strict concerns of Deut. 4:9-
14. This being the case, one need look no further for an explanation as to
why the divine Presence references contained in Exod. 19:3,[30] 21, 22 and
24 have not been included in Deut. 4:10-11.

The absence of reference to divine descent. So far Deut. 4:10-11 has
been compared with Exod. 19:17, since both appear to anticipate YHWH
as being in close proximity to the people immediately prior to the giving
of the law. It could also be compared with Exod. 19:9, since in both

---

[28] See above, p. 45.
[29] Cf. Nicholson (1973): "[I]n chapter 19, great emphasis is placed upon Moses and
his role as mediator between Israel and God" (p. 80).
[30] Note, however, that many scholars regard vv. 3b-8, with their reference to "the
LORD calling to [Moses] *out of the mountain*" (v. 3b), as deuteronom(ist)ic: Burns
145, Zenger (1978) 191, Mittmann 157, Childs (1974) 360-361, Michaeli (1974) 164,
Hyatt (1971) 200, Noth (1959) 126, Rylaarsdam 835; cf. Beer 12, McNeile (1908)
xxv, xxvii, 110-111.

places YHWH refers to the people's subsequent hearing of what he has to say:

Deut.	Exod.
"[T]he LORD said to me, 'Gather the people to me, that I may let them hear my words...'" (4:10)	[T]he LORD said to Moses, "Lo, I am *coming* to you *in a thick cloud*, that the people may hear when I speak with you..." (19:9)

However, while the latter describes YHWH as "coming...in a thick cloud", neither this, nor the three direct references to divine descent in vv. 11, 18 and 20a, finds any parallel in the deuteronomistic account. This omission is a little strange in view of the presumed visibility of the divine "vehicle",[31] the implication in Exod. 19:11 that the people did in fact witness the descent (לעיני כל־העם), and the clear appeal (in Deut. 4:9) to what the Israelites had *seen* with their own eyes. Whatever may be the reason, however, the absence of any reference to divine descent in this context is consistent with the absence of such references from the Deuteronomistic History as a whole.[32]

Nevertheless, while Deuteronomy makes no mention of YHWH's descent in its reflection on the events leading up to the giving of law, it does, by its references to the people *standing before* and being *gathered to* him, indicate that on that occasion the Deity was localized at Horeb in the immediate vicinity of the Israelites. In this respect it is no different from Exodus.

THE DECLARATION OF THE DECALOGUE

Although in Exodus it is clearly implied by the context of 20:1 that YHWH communicated the Decalogue while localized on Mount Sinai,[33]

---

[31] "Cloud" (Exod. 19:9) and/or "fire" (Exod. 19:18).

[32] Deut. 31:15, in which divine descent may be implied (see above, p. 23 n. 40), and 2 Sam. 22:10 (// Ps.18:10 [EVV 9]) are widely regarded as being *post*-deuterono–mistic: Preuß (1982) 162, Phillips (1973) 205, 207-208, Noth (1967) 40, Buis and Leclercq 17-18 (*re* Deut. 31:15); McCarter (1984) 475, Mayes (1983) 166 n. 12, Noth (1967) 62 n. 3, Weiser (1966) 155, Caird 862, 865 (*re* 2 Sam. 22:10). Cf. Mettinger 125: "[T]he primal theological datum of the D-Work is a theophany, although no mention is made of God's 'descent'."

[33] I.e. by the references to divine descent (19:18, 20), the dangers inherent in approaching him (19:21-22, 24), and the thick darkness "where God was" (20:21).

it is only in Deuteronomy that it appears to be stated *explicitly*, and in three ways. Each of these possible indications of divine Presence will be discussed in turn.

DEUT. 4:12; 5:4, 22 // EXOD. 20:1

Deut.	Exod.
"[T]he LORD spoke to you *out of the midst of the fire*... And he declared to you his covenant...that is, the ten commandments..." (4:12-13)	God spoke all these words, saying... (20:1)

"The LORD spoke with you...*out of the midst of the fire*...He said..." (5:4-5)

"These words the LORD spoke to all your assembly... *out of the midst of the fire, the cloud, and the thick darkness*..." (5:22)

As was pointed out earlier in the discussion of Deut. 4:9-14, Deut. 4:12-13 is generally regarded as being deuteronomistic.[34] Deut. 5:4-5 is usually thought to be either deuteronomic[35] or deuteronomistic,[36] though some scholars view v. 5 (except for its last word) as a post-deuteronomistic addition.[37] Deut. 5:22-27 also tends to be attributed to either deuteronomic[38] or deuteronomistic[39] authorship.

---

[34] See above, p. 46 n. 3.
[35] Clifford (1982) 2-3, Nelson 91-92, Seitz 49, 308, Watts (1970) 180-182, Noth (1967) 16, von Rad (1964) 7, Buis and Leclercq 16, Wright (1953) 316, 361.
[36] Preuß (1982) 48, 100, Mayes (1979) 161, Phillips (1973) 42, Nicholson (1967) 26, 31-32, 36, 108, de Tillesse 35, 43-44, 73.
[37] Preuß (1982) 48, Mayes (1979) 161, 166, Nicholson (1977) 431 n. 13, Seitz 49; cf. Cunliffe-Jones 49, Welch (1932) 18, Hölscher (1922) 169, Steuernagel (1900) 21, Bertholet (1899) 21, Dillmann 265-266, Robinson (n.d.) 84.
[38] Clifford (1982) 2-3, Nelson 91-92, Watts (1970) 180-182, Noth (1967) 16, von Rad (1964) 7, Buis and Leclercq 16, Wright (1953) 316, 361. Note that von Rad wonders whether vv. 6-22 are a later interpolation (p. 43).
[39] Mayes (1979) 42, 161, Phillips (1973) 3, Nicholson (1967) 26, 31-32, 36, 108, de Tillesse 35, 43-44, 73; cf. Preuß (1982), who describes Deut. 5:22-33 as "die (dtn)/dtr [*sic*] Ausführung" of Exod. 20:18-21 (p. 101).

However, in addition to Deut. 4:12-13 and 5:4-5, 22, which refer to YHWH speaking to the Israelites "out of the midst of the fire", there are in Deuteronomy a further seven instances of communication in this particular way:

> "Therefore take good heed to yourselves. Since you saw no form on the day that the LORD spoke to you at Horeb *out of the midst of the fire*, beware lest you act corruptly by making a graven image for yourselves..." (4:15-16)

> "Did any people ever hear the voice of a god speaking *out of the midst of the fire*, as you have heard, and still live?" (4:33)

> "Out of heaven he let you hear his voice, that he might discipline you; and on earth he let you see his great fire, and you heard his words *out of the midst of the fire*." (4:36)

> "[A]nd you said, 'Behold, the LORD our God has shown us his glory and greatness, and we have heard his voice *out of the midst of the fire*; we have this day seen God speak with man and man still live.'" (5:24)

> "'For who is there of all flesh, that has heard the voice of the living God speaking *out of the midst of fire*, as we have, and has still lived?'" (5:26)

> "And the LORD gave me the two tables of stone written with the finger of God; and on them were all the words which the LORD had spoken with you on the mountain *out of the midst of the fire* on the day of the assembly." (9:10)

> "And he wrote on the tables, as at the first writing, the ten commandments which the LORD had spoken to you on the mountain *out of the midst of the fire* on the day of the assembly; and the LORD gave them to me." (10:4)[40]

---

[40] The references in 4:12 and 5:4, 22 to this particular mode of communication fulfil a basically *narrative* function, i.e. in connection with the first giving of the law, whereas those in the seven additional instances perform a variety of roles. In 4:15 the Israelites' lack of perception of any divine form (in the fire?) is made the basis of a discourse on the prohibition of images. In 4:33 the people are invited to reflect on the significance of having survived hearing YHWH speak from the fire, and in 4:36 his having allowed them to hear his words in this way functions as part of an argument for keeping his statutes and commandments. In 5:24 and 26 Moses reminds Israel of their immediate reaction to the experience, and finally, in 9:10 and 10:4, YHWH's addressing them out of the fire is used to specify more closely what was written on the two sets of tables.

Thus before considering the significance of YHWH's speaking "out of the midst of the fire", it will be necessary to mention the sources to which these seven other instances of the expression have been allocated. Deut. 4:15-24 is generally regarded as being deuteronomistic,[41] though a minority of scholars exclude those parts of it which use the singular form of address (vv. 19, 21bβγ and 23bβ-24).[42] Their removal, however, would make little difference to the argument presented below. Deut. 4:32-40 is also usually thought to be deuteronomistic,[43] though some scholars believe the whole of it to be a post-deuteronomistic addition.[44] Deut. 9:10 and 10:4 are considered to be either deuteronomic[45] or deuteronomistic.[46]

It can therefore be seen that the above six sections are regarded by the majority of scholars as being either deuteronomic or deuteronomistic. None is generally agreed to be more recent, and so all ten instances of divine communication out of the fire occur in deuteronom(ist)ic contexts.

Exod. 20:1

In contrast to Deut. 4:12; 5:4 and 22 (in the quasi-narrative sections of Deuteronomy), Exod. 20:1 contains no reference to YHWH speaking "out of the midst of (מתוך) the fire". It merely records that "God spoke all these words". Neither is there mention of this particular mode of commu-

---

[41] Clifford (1982) 2, Preuß (1982) 47, Nelson 94 (assuming that he ascribes the "somewhat later addition" of vv. 15-18, 23-28 to one of the "later Deuteronomists" [p. 92]), Mayes (1979) 44, 45, 148, Levenson (1975) 221, Rose 149, Phillips (1973) 3, 12, Watts (1970) 182, 200, Cazelles (1967) 219, Nicholson (1967) 20, 31-32, 36, 108, Lohfink (1965) 18, 91, 92, 93, 96, 100, von Rad (1964) 7, Buis and Leclercq 57 (contrast 16, in which 4:1-28 is attributed to the "première rédaction" before "L'École deutéronomique"), de Tillesse 32-33, Wright (1953) 316, 317, 351. Note that with the exception of vv. 22-23a, which he attributes to Dtr, Noth (1967) regards the section as *post*-deuteronomistic (pp. 37-39).

[42] Preuß (1982) 47, Cazelles (1967) 213-219; cf. Noth (1967) 38, de Tillesse 33 n. 3.

[43] Clifford (1982) 2, Mayes (1979) 44, 45, 148, Levenson (1975) 221, Rose 149, Phillips (1973) 3, 12, Watts (1970) 182, 200, Nicholson (1967) 20, 31-32, 36, 108, Lohfink (1965) 18, 91, 92, 93, 96, 100, von Rad (1964) 7, Buis and Leclercq 17-18, 61, Wright (1953) 316, 317, 351.

[44] Preuß (1982) 47, Nelson 94, Noth (1967) 37-39, de Tillesse 33 n. 3.

[45] Watts (1970) 180-181, Noth (1967) 16, 17, Cazelles (1966) 15, Wright (1953) 316, 317, 361.

[46] Preuß (1982) 49-50, 102, Mayes (1979) 42, 195, Phillips (1973) 12, 69, Nicholson (1967) 30-31, Buis and Leclercq 17, 89, 91 (contrast 16, in which 5:1-9:10 is attributed to the "première rédaction" before "L'École deutéronomique"), de Tillesse 45-46, 56-63, 83; cf. von Rad (1964) 7, 54-55.

nication in any of the three chapters (Exod. 19-20, 24 [and 31:18]) devoted to the events accompanying the initial giving of the law, even
though fire is described as the vehicle of YHWH's descent on to Sinai
(Exod. 19:18). In fact, there is only one such instance in the book as a
whole, i.e. in the account of Moses and the burning bush:

> When the LORD saw that he turned aside to see, God called to
> him out of (מתוך) the bush... (3:4)[47]

Within its own version of the first giving of the law, the nearest that Exodus approaches to this kind of divine communication is in 24:16, where
YHWH is represented as calling to Moses "out of the midst of (מתוך)" a
cloud. It is important to note, however, that although fire *is* mentioned in
the immediate context, it is not portrayed as the medium from which
YHWH speaks, but as that to which the divine glory could most appro-
priately be compared: "[T]he appearance of the glory of the LORD was
like a devouring fire (כאש אכלת)" (v. 17). Thus, although Exodus as a
whole contains closely related ideas, it is only in Deuteronomy's account
of the first giving of the law that reference is made to YHWH's speaking
"out of the midst of the fire".

Communication "out of the midst of the fire"

Characteristics. With regard to the ten instances of divine communication "out of the midst of the fire" a number of points can be made.[48]
First, the idea is expressed either by reference to YHWH's *speaking* (דבר
[Piel]),[49] or by the people *hearing* (שמע) his words or voice[50] "out of the
midst of the fire", or by a combination of the two.[51] Secondly, eight of
the ten instances specify the site at which the communication took place,
either themselves (4:15 ["at Horeb"]; 5:4, 22 ["at the mountain"];[52] 9:10;
10:4 ["on the mountain"]) or in their immediate context (4:12, cf. vv. 10
["at Horeb"], 11 ["the mountain"]; 5:24, 26, cf. vv. 22 ["at the mountain"], 23 ["the mountain"]). The other two (4:33, 36) make no such

---

[47] Cf. "[T]he angel of the LORD appeared to him in a flame of fire out of the midst
of (מתוך) a bush" (v. 2).
[48] The discussion will include reference to *all* the instances of such communication
in Deuteronomy.
[49] Deut. 4:15; 5:4, 22; 9:10; 10:4.
[50] Deut. 4:36; 5:24.
[51] Deut. 4:12, 33; 5:26.
[52] Identified as Horeb in v. 2.

58   *Out of the Midst of the Fire*

identification, but it would seem reasonable to presume that the writer
has the same site in mind. Thirdly, the majority of cases indicate that it
was the initial giving of the law which occurred "out of the midst of the
fire".[53] The other two instances (4:33, 36) make no clear reference to the
content of the revelation, either themselves or in the surrounding context.
The emphasis in 4:33 seems to be on the fact of hearing YHWH's voice
rather than on what was actually said, and the same may be true in 4:36
of the people's hearing "his words" (דבריו). The latter, however, may represent an allusion to the law, since in Hebrew the commandments are
usually referred to as the ten *words*.[54] Fourthly, in all ten instances the
emphasis is on the *people* as those who have experienced the divine
communication "out of the midst of the fire". Moses points this out to
them himself in 4:12, 15, 33, 36; 5:4, 22; 9:10; 10:4, and in addition reminds them of their own earlier acknowledgement of that experience in
5:24, 26. There are no examples of such communication to Moses himself, whether alone or in company with the Israelites.[55] The focus of attention is solely on the people. Fifthly, the expression "out of the midst
of the fire" is used to qualify the majority of the references to YHWH's
audible communication of the law to the people at Horeb. Apart from the
ten instances under discussion there are only three clear examples of his
addressing (דבר [Piel], אמר) the Israelites at Horeb, and only five references to the people hearing (שמע) him there. Of the three other instances
of divine communication to the people, two are in close proximity to one
of the ten already mentioned,[56] and so can reasonably be understood as
themselves occurring "out of the midst of the fire": 5:5 (אמר, cf. v. 4),
5:24b (דבר [Piel], cf. v. 24a). The third instance is in 1:5-6:

---

[53] Deut. 4:12, 15, cf. v. 13 ("[H]e declared to you his covenant, which he commanded you to perform, that is, the ten commandments; and he wrote them upon two
tables of stone"), 5:4, cf. vv. 2, 5-6 ("The LORD our God made a covenant with us...
He said: 'I am the LORD your God...'"), 5:22, 24, 26, cf. v. 22 ("These words [i.e.
vv. 6-21] the LORD spoke to all your assembly...out of the midst of the fire...And
he wrote them upon two tables of stone"), 9:10 ("[T]he LORD gave me the two
tables of stone written with the finger of God; and on them were all the words which
the LORD had spoken with you...out of the midst of the fire"), 10:4 ("[H]e wrote on
the tables...the ten commandments which the LORD had spoken to you...out of the
midst of the fire").
[54] Cf. עשרת הדברים in Exod. 34:28; Deut. 4:13; 10:4.
[55] Note the absence from Moses' lips of affirmations such as "YHWH spoke to *us*" or
"*we* heard his voice" מתוך האש.
[56] See above, p. 55.

> Moses undertook to explain this law, saying, "The LORD our God said (דבר [Piel]) to us in Horeb, 'You have stayed long enough at this mountain...'"

In this case, however, the context contains neither reference to YHWH speaking from the fire nor to fire itself, and the divine remark is directed at Moses as well as the people (אלינו). These differences from the ten texts under consideration may be accounted for by the observation that while the site referred to is Horeb, the occasion is not the giving of the law but YHWH's instruction to Moses and the people to depart from the mountain, i.e. after the law-giving has been completed. Similarly, of the five other examples of the people hearing YHWH at Horeb, three are in close proximity to one or more of the ten under discussion, and so also can reasonably be understood as involving divine communication from the fire: 4:10 (שמע [Hiph.], cf. v. 12); 5:23,[57] 25 (שמע, cf. vv. 22, 24, 26). 18:16 (שמע), however, has no such instances in its context, though fire is mentioned,[58] and 4:36 (שמע [Hiph.]) refers to the people hearing YHWH's voice "*out of heaven*". While the significance of the latter will be discussed in detail below,[59] suffice it to note here that it too is mentioned in the context of divine communication "out of the midst of the fire".[60]

Thus, apart from 4:36, which refers in addition to the people hearing YHWH's voice "out of heaven", and 18:16, which mentions fire but no divine speech coming from it, all other references to the Deity declaring the law to the people, or to their hearing that law by means of his voice or words, specify (either explicitly or in context) that the divine communication proceeded from the fire. It seems, therefore, that for Deuteronomy/the Deuteronomist it was important not only to indicate that at

---

[57] Deut. 5:23 refers to the people hearing the voice "out of the midst of the *darkness* (החשך)". That this is sandwiched between two verses (vv. 22, 24) indicating that YHWH's communication was "out of the midst of the *fire*", implies that the two phenomena were closely related. Cf. v. 22: "[T]he LORD spoke...out of the midst of the fire, the cloud and the thick darkness (הערפל)".

[58] "[J]ust as you desired of the LORD your God at Horeb on the day of the assembly, when you said, 'Let me not hear again the voice of the LORD my God, or see this great fire any more, lest I die.'"

[59] Pp. 66-73.

[60] "Out of heaven he let you hear his voice, that he might discipline you; and on earth he let you see his great fire, and you heard his words out of the midst of the fire."

Horeb YHWH conveyed his law to the people, but also that he did so
"out of the midst of the fire".

Its plain implication. If YHWH is represented as speaking "out of the
midst of" a fire, then that would seem to suggest, *a priori*, that he is considered to be present within that fire. The same could be said when the
people are portrayed as hearing either his voice or his words "out of its
midst".[61]

Usage elsewhere. Within the OT as a whole there are six other instances
of communication out of or in "the midst of" something. Four refer to
human, and two to divine, speech. Of the former group three involve תוך
in combination with ב,[62] but the fourth employs מן:

> "The mighty chiefs shall speak of [the multitude of Egypt],
> with their helpers, out of the midst of (מתוך) Sheol: 'They have
> come down, they lie still, the uncircumcised, slain by the
> sword.'" (Ezek. 32:21)

While many scholars make no clear comment as to the significance of
the chiefs speaking "out of the midst of" Sheol,[63] those that do indicate
that they consider them to be present there themselves.[64] In addition,
both instances of *divine* communication involve מן, the Deity being represented as calling to Moses "out of the midst of" (מתוך) a bush (Exod.
3:4) and a cloud (Exod. 24:16) respectively.[65] In each case it is generally
thought, either explicitly or by implication, that the writer is affirming

---

[61] Note, however, that these alternative expressions of the people's experience are
more susceptible of being understood in terms of YHWH as divine ventriloquist, in
heaven but projecting his voice/words through the fire on the mountain. Cf. Weinfeld
(1972a) 206-207, McBride 2.

[62] Pss. 22:23 (EVV 22): בתוך, 109:30: ובתוך, and 116:19: בתוככי.

[63] Fuhs 177, Cody 153-154, Wevers 244-246, Zimmerli (1969) 786, Stalker 233-234,
Eichrodt (1966) 301-303, Cooke 350-352.

[64] Allen 137: "It may be that...the valiant ones...greet the newcomers and from their
own more comfortable quarters [i.e. in Sheol] point to the lower regions, where the
Egyptians were to go", Carley 216: "[T]hose already in Sheol greet with scorn the
mighty ruler who descends among them", Taylor 211: "[Egypt's] arrival is greeted by
mocking words of welcome from the mighty chieftains who are already [in the
underworld]", Fisch 218: "The leaders of the nations already in Sheol are represented
as speaking about Pharaoh and his allies on their appearance in their midst", Heinisch
(1923) 153: "Wenn...der Pharao [in die Unterwelt] ankommt, werden die 'Helden'...
ihn mit Hohn empfangen. Sie halten ihm vor...Er muß weiter hinab in die Tiefen des
Hades...bei 'Unbeschnittenen', seine Stelle einzunehmen."

[65] See above, p. 57.

the Presence of the Deity within that from which he speaks.[66],[67] In view
of this, it would seem reasonable to presume that in the eight deuterono-

---

[66] *Re* Exod. 3:4: Scharbert 21: "Dem Leser verrät J, daß es sich um eine Gotteser-
scheinung handelt", Durham 31: "Finally, in the ultimate certification of a theophanic
site, a place where God is present, Moses is told that he stands…on holy ground",
Burns 45: "When Moses turned to investigate the fire, he did not yet know he was in
the presence of God", Gispen 52: "The Lord Himself was in the bush", Zenger (1978)
44: "In 3,1-6 stammt die Erzählung von der Erscheinung Jahwes aus dem Dorn-
strauch vom jehowistischen Erzähler, in dessen Geschichtsdarstellungen Gotteserscheinungen an heiligen Orten eine wichtige Rolle spielen", Jeremias (1976) 897:
"Moses (Exod. 3:1ff.)…[was] called and commissioned through [an] appearance of
God at a holy place", Knight 21: "The living God is in the Bush"; Michaeli (1974)
48: "Dieu avait choisi un buisson d'épines…pour marquer sa présence", Clements
(1972) 20: "[T]he fire here is…a sign of the presence of God"; Schnutenhaus 12: "An
seiner Stätte war der Gott anwesend, wie z.B. Ex 3:5 zeigt", Davies (1942) 15: "J introduces certain limitations into the manifestation of Yahweh…[he] is veiled in the
bush", Beer 26: "Jahwes Gegenwart bekundet sich im brennenden Dornbusch",
Heinisch (1934) 49: "Moses soll zum Zeichen, daß er in der Gegenwart Gottes rein
sein muß, seine Sandalen ablegen", Driver (1911) xix: "Jehovah appears to Moses in
the burning bush", Morgenstern (1911) 166: "[Exod. 3:2-4a] pictures Jahwe as re-
vealing Himself to Moses in the midst of the bush", McNeile (1908) 16: "It was a frequent conception among the ancients that the divine presence shewed itself by an appearance of fire"; cf. the characterization of the event as involving a theophany by:
Tournay 54, Cohn 47-48, Terrien (1978) 109-112, Childs (1974) 53, 60, 70, 72-74,
Cassuto 31, Lindblom 103, Noth (1959) 21, 25, Holzinger (1900) 10.

[67] *Re* Exod. 24:16: Scharbert 101: "Mose geht in die Wolke hinein…während das
Volk die Gegenwart Jahwes in der leuchtenden Wolke wahrnimmt", Gispen 241:
"God descended and was present on this mountain…the Lord Himself dwelled tem-
porarily on Mount Sinai", Mann 154: "Moses is allowed to enter the cloud, which
conceals the divine presence", Knight 159: "'[S]ettled'…described the 'resting' of the
special presence of God at a chosen spot", Clements (1972) 160: "God's glory…rep-
resents God's presence…and is intended to affirm that his presence was with Israel",
Weinfeld (1972b) 1016: "The cloud serves as an envelope which screens the Deity
from mortal view", Hyatt (1971) 258: "[The] glory of the LORD…is one of the terms
used for the visible manifestation of the Deity…The Priestly narrative uses the term
to express various appearances of Yahweh", Cassuto 316: "[Vv. 16-18] portray…the
theophany on Mount Sinai and Moses' approach to the site of the Divine manifestation", Davies (1967) 197: "[T]he cloud covers Sinai to show that God is in residence…on this mountain", Noth (1959) 162: "[D]ie 'Herrlichkeit' Jahwes, die die
göttliche Gegenwart repräsentiert…sich nieder[läßt auf dem in einer Wolke verhüll-
ten Berg]", Heinisch (1934) 196: "Josue [durfte] ihm nur ein Stück des Weges folgen
bis zu der Wolke, welche die göttliche Gegenwart anzeigte", McNeile (1908) 149:
"[T]he glory of Yahweh [is] the visible manifestation of His presence", Holzinger
(1900) 106: "[I]n der Hülle der Wolke verbirgt [Gott] sich…Auch Mose darf nicht
ohne weiteres aus dem Alltäglichen heraus in die Nähe Gottes kommen, sondern
muss…6 Tage lang warten"; cf. Terrien (1978) 172, 423-424, 425-426, Childs (1974)
508, Jeremias (1965) 103, 104.

m(ist)ic references to YHWH's speaking to the people "out of the midst of (מתוך)" the fire[68] he is likewise to be regarded as being present within the fire.

The significance of seeing no form. The use to which the deuteronomistic 4:15-24 puts Moses' reminder that the people saw no form when they heard the divine words (v. 12) would most naturally imply that YHWH himself was present within the fire. Before arguing the point, however, it will be useful to consider the views of two scholars who appear to regard the absence of any visible form as evidence for the *opposite* conclusion. Mettinger and Weinfeld emphasize what they describe as the non-corporeal and even abstract conceptions involved in the deuteronom(ist)ic representation of the Deity at Horeb:

> Deuteronomistic theology is programmatically abstract: during the Sinai theophany, Israel perceived no form...she only heard the voice of her God (Deut. 4:12, 15). The Deuteronomistic preoccupation with God's voice and words represents an auditive, non-visual theme.[69]

> [I]t was the deuteronomic school that first initiated the polemic against the anthropomorphic and corporeal conceptions of the Deity...It is by no means coincidental that the only passages which reflect a *quasi*-abstract conception of the Deity and negation of his corporeality are to be found in Deuteronomy... Deut. 4:12: "You heard the sound of words, but saw no form"...[70]

While in the context of such reflections neither scholar gives any explanation as to *why* no form was seen, it is clear from their remarks vis-à-vis Deut. 4:36 that both of them consider YHWH to be portrayed as be-

---

[68] Deut. 4:12, 15, 33; 5:4, 22, 26; 9:10; 10:4.

[69] Mettinger 46; cf. p. 124.

[70] Weinfeld (1972a) 198. He considers that: "These later conceptions [found in Deuteronomy and elsewhere] are diametrically opposed to the earlier views articulated in the JE and P documents" in which "in Exod. 24:9-11 we read about the leaders, elders, etc. seeing God; in Exod. 33:23 Moses is said to have *beheld God's back*, and Num. 12:8 speaks even more strikingly of Moses as gazing upon 'the *form*...of the Lord'". The contrast, however, is inappropriate, since like is not being compared with like. As Fretheim (1984) observes: "Num. 12:8 speaks of Moses beholding 'the form of the Lord'...Deut. 4:15 - 'you saw no form' at Sinai - does not contradict this conclusion. It speaks not of Moses but of *the people* [our italics] not seeing any form" (p. 96).

ing other than in the fire,[71] and thus not actually present.[72] No form was seen because the Deity was elsewhere. Now, it is certainly true that in Deuteronomy there is less implication of YHWH's corporeality than there is in other parts of the OT. However, at the same time, in the deuteronom(ist)ic presentation of the law-giving at Horeb it is important to distinguish between an affirmation of YHWH's absence and one of Israel's *non-perception* of his Presence as corporeal. There is no reason why YHWH could not have been present within the fire, but invisible or veiled,[73] since this also would account for the people seeing no form.[74] In fact, as stated at the beginning of this section, the lesson drawn from the people's non-perception of that form most naturally implies that such was indeed the case:

> "Since (כי) you saw no form...beware lest you...[make] a graven image..." (4:15-16)

---

[71] Mettinger 48, Weinfeld (1972a) 206-208; see below, pp. 66-67.

[72] Curiously though, both scholars refer to the Horeb/Sinai event (in its Deuteronomy version) as a "theophany": Mettinger 46, 124 (*re* 4:12), 46 (*re* 4:15), 48 (*re* 4:11, 36; 5:4, 22), Weinfeld (1972a) 206-208 (*re* 4:33, 36).

[73] Cf. remarks made about related phenomena: "[T]he flame of fire [in Exod. 3:2] is not to be identified as the form of the divine self-manifestation, but only as a veil or envelope for the...form of the divine appearance" (Fretheim [1984] 95, " [I]n the Bible...the cloud is a sort of camouflage for the divinity himself" (Weinfeld [1983] 145), "[D]uring the Sinai theophany, the cloud conceals the essence of Yahweh from the people at the same time that it reveals his presence" (Cohn 50), "The term [ערפל] admirably fitted the ambiguity of the Hebraic theology of presence, for the meaning which it carried...conveyed the symbol of the hiddenness of God at the exact moment of his proximity" (Terrien [1978] 194; cf. p. 128),"[T]he ritual cloud of incense...masks but reveals the presence of Yahweh" (Mendenhall [1973b] 212), "[T]he [Biblical] theophany is limited to a partial disclosure of the deity. The hiddenness of God does not exclusively relate to his sublime status far above the stage of human life; the hiddenness applies equally to his divine presence *in* the world" (Kuntz: 38), "The understanding [i.e. of the priestly *kabod* conception] seems to be...of a veiled appearance, an appearance in a manner in which no precise lineaments of form can be discerned" (Barr 35), "[T]hese pillars of cloud and fire...are merely the envelope or cloak in which Jahwe has shrouded Himself, so that His actual, sacred presence shall not be seen" (Morgenstern [1911] 153-154).

[74] Cf. Fretheim (1984) 96: "Deut. 4:15...speaks...of the people *not seeing* any form; in particular, it says nothing about the possible absence of form altogether", Ridderbos 85: "Moses does not say [*re* Deut. 4:12] that it would have been impossible to see a form of God...[he] simply observes that this did not happen". Contrast Weinfeld [1991] 204: "[A]ccording to Deuteronomy [4:12] there was nothing to see: God revealed himself by sound of words only", Carroll 55: "[T]he people saw nothing, but only heard a voice. Therefore *there was no form* [our italics] to make into an image".

This prohibition seems to assume that YHWH himself *was actually present* at Horeb, and that as a result of the people perceiving that Presence they may have been tempted to make an image of him. Certainly if he were not present on that occasion there would seem to be little reason why the people's lack of perception of his form (i.e. as opposed to a denial of his Presence) should provide the basis for a section on the prohibition of images, or indeed why in that connection their experience at Horeb should be appealed to at all. On the other hand, if YHWH *was* present within the fire, then such an appeal would provide good grounds ˏfor the prohibition, since the people's non-perception of his form would render it impossible for them to reproduce an appropriate image. The Israelites are therefore forbidden either to make images based on the creatures listed in vv. 16b-18, or to worship any of the luminous[75] heavenly bodies referred to in v. 19. It thus appears that in arguing against the making of images the writer is crediting the people with having had at Horeb a genuine encounter with the divine Presence.

The people's response to the phenomenon. The response of the people both to the fire out of which YHWH's voice was heard and to the voice itself is consistent with YHWH himself being present within the fire. Their fear, referred to by Moses,[76] their surprise at having survived both seeing [*sic*] God speak with man and hearing his voice,[77] and their conviction that continued exposure to the fire and voice would be fatal[78,79]

---

[75] Fire-like?

[76] "[Y]ou were afraid because of the fire" (5:5).

[77] "[W]e have this day seen God speak with man and man still live" (5:24), "For who is there of all flesh, that has heard the voice of the living God speaking out of the midst of fire, as we have, and has still lived?" (5:26); cf. Moses' expression of the same point (4:33).

[78] "Now therefore why should we die? For this great fire will consume us; if we hear the voice of the LORD our God any more, we shall die" (5:25). "Let me not hear again the voice of the LORD my God, or see this great fire any more, lest I die" (18:16).

[79] Cf. Weinfeld (1972a) 192: "Drawing nigh to the Deity [i.e. in the sanctuary] signifies entrance into the actual sphere of the divine presence and for this reason is fraught with great physical danger", Eichrodt (1939) 19: "[D]ie Begegnung mit dem einen Herrn der göttlichen Welt [muß] wirklich als die absolute Infragestellung des menschlichen Daseins empfunden werden".

are all reminiscent of the reactions experienced by those coming into close contact with the divine Presence.[80,81]

Consistency with other indications of divine Presence. Such an interpretation of YHWH's communication "out of the midst of the fire" is consistent with other indications of divine Presence in the contexts of two of the relevant verses: 4:12 (cf. "[O]n the day that you stood *before the LORD your God*[82] at Horeb, the LORD said to me, 'Gather the people *to me*[83]'" [v. 10]) and 5:4 (cf. "The LORD spoke with you *face to face*[84] at the mountain...while I stood *between the LORD and you*[85] at that time" [5:4-5]).

Significance in Deuteronomy. There are thus several grounds for considering that these deuteronom(ist)ic references to divine communication from the fire express the belief that YHWH himself was in some sense localized within the fire. Elsewhere in the OT the plain meaning of the expression operates in all three instances of similar communication and entails the presence of the speaker within that "out of the midst of" which he speaks. That such an understanding also pertains in the case of Deuteronomy is clear both from the lesson drawn from the people's non-perception of any form within the fire and from their reactions to the phenomena associated with it. Moreover, in relation to two of the three texts concerned,[86] this interpretation is consistent with other indications of divine Presence in their immediate context. There is therefore a strong case

---

[80] Terrien (1978) 378: "[I]n Hebraic faith, the fear of Elohim represents man's ambivalent reaction to the nearness of the holy", cf. (1962) 257-258, Kuntz 43: "[*T*]*he [Old Testament] theophany is inclined to link the approaching nearness of the deity with a response of fear and dread that is induced in man who attends it*", Eichrodt (1939) 18: "Das Erzittern angesichts der göttlichen Gegenwart...durchdring[t]...die Berichte aus der altisraelitischen...Zeit", Hempel 6: "Die Furcht vor dem Heiligen ist natürlich da am stärksten, wo der Mensch der Gottheit selbst begegnet".

[81] Note that in Deut. 5:5 the people's fear of the fire is given as the reason for (כי) Moses' standing between them and *YHWH*. This implies that the person of the latter was in some way associated with the fire.

[82] See above, pp. 47-49.

[83] See above; pp. 49-50.

[84] See below, pp. 76-78.

[85] See below, pp. 78-81.

[86] Deut. 4:12; 5:4.

for understanding YHWH's speaking "out of the midst of the fire" in terms of his own Presence within that fire.[87]

The impact of Deut. 4:36

> "Out of heaven he let you hear his voice, that he might disci-
> pline you; and on earth he let you see his great fire, and you
> heard his words out of the midst of the fire."

Earlier views. A number of scholars regard the first half of the verse as locating YHWH in heaven, and therefore by implication deny his Presence on earth:

> [P]re-Deuteronomistic materials speak expressly of God's *de-*
> *scent*...from heaven...while the D-Work, in sharp contrast,
> contains no hint of such usage. Admittedly, the Lord is said,
> with reference to earlier traditions, to speak "from the moun-
> tain" (Deut. 5:4, 22), but the mountain itself is said to burn
> with fire "to the heart of heaven" (Deut. 4:11), and in exten-
> sion of this we read the typically Deuteronomistic expression,
> "out of heaven he let you hear his voice" (Deut. 4:36).[88]

---

[87] Cf. Curtis 283: "God's presence was clearly evident...in the fire", Craigie (1976) 134: "[The Israelites] had...sensed the awe of [God's] presence in the fire", Thompson (1974) 119: "[T]he heads of the tribes and...elders, moved by deep fear in the divine presence...asked that in future they should be represented before God by Moses", Watts (1970) 206: "[T]his proximity of Yahweh to his people is expounded in terms of the voice speaking from the fire at Sinai", Rennes 233: "[C]e grand feu qui fait naître la crainte...est le signe de la présence de Yahweh", Jeremias (1965) 108: "[I]n allen diesen Texten der Sinai-tradition ist das Feuer Begleiterscheinung oder Mittel der Erscheinung Jahwes bei seinem Kommen", Lohfink (1965) 117: "[D]as Feuer, in dem Jahwe erschien, habe bis ins Herz des Himmel gelodert", Buis and Leclercq 26: "[Le Deutéronome] insiste beaucoup sur la théophanie de l'Horeb où Yahwé est apparu à tout le peuple, mais 'dans le feu', sans aucune forme perceptible", Davies (1962a) 272: "Horeb with all its glory of fire and darkness and cloud - a condescending Presence, invisible as to form, but luminous in spoken revelation", Wright (1953) 354: "[W]hile God was obviously present as his words clearly indicated, no one saw him", Clamer 557: "[M]ieux valait ne plus se retrouver en présence de la majesté divine. C'était en effet une croyance, maintes fois exprimée dans l'Ancien Testament, que l'homme ne pouvait paraître en présence de Yahweh sans mourir de crainte et de frayeur", Reider 50: "God being surrounded by fire and invisible to the human eye", Junker 45-46: "Die Bitte der Ältesten geht von der Vorstellung aus...daß der Mensch die sichtbar in die Erscheinung tretende Gegenwart Gottes nicht zu ertragen vermag", Steuernagel (1900) 16: "Zwar erschien Feuer, aber dies war nur die Hülle Jahves, nicht er selbst"; cf. Ridderbos 111, Mayes (1979) 173.
[88] Mettinger 48.

> In contrast to the account in Exod. 19 of God's descent upon
> Mt. Sinai (19:11 and 20)...the commandments were heard
> from out of the midst of the fire that was upon the mount, but
> they were uttered by the Deity from heaven.[89]

> [T]he JE narrative leaves it perfectly clear that...[Yahweh]
> came down to Sinai...As Deuteronomy tells of these events
> [i.e. in Deut. 4:11-12, 36] there is no mention at all of a de-
> scent by Yahweh from heaven to the mountain...but only of
> the appearance of fire and of a voice out of the fire.[90]

The absence of any reference to divine descent and/or an interpretation
of 4:36a in terms of YHWH's whereabouts when he let the Israelites hear
his voice is thus taken to indicate that the Deuteronomist portrays the
Deity as present *in heaven* for the declaration of the law and therefore
not upon the earth at the time in question.[91] In view of this, it will be
necessary to consider whether the mention of heaven in Deut. 4:36 does
in fact necessitate a denial of YHWH's Presence within the fire.

The structure of Deut. 4:36. Examination of the Hebrew suggests that the
first four words of each half of the verse are meant to be parallel:

4:36a: מן־השמים השמיעך את־קלו
4:36b: ועל־הארץ הראך   את־אשו הגדולה

First, each half begins with an adverbial phrase, involving either "from"
(מן) or "upon" (על), the definite article (ה) and one of the pair of contrasting nouns "heaven" (שמים) and "earth" (ארץ). Secondly, this is then followed by the verb, which in each case is in the Hiphil, and incorporates
within it the indirect object as a second person singular suffix: "he let
you hear" (השמיעך) or "he let you see" (הראך). Finally, there is the direct
object, which in each case is introduced by the object marker (את) and incorporates within it the third person singular suffix: "his voice" (קלו) or
"his fire" (אשו). This last point is particularly significant, since while "his
voice" occurs in a number of places in Deuteronomy,[92] "his fire" is found
only at 4:36b. Apart from this one instance, all other references in Deu-

---

[89] Weinfeld (1972a) 206-207; cf. "The Israelites saw only 'his great fire'...whereas
God himself remains in his heavenly abode" (pp. 207-208).
[90] Clements (1965) 90.
[91] Contrast Clements' more recent remark: "[W]hen God revealed his will to Israel at
Mount Horeb...he was hidden in fire" ([1989] 51); cf. above, p. 63 n. 72.
[92] 4:30; 5:24; 9:23; 13:5 (EVV 4); 26:17; 30:2, 20.

teronomy to the Horeb fire involve the article ה, either with[93] or without[94] the preposition ב. Thus, that the only instance of אש with the third
person singular suffix occurs at 4:36b is strongly suggestive of it having
been placed there deliberately, with the intention of further emphasizing
the parallelism between the beginnings of the two halves of the verse.[95]

The interpretation of Deut. 4:36. Assuming the observed parallelism to
be intentional, it would seem reasonable to presume that the interpretation of each half of the verse should proceed along similar lines. In the
first half of the verse the opening adverbial phrase "out of heaven" must
therefore qualify either the subject or the object of the main clause. If it
qualifies the object, then it indicates the place from which YHWH's
voice was transmitted.[96] This, however, must be rejected, since not only
v. 36bβ but also the other nine references to this event indicate that it occurred not "out of heaven" but *from the fire.*[97] This means that the phrase
must qualify the subject. In which case it indicates the place from which
YHWH spoke. It tells us where YHWH himself was when he "let [the
people] hear his voice". This interpretation agrees with Mettinger et al. in
locating YHWH in heaven.[98] The corollary to this, however, if our inter-
pretative methodology is to be consistent, is that the opening adverbial
phrase of the *second half* of the verse must qualify the subject of *its* main
clause. This means that v. 36bα tells us where YHWH was when he "let
[the people] see his great fire", i.e. he was *on the earth*. Thus, taking into
account the clear parallelism between the two halves of the verse, the
consistent application of this approach locates YHWH both in heaven
and on earth.[99] Deut. 4:36 therefore poses no threat to an understanding
of communication "out of the midst of the fire" in terms of YHWH being

---

[93] 4:11; 5:23; 9:15.

[94] 4:12, 15, 33, 36bβ; 5:4, 5, 22, 24, 25, 26; 9:10; 10:4; 18:16.

[95] Cf. Van Seters 121 "[I]n Deut. 4:36 we have this...speaking 'from heaven' set in
parallel structure to God's speaking from the midst of the fire", Knapp 106:
"V. 36abα besteht aus zwei parallelen Teilen...Himmel und Erde, Hören und Sehen,
Stimme und Feuer korrespondieren miteinander".

[96] This would have the advantage that when the same principle of interpretation is
applied to v. 36bα, the result is consistent with what we know to be true, namely that
"on earth" indicates the place where "his great fire" was located.

[97] 4:12, 15, 33; 5:4, 22, 24, 26; 9:10; 10:4.

[98] See above, pp. 66-67.

[99] That *both* parts of the verse (36abα and 36bβ) represent the Deity as being present
on the earth tends to undermine the view of v. 36bβ as a later addition. Cf. Knapp 40,
Mittmann 123, 184.

present at Horeb, since while it does indeed locate him in heaven, by the same token it also locates him on the earth.[100]

Now, if our understanding of Deut. 4:36 is correct, then the verse represents YHWH as being in two places at once, and thus contains what a number of scholars describe as a "mythical concept of space". Such a notion is characterized by two different places being represented as possessing the same content, and is taken to imply an eradication of the distinction between them.[101] It is frequently detected in connection with the Jerusalem temple. Mettinger's comment, for example, would be fairly typical:

> [A]s expressed in the pre-exilic Zion tradition, the concept seems to imply unity or identity, the Temple is the site at which the category of space is transcended. Here the distinction is obliterated between the heavenly and the earthly, in that both are subsumed under a higher mystical identity.[102]

---

[100] Cf. Nicholson (1977) 425: "Yahweh...is both transcendent and immanent, for he has spoken to his people 'from heaven' and has revealed his will on earth below, speaking to his people 'from the midst of the fire'", Watts (1970) 206: "Verse 36 maintains the balance of transcendence-immanence. The voice from heaven and the epiphany in fire on earth together were the teachers of God's being and way'.

[101] Childs (1960) 86: "[T]here is evidence of the mythical understanding of space in the identification of Zion with Eden. When two spaces possess the same content, then distance is transcended. These are not two different spaces, but one".

[102] P. 30; cf. Hendel 375: "The ark...constitutes Yahweh's throne; it is the earthly image of the heavenly throne. Yahweh, of course, rules from both thrones simultaneously, according to the mythic parallelism of the earthly and heavenly shrine", Levenson (1985) 123: "[T]he Temple could serve as...the 'meeting place of heaven and earth'", Cohn 39: "With the mountain symbol the biblical authors can express the paradox of Yahweh dwelling simultaneously in heaven and on earth...At Mount Zion the boundary between heaven and earth is erased", Clifford (1972) 3: "[I]n the Hebrew Bible, some mountains...can be...the meeting place of heaven and earth, the place where effective decrees are issued", Weinfeld (1972a) 197 n. 3: "The belief of the divine presence in the sanctuary did not...preclude the belief in the Deity's heavenly abode. Israel appears to have shared this dialectical conception of the divine abode...with other peoples of the Ancient East", Metzger 144: "Die Vorstellung, daß im Bereich des Heiligtums die Grenzen zwischen Himmlisch und Irdisch aufgehoben sind, ist auch für das Jerusalemer Heiligtum bezeugt", Terrien (1970) 333-334: "It was...the belief in the myth of Zion as the cosmic umbilic - the eternal bond between heaven and earth - which...", Clements (1965) 94: "[T]he...mythology, by which Yahweh's abode on earth was thought to be united to his abode in heaven...". See also Eliade 30-37, where Zion is regarded as an example of "[une] Montagne Sacrée - où se rencontrent le Ciel et la Terre" (p. 30).

He goes on to reflect that the concept "may help to explain those passages which so unconcernedly locate God simultaneously *on earth and in heaven*" (our italics),[103] cites a number of examples, mainly from the Psalms,[104] and concludes that:

> The heavenly and the earthly may not be regarded as two opposed poles in a field of tension; rather, heaven and earth become one in the sacred space of the sanctuary. Thus the Psalmist can say in synonymous parallelism, The Lord is in his holy temple...the Lord's throne is in heaven. (Ps. 11:4).[105]

As far as the present discussion is concerned, it is important to note that Mettinger is prepared to accept that the Psalmist can, without any sense of incongruity, "locate God simultaneously on earth and in heaven." Hence, given that such can be predicated of God in the Psalms, without any appeal to multiple authorship (i.e. to account for the apparent contradiction), the way is then clear for acceptance of a similar notion in Deuteronomy. The interpretation of Deut. 4:36 in terms of YHWH being present both in heaven and upon earth for the first giving of the law cannot be dismissed on the grounds of self-contradiction.

Deut. 4:36 in its immediate context (vv. 32-40). Before considering the role of Deut. 4:36 within the surrounding context, it will be necessary to examine the structure and purpose of that context. First, Deut. 4:32-39 subdivides into two very similar sections: vv. 32-35 and vv. 36-39.[106] Both refer to the people hearing the divine communication out of the midst of the fire (v. 33 // v. 36), to YHWH's choice of Israel and bringing about the Exodus (v. 34 // v. 37), and to the purpose for which these things occurred (v. 35 // v. 39):

vv. 32-35	vv. 36-39
"Did any people ever hear the voice of a god speaking out of the midst of the fire, as you have heard...?" (v. 33)	"[Y]ou heard [YHWH's] words out of the midst of the fire." (v. 36)

---

103 P. 30.
104 E.g. 14:2, 7; 20:3, 7 (EVV 2, 6); 76:3, 9 (EVV 2, 8).
105 P. 31. Cf. Levenson's (1985) comment on the same verse: "[T]he Hebrew Bible is capable of affirming God's heavenly and his earthly presence without the slightest hint of tension between the two" (p. 140).
106 For their relation to v. 40, see below, p. 73.

vv. 32-35	vv. 36-39
"Or has any god ever attempted to go and take a nation for himself from the midst of another nation...according to all that the LORD your God did for you in Egypt...?" (v. 34)	"[YHWH] loved your fathers and chose their descendants after them, and brought you out of Egypt..." (v. 37)
"To you it was shown, that you might know that the LORD is God; there is no other besides him." (v. 35)	"[K]now therefore...that the LORD is God in heaven above and on the earth beneath; there is no other." (v. 39)

Secondly, however, the two sections have significantly different purposes. In v. 35 the intention is that the Israelites might know that "the LORD is God", whereas in v. 39 it is that they might know that "[He] is God *in heaven above and on the earth beneath*", and it is this qualification which gives a clue to the different thrust of the second section. Thus, in vv. 32-35, the highlighting, by means of rhetorical questions,[107] of the uniqueness of YHWH's action (i.e. in speaking from the fire, and bringing about the Exodus) is intended to point both to the uniqueness of YHWH himself and to the people's privileged position in witnessing such events. These two aspects are made explicit in the section's stated purpose (v. 35), which is not to establish in the abstract that YHWH is God, but rather to establish it *in the minds of the people*:

> "To *you* it was shown, that *you might know* that the LORD is God; there is no other besides him."

In vv. 36-39, however, there are no rhetorical questions. Once Israel has been brought to the point of realizing that YHWH is God (in a *general* sense) no more are needed. Rather, the section contains a series of statements about what this YHWH (who is God) has done for the people. It is true that vv. 32-35 also refer to what he has done for them, but to nowhere near the same extent, as can be seen by noting the much greater in-

---

[107] Vv. 33, 34.

cidence of "you" (cf. also "your") as either the object or indirect object of
actions carried out by YHWH:[108]

vv. 32-35	vv. 36-39
"[A]ll that the LORD your God did for *you*...To *you* it was shown..."	"[YHWH] let *you* hear[109]... that he might discipline *you*...he let *you* see...he loved *your* fathers...and brought *you* out...to bring *you* in, to give *you* their land..."

Moreover, as in the case of vv. 32-35, it is on the information given in
the main body of the section that its conclusion is based. The various
statements of what YHWH has done for the people are meant to illustrate
from their own experience the two spheres in which YHWH's unique
Deity is operative. He is God "in heaven above" because it was from
there that "he let [them] hear his voice" (v. 36a). And he is God "on the
earth beneath" because it was on earth that "he let [them] see his great
fire,[110] and [they] heard his words out of the midst of the fire" (v. 36b).
Indeed, the whole presentation in vv. 37-38 strongly implies his personal
involvement in, and presence with,[111] his people on the earth. These ob-

---

[108] Alternatively, one can note the number of extra actions which vv. 36-39 record YHWH as having carried out on the people's behalf.

[109] Note that this is the only instance of the people being portrayed as the *direct object* (השמיעך) of the communication from the fire.

[110] 4:36 is the only reference in Deuteronomy which mentions "the earth" in connection with the fire at Horeb.

[111] Note that while the occasional scholar regards YHWH's פנים (v. 37) as some kind of representative of the Deity (Steuernagel [1923] 69; cf. Bertholet [1899] 19-20), there are those who view it as standing for YHWH himself: Ridderbos 93: "[T]he 'Presence of the Lord' is the pillar of cloud and fire, in which the Lord is present in a special sense", Reindl 78: "Will man...das בפניו übersetzen, dann am besten mit einer Umschreibung 'durch sein (persönliches) Eingreifen', 'durch seine Gegenwart'", Jacob (1968) 63: "[L]'expression désigne la personne, c'est-à-dire Dieu lui-même et non un de ses représentants", Clements (1965) 94 n. 4: "The older ideas of Yahweh's accompanying presence...are to be found in...Deut. iv. 37", Johnson (1947) 159: "The most important examples of this use of the term פנים [i.e. involving "the employment of synecdoche (*pars pro toto*)" - see p. 157]...are to be found in association with the person of Yahweh...Deuteronomy iv. 37", Phythian-Adams (1942) 19: "Jahweh... brought Israel out of Egypt by His Presence (iv. 37)", Eichrodt (1935) 14: "[Die] selbständige Geltung [der panîm] als Erscheinungsform Gottes...scheint...noch durchzuleuchten"; cf. Mayes (1979) 158, Gulin 27, Robinson (n.d.) 81.

servations lead to the conclusion that both in heaven where he is present, and on earth where he is also present, *YHWH* is God (v. 39). It is therefore clear that the affirmation in v. 36 of his simultaneous location in heaven and upon earth functions within its context as part of the evidence on which such a conclusion is based.

Finally, in v. 40 there is an exhortation to obedience arising out of what has been established:

> "Therefore you shall keep his statutes and his commandments, which I command you this day, that it may go well with you, and with your children after you, and that you may prolong your days in the land which the LORD your God gives you for ever."

The people are to keep YHWH's commands because, being God in heaven, he alone has the authority to demand such obedience, and because, being at the same time God on the earth, he alone can ensure both the well-being of themselves and their descendants and also their continuance in the land which he has given them.

The above analysis has cast doubt on the assumption that the affirmation in Deut. 4:36 of YHWH's Presence in heaven necessarily entails his absence from the earth. The parallelism within the verse suggests, rather, that YHWH is portrayed as being in heaven *and also* on the earth. It therefore contains a deuteronomistic example of a phenomenon found particularly in the Psalms, and characterized by many scholars as representing a "mythical concept of space". Consequently, its reference to YHWH letting the people hear his voice "out of heaven" poses no threat to an understanding of his communication "out of the midst of the fire" in terms of his localized Presence at Horeb.

The emphasis on divine communication "out of the midst of the fire"

It was demonstrated above that the majority of the deuteronom(ist)ic instances of YHWH's communication of the law to the people or to the people's hearing of that law by means of his voice or words are either specified as taking place "out of the midst of the fire" or are found in contexts which make it reasonable to suppose that such was the case.[112] This is in complete contrast to the Exodus account, and raises the question as to why such qualification occurs.

---

[112] Pp. 58-60.

Some observations on the data. First, as shown earlier, in all ten instances of the expression, the emphasis is on the *people* as the ones to
whom the divine communication "out of the midst of the fire" is directed.[113] And secondly, over half of all the references to that particular
fire, i.e. in Deuteronomy,[114] are accompanied by an insistence that those
whom Moses is now addressing experienced either the fire (by seeing) or
the voice that proceeded from it (by hearing) *themselves*. Thus, Deut.
4:11 and 12 are part of the brief report (vv. 10-14) given to remind the
Israelites of what they themselves had *seen* (v. 9) and were on no account
to forget. The subject of the verb ראו is "your eyes", i.e. as opposed to
"you", and this would seem to suggest that appeal is being made specifically to the people's *visual* rather than general perception.[115] Of the phenomena referred to and susceptible of being experienced in this way, the
fire from which YHWH addresses the people would appear to be the
most significant. In addition, the observation that "the LORD spoke to
you out of the midst of the fire" is followed by the reminder that "*you
heard* (שמעים) the sound of words" (v. 12). It therefore seems likely that
in vv. 11-12 the writer is appealing to the people's experience both of the
sight of the fire and of the sound of the voice which proceeded from it. In
Deut. 4:15 also appeal is made to the people's visual experience ("Since
you saw [ראיתם] no form..."),[116] though there is no explicit reference to
their having seen the fire or heard the voice. The former, however, is im-
plicit in the (negative) experience to which Moses refers. The location of
the divine form (had it been both present and visible) would presumably
have been the place from which YHWH spoke. That the Israelites did not
see one clearly implies that they looked at the fire. Deut. 4:33 and 36
contain obvious reminders of the people's experience both of seeing the
fire (v. 36)[117] and of hearing the voice (vv. 33, 36 [2x]) associated with
it: "Did any people ever hear the voice of a god...as *you have heard*
(שמעת), and still live?" (v. 33) and "[o]ut of heaven *he let you hear*

---

[113] See above, p. 58.

[114] 4:11, 12, 15, 33, 36 (2x); 5:4, 5, 22, 23, 24, 25, 26; 9:10, 15; 10:4; 18:16.

[115] Contrast, for example, Deut. 5:24, where ראינו could equally well be rendered
"perceived". Cf. Staton 197 n. 47.

[116] Note that the prohibition is based not on the objective absence of any form
("Since there was no form..."), but on the people's non-perception of the same.

[117] There may also be an allusion to their having seen the fire in the explanation as to
why YHWH allowed them to experience both his speaking from it and the deliverance from Egypt: "*To you it was shown* (אתה הראת)..." (v. 35).

(השמיעך) his voice...and on earth *he let you see* (הראך) his great fire, and *you heard* (שמעת) his words out of the midst of the fire" (v. 36). Deut. 5:23, 24, 25 and 26 are found within Deut. 5:23-27, Moses' reminder to the people of both the context (v. 23) and the content (vv. 24-27) of their reaction to the divine revelation at Horeb. He makes no mention of their having seen the fire,[118] but quotes them as having several times referred to hearing the divine voice which came from it: "[W]*hen you heard* (כשמעכם) the voice out of the midst of the darkness...you said '...*we have heard* (שמענו) his voice out of the midst of the fire...if *we hear* the voice of the LORD our God any more (אם־יספיםאנחנולשמע)...For who is there... that has heard the voice of the living God speaking out of the midst of fire, *as we have* (כמנו)...?'" (vv. 23-26). Finally, Deut. 18:16 occurs in the section (vv. 15-19) dealing with YHWH's future raising up of a prophet like Moses. The latter tells the people that when this happens they must listen to such a one in the same way that on Horeb they (by implication) listened to Moses. Moses justifies this by reminding them of the reasons which they originally gave for preferring to receive the divine revelation mediated (through himself) rather than direct from YHWH: "*Let me not hear again* (לא אסף לשמע) the voice of the LORD my God, or *see* this great fire *any more* (לא־אראה עוד), lest I die" (v. 16). Such a reminder clearly constitutes a further explicit appeal to the people's experience of both hearing the voice and seeing the fire.

Thus, within Deuteronomy a significant proportion of the references to the fire on Horeb claim that Moses' present audience personally experienced the divine revelation on that occasion. One of the ways in which they do so is by reminding the people that they themselves saw the fire (4:9 [referring to vv. 11 and 12], 15 [by implication], 36bα; 18:16bβ) and/or heard the voice that proceeded from it (4:12, 36a, 36bβ; 5:23, 24, 25, 26; 18:16bα).

Explanation. The dual claim that the people both saw the fire and heard the voice associated with it constitutes an appeal to an experience of *objective* phenomena. Any reminder of either experience would thus serve to emphasize to the Israelites the reality of what had happened at Horeb.

---

[118] Unless the confession to having "*seen* [sic] God speak with man" refers to the Israelites' sight of the fire from which he spoke, the verb would be better translated "perceived". Note, however, that the Israelites do make some reference to their *visual* experience: "the LORD our God *has shown us* (הראנו) his glory and greatness" (v. 24).

YHWH really did speak to them then because they themselves heard his
voice and saw the fire from which it came. If this be granted, then it is
reasonable to presume that in those instances of divine communication
qualified by "out of the midst of the fire" but which refer neither to the
people seeing the fire nor hearing the voice (5:4, 22; 9:10; 10:4), the
qualification serves to bring to the Israelites' mind the reality of their experience of the divine revelation.

DEUT. 5:4 // EXOD. 20:1

	Deut.	Exod.
	"The LORD spoke with you	God spoke all these words,
	*face to face...*He said..."	saying... (20:1)
	(5:4-5)	

Many scholars do not comment on the expression "face to face" in
Deut. 5:4,[119] while those who do tend to regard it as indicating either that
YHWH spoke *directly* to the people, i.e. without the mediation of another person,[120] or that the covenant was made in the area of personal
rather than purely legal relationships.[121] Few reflect on whether the
phrase has any bearing on the location of the divine Presence,[122] though
some imply in their more general discussion of vv. 1/2-5 that YHWH
was present on that occasion.[123]

Communication "face to face"

Its plain implication. The sheer intimacy[124] of the expression would
seem to imply that when it is used to qualify an activity predicated of A

---

[119] Braulik (1986) 49, Clifford (1982) 41-42, Phillips (1973) 44, Cazelles (1966) 43,
von Rad (1964) 40, Davies (1962a) 273, Wright (1953) 363, Cunliffe-Jones 49.

[120] Christensen 111, Mayes (1979) 165-166, Craigie (1976) 148, Childs (1974) 351,
Watts (1970) 207, Rennes 40, Clamer 549, Junker 42, Nötscher 23, Steuernagel
(1923) 72, Smith (1918) 80-81, Bertholet (1899) 21, Dillmann 265; cf. Terrien
(1978) 90-91.

[121] Thompson (1974) 113, Buis and Leclercq 63.

[122] See, however Reindl 215: "Zwar spricht auch Dtn 5,4 (פנים בפנים) von der Unmit-
telbarkeit der Gottesbegegnung Israels; aber diese Nähe Gottes..." (cf. pp. 73-74),
Reider 62: "*face to face*, i.e. in close proximity, without the intervention of another".

[123] Wright (1953) 363, Steuernagel (1900) 21.

[124] Cf. Simian-Yofre 639, Mann 258.

in relation to B, then regardless of whatever else might be involved,[125] A and B are in close proximity to one another.

Usage elsewhere. In the form in which it is used in Deut. 5:4, i.e. with the preposition ב, "face to face" (פנים בפנים) occurs nowhere else in the OT. There is, however, a very similar expression (פנים אל־פנים) which generally seems to be regarded as having the same meaning.[126] Its five occurrences, all of which involve the Deity, will therefore be examined in turn to see whether at the same time he is portrayed independently as being present.

First, regardless of whether Gen. 32:31 (EVV 30) originally belonged to the account of Jacob's nocturnal wrestling-match or not,[127] it is difficult to escape the conclusion that in its present context the verse identifies the God whom Jacob saw "face to face" with the "man" with whom he had wrestled.[128] Secondly, in view of the reference to the descent of the pillar of cloud in Exod. 33:9, it is generally considered that YHWH was present on those occasions when he is described as speaking to Moses "face to face".[129] Thirdly, there are no indications of divine Presence in the context of Deut. 34:10. YHWH's "face to face" knowledge of Moses is frequently understood as an expression of the intimacy of the unique relationship which existed between them,[130] but few if any scholars relate it *explicitly* to an experience of the divine Presence. Fourthly, that the angel of the LORD whom Gideon saw "face to face" was originally present is clear from several indications within Judg. 6:11-24. He "sat under the oak at Ophrah" (v. 11), he "appeared" to Gideon

---

[125] E.g. When YHWH interacts with a human being "face to face" the question as to whether the latter is regarded as in any sense *seeing* the divine visage.

[126] E.g. Reindl 255 n. 154: "Gegenüber פנים אל־פנים [ist פנים בפנים] nur eine sprachliche Variante"; cf. Simian-Yofre 639, van der Woude (1976) 448, BDB 815.

[127] It is regarded as a subsequent addition by Westermann (1981) 625, 632-633.

[128] Brueggemann (1982) 267, Maher 189, 190, Terrien (1978) 89, 90, 91, Vawter 349, 351, Reindl 70-71, Kidner 169, 170, Johnson (1961) 28, Leupold (1953) 875, 876, 881, von Rad (1953a) 280-281, 283, Davies (1942) 12, Eichrodt (1935) 4, 12, Skinner (1930) 408, 409-410, 411. For an alternative view, see Westermann (1981) 633; cf. Barr 32.

[129] Durham 440, 442, Curtis 285, Terrien (1978) 177-178, Mann 145, Knight 194, Childs (1974) 592, 593, Cole 223, Mendenhall (1973a) 59, Clements (1972) 213, Hyatt (1971) 314, 315, Reindl 303 n. 608, Schnutenhaus, 6, 12, 13, Barr 35, Morgenstern (1911) 156.

[130] Cairns 306, Simian-Yofre 639, Thompson (1974) 320, Buis and Leclercq 214; cf. Craigie (1976) 406, Reindl 72, Cunliffe-Jones 190.

(v. 12), the latter's request to him not to depart "from here" is met by a promise that he would "stay" until Gideon returned (v. 18), and then, after "touch[ing] the meat and the unleavened cakes" with his staff he "vanished from [Gideon's] sight" (v. 21). Finally, YHWH's promise that he will enter into judgement with Israel "face to face" (Ezek. 20:35) has no indications of divine Presence in its immediate context.

Thus three out of the five other OT instances of "face to face" encounters are found in contexts which indicate that the parties concerned are in close proximity. Jacob wrestles with God, YHWH descends to the tent which Moses has entered, and the angel touches the food which Gideon sets before him. While the other two instances do not spell out the idea of spatial proximity, neither do they rule it out, and the basic literal sense may not be far from view.

Significance in Deut. 5:4. On the basis of what is implied by the expression itself, the OT usage elsewhere, and the other references to divine Presence in its immediate context,[131] it would seem reasonable to presume that when YHWH is described as having spoken with the people "face to face", he did so in their immediate vicinity. Such a qualification therefore constitutes a further deuteronom(ist)ic indication of his localized Presence at Horeb.

DEUT. 5:5 // EXOD. 20:1

Deut.	Exod.
"The LORD spoke with you...while I stood *between the LORD and you* at that time...He said..." (5:4-5)	God spoke all these words, saying... (20:1)

In general, scholars regard Moses' "[standing] between the LORD and [the people]" in Deut. 5:5 as designating his role as a *mediator* between YHWH and the Israelites.[132] Some see it as implying that only *he* heard

---

[131] I.e. those to YHWH's speaking "out of the midst of the fire" (v. 4; see above, pp. 60-66), and to Moses' standing between him and the people (v. 5; see below, pp. 79-81). Note that the context still contains independent evidence of the divine Presence even if v. 5 is taken as an addition (see above, p. 54 n. 37).

[132] Staton 197, Braulik (1986) 49, Clifford 42, Craigie (1976) 148, Thompson (1974) 113, Phillips (1973) 44, Watts (1970) 207, von Rad (1964) 40, Buis and Leclercq 63, Reider 62, Welch (1932) 18, Driver (1902) 83, Steuernagel (1900) 21, Bertholet (1899) 21, Dillmann 265, Robinson (n.d.) 84.

the divine words but then passed them on to the people,[133] while others consider it to be at variance with v. 4, which seems to represent the Deity as having spoken to them *directly* ("face to face"). This perceived dichotomy is usually resolved by postulating either that the Israelites heard the sound of the divine voice but not what it said (though Moses did, and subsequently relayed it to them),[134] or that v. 5 is an addition,[135] or both.[136] However, while scholars generally agree that Moses' "standing between the LORD and [the people]" refers to his mediation, their comments seem to imply that they view it primarily in a metaphorical sense. Few have addressed the specific question as to whether the "standing between" is at the same time to be understood in its literal, *locative*, meaning.[137]

The act of "standing between"

Its plain implication. If the verb עמד is taken in its literal sense, then when A stands "between" (בין) two sets of *people* (i.e. as opposed to places) it is usually understood that each of the two groups is situated at a particular spot, and that A is in reasonably close proximity to both of them. If this is true of Deut. 5:5, then it implies the localization of YHWH at a site both known to and not far from Moses such that he was then able to position himself "between the LORD and [the people]".

Usage elsewhere. Apart from Deut. 5:5 the combination עמד בין occurs only three times in the OT. Each instance will be briefly examined in turn:

> [T]he pillar of cloud moved from before them and *stood* (ויעמד)
> behind them, coming *between* (בין) the host of Egypt and (ובין)
> the host of Israel... (Exod. 14:19-20)

From the sheer amount of spatial information associated with the movements of the pillar of cloud, it is clear that the "standing between" is intended to be understood in the locative sense. The two hosts are known to be earthbound and in close proximity to one another, and the change

---

[133] Watts (1970) 207, von Rad (1964) 40.

[134] Phillips (1973) 44, Clamer 549, Reider 62, Driver (1902) 84; cf. Ridderbos 99, Craigie (1976) 148.

[135] See above, p. 54 n. 37.

[136] Smith (1918) 81, Dillmann 265-266.

[137] Though Braulik (1986) refers to "die örtliche Position des Mose zwischen Jahwe und Israel" (p. 49).

in the pillar's position (i.e. from being "before" Israel to standing "behind" them) would suggest that only a literal interpretation is possible.

> [H]e *stood between* (ויעמד בין) the dead and (ובין) the living;
> and the plague was stopped. (Num. 17:13 [EVV 16:48])

Aaron's act of atonement for the people takes place in their midst (17:12aα [EVV 16:47aα]), and since both the dead and the living can be presumed to have been present at the time (the plague had already started, 17:12aβ [EVV 16:47aβ]), then here also the "standing between" is most naturally understood in a locative sense. In this case, however, it may be that בין would be better rendered as "among".[138]

> David lifted his eyes and saw the angel of the LORD *standing between* (עמד בין) earth and (ובין) heaven, and in his hand a drawn sword stretched out over Jerusalem... (1 Chron. 21:16)

Scholars who comment on the "angel...standing between earth and heaven" generally consider him to have been suspended in mid-air,[139] an interpretation which clearly views the "standing between" in a locative sense.

Before we return to Deut. 5:5, it is important to note that in none of these three instances is there any indication that who/whatever "stands between" fulfils a mediating role between the other two parties(?) concerned. In Exod. 14:19-20, the pillar of cloud "stands between" the two hosts, presumably to prevent the Egyptians from approaching any closer to the Israelites, and possibly to conceal the latter from view. In Num. 17:13 (EVV 16:48), Aaron "stands between" the dead and the living, not to mediate between the two groups, but to do so between *YHWH* and the living. Finally, in 1 Chron. 21:16, the angel "standing between" earth and heaven is in no sense acting as a mediator between man and God, but rather as the Deity's agent of judgement upon Jerusalem. There are thus no OT examples of עמד בין being used in the sense of a go-between. All three instances cited above are to be understood literally, and none of them involve any hint of mediatorial activity on behalf of who/whatever is stood between.

---

[138] See BDB 107, which includes this as a possible meaning.
[139] Williamson (1982) 147, Michaeli (1967) 111, Myers (1965a) 148, Goettsberger 156, Curtis and Madsen 251.

Significance in Deut. 5:5. It has been shown that there is no OT precedent for עמד בין *of itself* being understood in the metaphorical sense of
mediation. In Exod. 14:19-20; Num. 17:13 (EVV 16:48) and 1 Chron.
21:16 the expression carries a *literal* meaning. It is therefore reasonable
to presume that in Deut. 5:5, Moses' "standing between" YHWH and the
people is intended to be taken in the same locative sense. The verse thus
portrays Moses as occupying the physical space which separates the Israelites from the Deity, who is thereby represented as being localized in
their immediate vicinity.[140] In fact Moses does also mediate between
YHWH and the people, but not simply by virtue of being between them,
but rather because of what he does when he stands there, i.e. declares to
the Israelites the divine word.

Thus, on the basis of its usage elsewhere in the OT, עמד בין in Deut.
5:5 is best understood in a locative sense. This interpretation is consistent
with the other indications of divine Presence in the immediate context.

CONCLUSION

It has been argued that, whereas in Exod. 20:1 YHWH's Presence on
the mountain for his delivery of the Ten Commandments has to be *deduced from the context*, in Deut. 4:12-13; 5:4-5 and 5:22 it is strongly
implied within the verses themselves, i.e. by the references to his speaking with the people "face to face" and "out of the midst of the fire", and
to Moses' standing between God and the people. Far from being an
elimination, this clearly represents a heightened emphasis on divine Presence in this particular part of Deuteronomy.

THE PEOPLE'S REACTION TO THE DECLARATION OF THE
DECALOGUE

DEUT. 5:23-27 // EXOD. 20:18-19

Given that references to divine communication "out of the midst of
the fire" localize the Deity within the fire, then it is only in the deuter-
onom(ist)ic[141] account of the people's reaction to the declaration of the
Decalogue that YHWH's Presence is indicated.
By the narrator (Moses):

---

[140] See above, p. 65 n. 81.
[141] See above, p. 54.

Deut.	Exod.
"[W]hen you heard the voice *out of the midst of the darkness*, while the mountain was burning with fire, you came near to me...and you said..." (5:23-24)	[W]hen all the people perceived the thunderings and the lightnings and the sound of the trumpet and the mountain smoking, the people were afraid and trembled; and they stood afar off, and said to Moses... (20:18-19)[142]

By the people themselves:

Deut.	Exod.
"[Y]ou said, '...we have heard [the LORD's] voice *out of the midst of the fire*...if we hear the voice of the LORD...any more, we shall die. For who is there...that has heard the voice of the living God speaking *out of the midst of fire,* as we have, and has still lived? Go near, and hear all that the LORD...will say; and speak to us all that the LORD...will speak to you; and we will hear...'" (5:24-27)	[The people] said to Moses, "You speak to us, and we will hear; but let not God speak to us, lest we die." (20:19)

Two features stand out. First, while both accounts portray the people's words to Moses (i.e. in Deut. 5:24-27 and Exod. 20:19) as their immediate reaction to having experienced some aspect of the revelation of the Ten Commandments, only Deuteronomy represents them as the Israelites' response to hearing the divine voice "out of the midst of the darkness" (5:23), an expression which, as has been argued above for the related one involving "fire", implies the divine Presence within the darkness and thus on the mountain itself.[143] In Exodus, however, the people's words are a response, not to the sound of YHWH's voice, but to the natural phenomena associated with the theophany (the thunderings and lightnings, etc.). Secondly, both accounts portray the people as not wishing

---

[142] Exod. 20:18-21 is generally attributed to E. See below, p. 86 n. 159 and p. 91 n. 182.

[143] Pp. 60-66.

the Deity to speak to them for fear that they will die, and consequently as entreating Moses to listen in their stead (in Exodus by implication), and to pass on to them whatever YHWH says to him. In Deuteronomy, however, by way of explanation, the Israelites twice express their amazement at already having survived hearing YHWH's voice (in 5:24 and 26), and both times indicate that the voice came from the fire. By contrast, in Exodus they themselves give no such reason for their request.

Thus, only in the deuteronom(ist)ic account do narrator and people refer to the voice emanating from either the darkness or the fire, and so represent the Deity as being on the mountain itself. At this juncture of the narrative there is clearly a heightened interest in divine Presence in Deuteronomy as compared with Exodus.

MOSES' RESPONSE TO THE PEOPLE'S REQUEST

--- // EXOD. 20:20-21

Deut.	Exod.
_____	And Moses said to the people, "Do not fear for; God *has come* to prove you, and that the fear of him may be before your eyes, that you may not sin." And the people stood afar off, while Moses drew near to *the thick darkness where God was.* (20:20-21)

Exod. 20:20-21

At this point in the narrative Exod. 20 records both Moses' reply to the people's request: "Do not fear; for God *has come* to prove you" (v. 20), and his compliance with what is implied by it, i.e. that he should first listen to God before speaking to them: "And the people stood afar off, while Moses drew near to *the thick darkness where God was*" (v. 21). Here God's localized Presence at Sinai is indicated by the references to his having "come" (בא) and his being in the thick darkness (הערפל אשר־שם האלהים), neither of which has any parallel in Deut. 5.

Deut. 5

In fact, the deuteronom(ist)ic account omits all reference to Moses' response, and goes straight on to deal with that of YHWH himself (vv. 28-31). Nevertheless, with regard to the omission a number of points

can be made. First, it constitutes a further example of a concern to concentrate on the experience of the *people* rather than on that of Moses.[144]
Secondly, while Deuteronomy makes no mention anywhere of YHWH's
"coming" to Horeb, i.e. in the sense of motion towards it (however expressed),[145] but only of his Presence there, the particular omission in
question may not be *that* significant. A number of scholars have suggested that in combination with a second verb, בוא merely fulfils the aux-
iliary function of introducing the other activity.[146] Thus, when in Exod.
20:20 it is combined with נסה ("to prove"), it lacks the full sense of a literal "coming" (and consequently any clear reference to the divine Presence).[147] Thirdly, Deuteronomy *does* allude to YHWH's Presence within
the "thick darkness", though in a different way and in a different context.
5:22 refers to his speaking "out of the midst of...the thick darkness
(הערפל)", and this implies, as has already been suggested, the divine
Presence within it.[148] It would thus appear unlikely that Deut. 5 has omitted the Exodus reference to "the thick darkness where God was" because
of any aversion to the concept of divine Presence expressed by it.[149]

It is therefore clear that at this juncture of the Sinai/Horeb narrative
the Exodus account betrays a heightened interest in divine Presence. At

---

[144] Already noted for Deut. 4:10-14 in relation to Exod. 19 (pp. 51-52). See also
below, pp. 100-101.
[145] This particular activity is predicated of YHWH in 1 Sam. 3:10 and 4:7, where he
is represented as having "come" (בוא) by the narrator and Philistines respectively.
Both instances are regarded as pre-deuteronomistic: *re* 1 Sam. 3:10: Klein (1983)
xxx, 31, Mayes (1983) 83-84, 105, McCarter (1980) 16-17, Noth (1967) 60-61,
Hertzberg (1965) 10-11, 32, Brockington (1962) 318, 319, Caird 856, 860; *re* 1 Sam.
4:7: Gordon (1986) 21, Klein (1983) xxx, 40, Mayes (1983) 83-84,, Nelson 123,
McCarter (1980) 14, 18-19, 23-26, Noth (1967) 54, Hertzberg (1965) 10-11, 35,
Brockington (1962) 318, 319.
[146] Preuß (1973) 538: "בוא steht auch als eine Art Hilfsverb in Kombination mit
einem zweiten Verb und drückt dann die Absicht aus", Jenni (1971) 267: "[Eine]
recht unbestimmten Wendung in Ex 20,20...vgl. Dtn 4,34, wo *bōʾ* ebenfalls nur sub-
sidiär als Basis für das folgende Verbum dient"; cf. Zorell 98b.
[147] Cf. Jenni (1970) 252.
[148] See above, p. 82.
[149] The association of YHWH with ערפל also occurs in the pre-deuteronomistic (De
Vries 122, Jones [1984] 192, 196, Terrien [1978] 193, Würthwein 85, Robinson
[1972] 96, Weinfeld [1972a] 195, Gray [1970] 203, 212, Noth [1967] 70) 1 Kings
8:12b, which mentions his "dwell[ing]" in thick darkness (בערפל)", and which is interpreted by a number of scholars as referring to that in the most holy place of the Temple: Jones (1984) 196-197, Mettinger 28, 47, 93, Rehm (1979) 94, Terrien (1978)
128, Slotki (1950) 59; cf. Robinson (1972) 97, Šanda (1911) 219.

the same time it seems likely that the absence from Deut. 5 of the two expressions concerned is due to a rejection not of the expressions themselves but rather of the context in which they are found. The principal actor in Exod. 20:20-21 is Moses, whereas Deut. 5 is primarily concerned with the people.

YHWH'S RESPONSE TO THE PEOPLE'S REQUEST

Deut. 5:28-31 and Exod. 20:22-21:1 have little in common, beyond the fact that each consists largely of YHWH's words to Moses, and leads up to a statement of the "commandment...statutes and...ordinances" (Deut.) / "ordinances" (Exod.) which Moses is to present to the people. Both passages contain one expression of localized Presence (in Deut. 5:31 and Exod. 20:24 respectively), though in different contexts, while Exodus also refers to YHWH as having talked with the people "from heaven" (20:22). The three instances will be dealt with in turn.

--- // EXOD. 20:22

Deut.	Exod.
"[T]he LORD said to me, '...Go and say to [this people], "Return to your tents."'" (5:28-30)[150]	[T]he LORD said to Moses, "Thus you shall say to the people of Israel: 'You have seen for yourselves that I have talked with you *from heaven*.'" (20:22)

The claim that YHWH addressed the people "from heaven" (מן־השמים) provides an interesting parallel to Deut. 4:36 ("Out of heaven [מן־השמים] he let you hear his voice"), and seems to represent an example from within another tradition of what is generally regarded as the *deuteronomistic* view of the location of the divine Presence. However, while many scholars make no comment about whether Exod. 20:22 is original in its

---

[150] Deut. 5:28-33 is generally considered to be either deuteronomic (Clifford [1982] 2-3, Seitz 308, Watts [1970] 180-181, Noth [1967] 16, von Rad [1964] 7, Wright [1953] 316, 361) or deuteronomistic (Mayes [1979] 42, 161, 173-174, Phillips [1973] 3, 12, 42, Nicholson, [1967] 31-32, 36, 108, de Tillesse 35, 43-44, 72-73).

present context,[151] a significant number consider it to be secondary,[152] and frequently from a deuteronom(ist)ic hand.[153] The reasons given to support such attribution include the absence from the Sinai sources of any previous notion of YHWH speaking from heaven,[154] the verse's independence of the J and E concepts of divine Presence,[155] and its positive exhibition of interests found in Deuteronomy and the Deuteronomic writings.[156]

These lines of reasoning are unsatisfactory on several grounds. First, their deduction of the secondary nature of Exod. 20:22 involves two assumptions which, although theoretically capable of demonstration, have not as yet been proved. They are that J and E think *solely* in terms of the Deity communicating from the mountain to which he has descended/on which he dwells, and that the notion of YHWH speaking from heaven is one *exclusive to* deuteronom(ist)ic writers. On this basis the very evidence which would point on the one hand to some complexity in the thought of the early sources and on the other to some continuity with that of the deuteronom(ist)ic school is disallowed at the outset of any discussion. Secondly, the distinction between the concepts of divine Presence represented in J and E is by no means as clear as some have suggested. The Elohistic[157] Exod. 33:9 refers to the descent of the pillar of cloud, and thereby implies the descent of YHWH himself within the cloud.[158] It thus appears that, at least in the case of E, its theology of divine Presence is more complex than is commonly believed.[159] Thirdly, on the basis of

---

[151] Durham 318-319, Clements (1972) 129, Cassuto 254-255, Davies (1967) 172-173, Beer 12, 105, Driver (1911) 206.
[152] Scharbert 87, Noth (1959) 141-142, Heinisch (1934) 14, McNeile (1908) xxviii, xxix, 124, Holzinger (1900) XVIII, 79; cf. Rylaarsdam 991.
[153] Zenger (1978) 217, Nicholson (1977) 429, Mittmann 157, Childs (1974) 465, Michaeli (1974) 191, Hyatt (1971) 27, 224-225; cf. Weinfeld (1972a) 206 n. 4.
[154] Holzinger (1900) 79.
[155] Entailing the Deity descending to and dwelling on the mountain respectively: Hyatt (1971) 224-225, Noth (1959) 141-142; see above, p. 3.
[156] Michaeli (1974) 191, Hyatt (1971) 27.
[157] Mann 151 n. 14, Knight 194, Hyatt (1971) 312, 314, Davies (1967) 237, 238, Beyerlin 30, 129-130, Beer 13, Heinisch (1934) 236, Eißfeldt (1922) 156-157, Driver (1911) xxviii, 358-360, McNeile (1908) xxxiv, 211-214; cf. Clements (1972), who attributes it to "E (or perhaps J)" (p. 213).
[158] Durham 442, Mettinger 81, Jeremias (1976) 897, Childs (1974) 593, Newman 66, 68, Noth (1959) 210, Beer 158.
[159] The Elohistic Exod. 20:18-21 (Clements [1972] 126-127, Hyatt [1971] 217, Newman 32-33, 40, 46, 119, Beyerlin 17-18, 159, 187, 190, Noth [1959] 135, Beer

Deut. 4:36, which represents YHWH as being heard both from heaven ("Out of heaven he let you hear his voice") and from the mountain ("you heard his words out of the midst of the fire"), there is no inherent objection to a similar representation by J, E or Exod. 19-20 as a whole.

It is thus possible that the early sources in Exod. 19-20 (taken either singly or together) also portray the Deity's words at Sinai as being spoken both from heaven and from the earth, and in so doing provide a link with the situation envisaged in Deut. 4:36.

--- // EXOD. 20:24

Deut.	Exod.
"[T]he LORD said to me, '...Go and say to [this people], "Return to your tents."'" (5:28-30)	[T]he LORD said to Moses, "Thus you shall say to the people of Israel: '...in every place where I cause my name to be remembered *I will come to you* and bless you.'" (20:22-24)

The promise that YHWH would "come" to the Israelites occurs in the course of a directive to Moses about the building of two different types of altar. There is no parallel in Deut. 5 to either the instructions or the promise. As indicated above, the deuteronom(ist)ic account of the revelation at Horeb refers only to his Presence at the mountain, and never to his journeying there.[160] It needs to be pointed out, however, that Exod. 20:24 entails, like Exod. 20:20, the use of בוא in conjunction with a second verb (ברך [Piel], "to bless"), and so may be intended in less than its full, literal sense.[161] Despite this, Exodus still exhibits a heightened interest in divine Presence at this point.

12, Driver [1911] 201) refers to God having "come" to prove the Israelites (v. 20). It uses the same verb (בוא) as that employed in the Yahwistic 19:9a (Hyatt [1971] 197, 199, Davies [1967] 153, Newman 42, Beyerlin 14, 160, 186-187, Beer 12, Driver [1911] 168) to describe YHWH's "coming" in the thick cloud, and thus appears to contrast with the usual idea of his dwelling on the mountain. However, as indicated above (p. 84), בוא in Exod. 20:20 may not possess its full, literal sense, and in any case, even if it does, the divine journey may have been *on* rather than *to* the mountain.

[160] P. 84.

[161] See above, p. 84 n. 146.

DEUT. 5:31 // ---

Deut.	Exod.
"But you, stand here *by me...*" (5:31)	_____

Very few scholars comment on the divine instruction to Moses to 'stand here by me', though those who do generally see it as referring to the divine Presence on the mountain.[162]

The act of "standing by"

Usage elsewhere. The instruction to "stand by me" is expressed in Hebrew by means of the verb עמד and the preposition עם, and occurs elsewhere in the OT a further six times.[163] In addition, and with the same preposition, נצב (Niph.) occurs once[164] and יצב (Hithp.) four times.[165] Of these eleven, eight appear to involve a literal "standing by",[166] and so indicate the physical proximity of the parties concerned. The remaining three are more metaphorical, being found in contexts involving war or aggression,[167] and in these cases the preposition would be more accurately rendered "against".[168]

Significance in Deut. 5:31. Aside from there being no hint of animosity between YHWH and Moses, a number of features in the context suggest the *literal* usage of עמד עם. First, the inclusion of the adverb "here" (פה) implies the locative sense of the preposition. Secondly, YHWH's promise that he will speak to Moses while the latter "stands by" him is consistent

---

[162] Braulik (1986) 54: "Mose...steht nicht mehr bloß zwischen Jahwe und Volk, sondern tritt nun ganz zu Jahwe", Ridderbos 112: "Moses...must...take his place in the immediate presence of God's manifestation", Craigie (1976) 166: "The people were...sent to their tents while Moses continued in the intimacy of the presence of God", Thompson (1974) 120: "Moses remained with God on the mountain".

[163] Deut. 29:14 (EVV 15); 1 Sam. 17:26; Neh. 12:40; 1 Chron. 20:4; 21:15 and 2 Chron. 5:12.

[164] 1 Sam. 1:26.

[165] Exod. 34:5; Num. 11:16; Ps. 94:16 and 2 Chron. 20:6.

[166] This includes Exod. 34:5 ("[He] stood with him there" [ויתיצב עמו שם]), which, regardless of whether the subject of the verb is YHWH or Moses, must be intended literally because of the divine descent mentioned immediately before.

[167] Ps. 94:16: "Who stands up (יתיצב) for me against (עם) evil-doers?", 1 Chron. 20:4: "[A]fter this there arose (ותעמד) war with (עם) the Philistines at Gezer", 2 Chron. 20:6: "In your hand are power and might, so that none is able to withstand you (ואין עמך להתיצב").

[168] Cf. BDB 767.

with such an understanding of the phrase as a whole.[169] And thirdly, the Deity is represented as being present in vv. 22, 23, 24 and 26.[170] It would therefore seem that in Deut. 5:31 YHWH is instructing Moses to move into close proximity to himself, and thus that the verse contains a further deuteronom(ist)ic allusion to the divine Presence.

AUDITORY VERSUS VISUAL PHENOMENA AT HOREB/SINAI

A number of scholars have characterized the Deuteronomy and Exodus accounts of the initial giving of the law according to the types of phenomena which accompany the divine revelation. They tend to perceive Deuteronomy as emphasizing the auditory,[171] and Exodus either as stressing the visual[172] or as containing elements of both.[173,174] However, while for Terrien the emphasis on the auditory appears to have no necessary bearing on the location of the divine Presence,[175] for Mettinger and Weinfeld it is linked implicitly with the stress on transcendence associated with Name Theology.[176] Mettinger, for example, in comparing the idea of God present in the Zion-Sabaoth theology with that in the Deuteronomistic History, comments:

> [D]uring the Sinai theophany, Israel perceived no form...she only heard the voice of her God (Deut 4:12, 15). The Deuteronomistic preoccupation with God's voice and words represents an auditive, non-visual theme.

> Deuteronomistic theology...emphasiz[ed] the transcendence of God; we could, if the expression be allowed, say that God became "relocated" to the heavens above.[177]

---

[169] Cf. for example, 1 Sam. 17:26, in which David speaks to the men who "stand by" him.

[170] Scholars generally attribute vv. 22-27 and 28-31 to the same hand. See the relevant source allocations on pp. 54 and 85 n. 150.

[171] Mettinger 46, 124, Terrien (1978) 121, 201-202, Weinfeld (1972a) 207-208.

[172] Weinfeld (1972a) 207.

[173] Terrien (1978) 121-136, Mann 137-138, Newman 47-49, 61.

[174] Some scholars (e.g. Terrien [1978] 121, 130-131, 172, Kuntz 93-94, 99-100) regard E as emphasizing the auditory and J the visual. Note, however, the reservations of Mann (pp. 137-138).

[175] In connection with Deut. 4:11-13 he refers to the "'spectacular' yet invisible descent of Yahweh upon the...mountain" ([1978] 202).

[176] See above, p. 7.

[177] Pp. 46-47.

And Weinfeld, in contrasting the deuteronomic account of the Sinaitic revelation with that in Exod. 19 remarks:

> Deuteronomy has...taken care to shift the centre of gravity of the theophany from the visual to the aural plane. In Exod. 19 the principal danger confronting the people was the likelihood that they might "break through to the Lord to gaze" (v. 21)... Indeed, the pre-deuteronomic texts always invariably speak of the danger of *seeing* the Deity...The book of Deuteronomy, on the other hand, cannot conceive of the possibility of seeing the Divinity. The Israelites saw only "his great fire"...God himself remains in his heavenly abode. The danger threatening the people here, and the greatness of the miracle, is that of *hearing the voice* of the Deity: "Did any people ever hear the voice of a god speaking out of the midst of the fire as you have heard, and survived?" (4:32; cf. 5:23).[178]

Thus, on the unspoken assumption that if God can be seen (as well as heard), he is present, but if he can only be heard, he is absent, these scholars are using a perceived emphasis on the auditory aspects of the revelation at Horeb to support the claim that Deuteronomy's account of that event represents YHWH as being absent from the mountain but present in heaven. It will therefore be necessary to evaluate both that underlying presupposition and the differing degrees to which the two accounts emphasize the visual and auditory aspects of the event. Weinfeld's comments will be used as the focus for discussion.

WEINFELD'S METHODOLOGY

For a valid contrast to be drawn between two accounts, it is preferable to compare material which is closely similar. This Weinfeld has attempted to do, in that his main point of comparison concerns some danger to which the people are exposed, whether that of seeing YHWH (Exod. 19:21) or of hearing his voice (Deut. 4:32 [*sic*]). However, he has failed to note that these references are found in contexts which are entirely different. That in Exodus occurs within the *narrative* dealing with the first giving of the law, is part of a conversation (19:21-24) between YHWH and Moses about access to the mountain, and takes place prior to the giving of the Decalogue. In contrast, the danger referred to in Deuteronomy occurs neither in 4:10-14 nor 5:4-33 (i.e. those sections closest

---

[178] (1972a) 207-208.

to straightforward narrative), but within Moses' *reflection* (4:32-35) on the significance of both the first giving of the law and the Exodus from Egypt, in which he argues that YHWH is unique and that the Israelites are privileged to have experienced the two events. Neither section has any parallel in the other account. It should thus be clear, partly for the reason given, and partly because in the case of *one* of the dangers cited there is more comparable material available,[179] that Weinfeld's contrast is hardly satisfactory.

As far as the danger of *seeing* YHWH is concerned, there is only one reference in the Exodus account to the possibility of fatality consequent upon this (19:21), and, as has been mentioned above,[180] it occurs in a section having no parallel in Deuteronomy. There is thus no way of knowing whether the author of the deuteronom(ist)ic account would have referred to the possibility of the people gazing at YHWH or not, had he chosen to deal with the question of access to the mountain. In the case of the other danger, however, there are five references in Deuteronomy to that of *hearing* the voice of YHWH (4:33; 5:24, 25, 26 and 18:16), three of which occur in a section (5:23-27) which *is* paralleled in the Exodus account (i.e. 20:18-19).[181] These passages are similar in that both represent the people's words to Moses as their immediate reaction to having experienced some aspect of the revelation of the Decalogue, and both culminate in a request to Moses that *he* rather than YHWH should speak to the Israelites. It is within this context that the three deuteronom(ist)ic references to the danger of hearing YHWH's voice occur. The people's surprise at having survived hearing him speak from the fire (vv. 24 and 26) finds no parallel in the Exodus account, but their conviction that "if we hear the voice of the LORD our God any more, we shall die" (v. 25) *is* mirrored in Exod. 20 by the *non*-deuteronom(ist)ic "but let not God speak to us, lest we die" (v. 19).[182] It is clear that had Weinfeld chosen

---

[179] Deut. 5:25 // Exod. 20:19. Both refer to the people's fear of hearing the divine voice. See below, the next paragraph.

[180] P. 52.

[181] See above, pp. 81-83.

[182] Exod. 20:18-21 is ascribed by Weinfeld himself to JE ([1972a] 205) but otherwise usually to E (see above, p. 86 n. 159, and the table in Zenger [1971] 212). There are, however, a few scholars who consider either that v. 19 *is* deuteronomistic or that it has been influenced in some way by the portrayal of the Horeb theophany in Deut. 4-5: Hossfeld 173-175, Ruprecht 171-172 (the reference to Exod. 19:18-21 [p. 171] is presumably meant to be to Exod. 20:18-21), Zenger (1971) 165, 175, 212; cf.

from Deuteronomy the one reference to the danger of hearing the divine voice which is paralleled in Exodus, he would have come to a different conclusion.

EVALUATION OF WEINFELD'S ARGUMENT

The "centre of gravity of the theophany"

> Deuteronomy has...taken care to shift the centre of gravity of the theophany from the visual to the aural plane.[183]

This statement involves two affirmations about the two accounts of the first giving of the law. First, that in Exodus the "centre of gravity" of the theophany is visual, and second, that in Deuteronomy it is aural. While both claims need to be examined, a major difficulty with any comparison of the two versions is the dissimilarity of the material contained within them. Several entire sections of the Exodus account (19:1-20:1; 20:18-22; 24:1-18; 31:18 [excluding legal matter]) are missing from the Deuteronomy account (4:10-14 and 5:4-5, 22-31) because, as has already been observed, they involve conversations between *Moses* and YHWH, whereas Deuteronomy tends to concentrate on those aspects which concern the *people*.[184] Despite this, there is common to both accounts enough material which can be examined in an attempt to ensure that the present visual/aural comparison *does* entail the comparing of like with like. They are: Deut. 4:10 // Exod. 19:9; Deut. 4:11 // Exod. 19:17-18; Deut. 4:12; 5:4-5, 22a // Exod. 20:1; Deut. 4:13b; 5:22b // Exod. 31:18, and Deut. 5:23-27 // Exod. 20:18-19. When *these* sections are examined it is found that there are a number of references to both visual and aural features which are roughly parallel in the two accounts. Visible phenomena are referred to in:

Perlitt 92 n. 5. It should be noted though, that, were this attribution to become commonly accepted, it would merely mean that *no* "comparable material" (see above, pp. 90-91) was available for Weinfeld to consider, and thus that no valid comparison could be made between the two accounts. The crucial criticism, i.e. that he has failed to compare material that is "closely similar" (see above, p. 90), would still stand.

[183] Weinfeld (1972a) 207.

[184] See above, pp. 51-52, 83-85.

Deut.	Exod.
"[T]he mountain burned with *fire*...wrapped in *darkness, cloud, and gloom*." (4:11)	Mount Sinai was wrapped in *smoke*, because the LORD descended upon it in *fire*; and the *smoke* of it went up... (19:18)
"[W]hen you heard the voice out of the midst of the *darkness*, while the mountain was burning with *fire*..." (5:23)	[W]hen all the people perceived...the *lightnings*...and the mountain *smoking*... (20:18)

Aural phenomena are mentioned in:

Deut.	Exod.
"Gather the people to me, that I may let them hear my *words*..." (4:10)	"I am coming to you...that the people may hear when I *speak* with you..." (19:9)
"[T]he LORD *spoke* to you... you heard the *sound of words*...there was...a *voice*." (4:12)	God *spoke* all these words, *saying*... (20:1)
"The LORD *spoke* with you...He *said*..." (5:4-5)	
"These words the LORD *spoke* to all your assembly... with a *loud voice*..." (5:22)	
"[W]hen you heard the *voice*..." (5:23)	[W]hen all the people perceived the *thunderings*...and the *sound of the trumpet*... (20:18)
"[I]f we hear the *voice* of the LORD...any more, we shall die." (5:25)	"[L]et not God *speak* to us, lest we die." (20:19)

Moreover, each group of sections contains some reference to features which have no parallel (i.e. in the sense referred to above)[185] in the other. Additional visual phenomena are alluded to by *both* groups: Exodus (the thick cloud [19:9]), Deuteronomy (the fire [4:12; 5:4, 5, 22, 24, 25, 26],

---

[185] P. 92.

the absence of any form [4:12], and the cloud and thick darkness [5:22]). So also are aural ones: Exodus (the mountain quaking [19:18] and YHWH talking with the people from heaven [20:22]), Deuteronomy (the sound of words [4:12], the divine voice [4:12; 5:22, 24, 26] and YHWH's speaking [5:24, 26, 27]). On the basis of such observations it should be clear that these extra instances in Exodus no more constitute an emphasis on the visual than do those in Deuteronomy on the aural.

The "principal danger confronting the people" in Exodus

> In Exod. 19 the principal danger confronting the people was the likelihood that they might "break through to the Lord to gaze" (v. 21)...[186]

It is not clear on what grounds Weinfeld considers there to be a *principal* danger confronting the people, since two others are mentioned in the account,[187] and all three are different. In 19:24 YHWH refers to the possibility of his breaking out against the people if they "come up to the LORD", but gives no indication whether such action would result from their seeing or hearing him, from their being proximate, or from their merely being disobedient to him. And in 20:19, as has been noted above,[188] the people, expressing the fear that otherwise they might die, request Moses: "let not God speak to us". Thus, since not only gazing at YHWH, but also coming up to him, and hearing him speak, are also represented as being dangerous to the people, it would appear that in the Exodus account both visual *and aural* aspects of the theophany are significant in this respect. It seems that there is little justification for Weinfeld's view of the former as being the most important.

The "possibility of seeing the Divinity"

> The book of Deuteronomy, on the other hand, cannot conceive of the possibility of seeing the Divinity.[189]

This remark, taken with the previous one, has behind it the idea that Exodus *can* conceive of the possibility of seeing the Deity, because it lo-

---

[186] Weinfeld (1972a) 207.

[187] In addition to that (resulting from not being consecrated) accruing to any priests who approached YHWH (19:22).

[188] P. 91.

[189] Weinfeld (1972a) 207.

calizes him on Sinai, whereas Deuteronomy *cannot*, because it represents him as being absent from Horeb. However, aside from the observation that Weinfeld's basic premise vis-à-vis the latter is mistaken (i.e. in that the book portrays YHWH as being *present* on the mountain), three points should be taken into account. First, Weinfeld's implication that Exodus *can* conceive of the possibility of seeing the Divinity requires some qualification. לראות ("to gaze") in Exod. 19:21 may be an infinitive of purpose,[190] and thus represent the *motive* for the people's "breaking through", i.e. as opposed to something they may actually accomplish. In this case, the question of the Deity's visibility or otherwise cannot be settled by an appeal to this verse since it is not clear whether it is the sight of YHWH or the attempt to gain such which would result in many of the Israelites perishing. It is also important to note that YHWH's descent "in the sight of all the people" (Exod. 19:11) is a *veiled* one, since it is described as being both "in a thick cloud" (v. 9) and "in fire" (v. 18). YHWH himself is not seen. Moreover, the one instance of God actually *being seen* (referred to in Exod. 24:10, 11) is itself regarded as anomalous by the narrator, since he reports it not without comment, but with the observation, "[God] did not lay his hand on the chief men of the people of Israel" (24:11). Even in Exodus the idea of man seeing the Deity is an unusual one. Secondly, it is difficult to see on what grounds Weinfeld could assert the *impossibility* of Deuteronomy conceiving of seeing the Deity. The book neither makes any affirmation to that effect, nor contains any parallels to the two sections of Exodus (i.e. 19:20b-25 and 24:1-2, 9-11) in which the references to gazing at/seeing the Deity occur, and with which a comparison might be expected to reveal some aversion to such a notion. Neither would it be satisfactory to claim the very absence of such parallels as evidence, since it can be argued that they have been omitted on grounds *other* than that of a dislike for the idea that the Deity can be seen. The omission of all reference to the content of Exod. 24:1-2, 9-11 from the deuteronom(ist)ic account of the first giving of the law is explicable on the same grounds as that of the omission of Exod. 19:20b-25 from Deut. 4:10-14, i.e. that its principal actors do not include the main subject of Deuteronomy's concern at this juncture, namely the people.[191] In any case, although YHWH's descent in the thick cloud

---

[190] GKC 348 §114f.
[191] See above, p. 52.

(Exod. 19:9) and fire (Exod. 19:18) has no strict parallel in Deuteronomy, such veiling of his Presence *is* implied elsewhere in the references to his speaking "out of the midst of" the thick darkness (Deut.
5:22) and fire (Deut. 4:12, 15; 5:4, etc.). Thirdly, it has already been argued that the references in Deut. 4:12 and 15 to the people seeing no
form cannot be cited as firm evidence that YHWH was conceived as being absent.[192] They are equally consistent with his being present but con-
cealed, which is, moreover, the understanding to which Moses' use of the
non-observation of any form seems to point.[193]

The "danger threatening the people" in Deuteronomy

> The danger threatening the people [in Deuteronomy]...is that
> of *hearing the voice* of the Deity...[194]

That the danger of hearing YHWH's voice is presented as a major emphasis in the deuteronom(ist)ic account is certainly true. Both Moses
(4:33) and the people (5:24, 26) express surprise that the latter have
heard YHWH's voice and survived, and the Israelites twice reveal their
fear that if they continue to do so they will die (5:25; 18:16). However,
two further points need to be made. First, this danger of hearing the divine voice is not a new concept which Deuteronomy has introduced into
its account by way of contrast with a supposed emphasis in Exodus on
the danger of seeing YHWH's Person. Rather, as has been pointed out
above, the idea is already present in Exod. 20:19.[195] Secondly, in the
same way that Exodus refers to both visual and aural dangers in connection with the theophany, so also does Deuteronomy. In addition to emphasizing the danger associated with the voice (an aural phenomenon), it
three times mentions that associated with the fire (a visual one). Those
aspects regarded as being dangerous are: unspecified in 5:4 ("[Y]ou were
afraid because of the fire"), its destructive effect in 5:25 ("[W]hy should
we die? For this great fire will consume us"), and the *sight* of it in 18:16
("Let me not...see this great fire any more, lest I die"). Thus, while the

---

[192] See above, pp. 62-64.
[193] See above, p. 64. Interestingly, the Exodus account makes no claim that the
people *did* see the divine form at Sinai. Cf. Staton: "In spite of [Exod.] 19:11 there is
no indication that the people were allowed to see God in any way" (p. 193).
[194] Weinfeld (1972a) 208.
[195] P. 91.

emphasis is clearly on the danger of *hearing YHWH's voice*, reference is also made to that of *seeing the fire* from which the voice was heard.

It should by now be clear that Weinfeld has overstated his case. First, there are no valid grounds for supposing the centres of gravity of the Exodus and Deuteronomy accounts of the first giving of the law to be visual and aural respectively. Over and above those aspects mentioned in common, they each refer to both kinds of phenomena, and so invalidate his neat generalization. Secondly, the distinction that Weinfeld makes, as to what in each account is regarded as dangerous, is by no means as clearly drawn as he would like, since while there *is* an emphasis in Deuteronomy on the aural, there is no such similar emphasis in Exodus on the visual. It also needs to be said that even were the distinction to exist, it would not prove his contention that "God himself remains in his heavenly abode",[196] since an emphasis on the dangers of hearing the divine voice is equally consistent with the earthly localization of a deity who is veiled. Thirdly, Weinfeld's assertion that Exodus can, whereas Deuteronomy cannot, conceive of the possibility of seeing the Deity rests on rather flimsy foundations, particularly in the case of Deuteronomy. It would thus appear that this whole line of reasoning has no adequate basis in the text, and, moreover, would be inconclusive even if it had. Our justification of the inadmissibility of the visual versus aural distinction thus contributes to the general thesis that we are arguing, namely that Deuteronomy does envisage the localization, as well as the transcendence, of YHWH in its depiction of Israel's wilderness encounter with him.

OVERALL COMPARISON OF THE DEUTERONOMY AND EXODUS ACCOUNTS

Before attempting an overall comparison of the two sections,[197] i.e. with a view to obtaining some insight into the purposes behind their composition, it will be useful to make a number of preliminary remarks about some obvious differences between them. First, the Exodus account consists of narrative about Moses and the people, and apart from the numerous instances of dialogue which it contains, is written in the third

---

[196] Weinfeld (1972a) 208.

[197] If most of the material dealing with laws and instructions for the building of the tabernacle is excluded, the Exodus account consists of 19:1-20:1; 20:18-22; 24:1-18 and 31:18, while that in Deuteronomy incorporates 4:10-14 and 5:4-5, 22-31.

person. In contrast, the deuteronom(ist)ic account, which also concerns Moses and the Israelites, does not consist of straightforward narrative, but is presented in the form of speeches by Moses to the people, and in consequence is written substantially in the first and second persons. Secondly, the Exodus version is almost three times as long as that in Deuteronomy (50 verses, as opposed to 17),[198] and includes a number of sections for which there are no parallels in the shorter account, namely 19:1-2, 3-8, 10-15, 20b-25; 20:20-21 and 24:1-18. It is clear that if the author of the deuteronom(ist)ic version did have a copy of the Exodus one in front of him, then he exercised a considerable amount of selectivity in composing his own. In the discussion below, we hope to shed some light on the principles guiding his choice.

THE FREQUENCY OF DIVINE PRESENCE REFERENCES

In sections common to Deuteronomy and Exodus

First, a comparison of those sections which Deuteronomy and Exodus have in common[199] reveals there to be nearly twice the incidence of divine Presence expressions in the deuteronom(ist)ic account as there are in the Exodus one: while 95%[200] of the verses in Deuteronomy contain such a reference, only 50%[201] of those in Exodus do so.[202] Secondly, the two versions have it in common that they both indicate (though in different parts of the narrative) that the people's assembling at the foot of the mountain is in close proximity to the Deity: in Deuteronomy YHWH tells Moses, "*Gather the people to me*" (4:10), and in Exodus Moses

---

[198] It could be argued that since some of these verses (e.g. Deut. 4:13a, 14 and 5:31b) refer to the commandments they should be excluded from the comparison. This would increase the ratio of the number of verses in the Exodus account to that in Deuteronomy.

[199] Deut. 4:10 // Exod. 19:9; Deut. 4:11 // Exod. 19:17-18; Deut. 4:12; 5:4-5, 22a // Exod. 20:1; Deut. 5:23-27 // Exod. 20:18-19.

[200] The ten and a half verses concerned contain ten references to divine Presence: in 4:10 (2x), 12; 5:4 (2x), 5, 22a, 23, 24 and 26.

[201] The six verses concerned contain three references to divine Presence: in 19:9, 17 and 18.

[202] If the *entire* "narrative" sections (see above, p. 97 n. 197) are compared, the incidence of divine Presence expressions in Deuteronomy is still significantly higher than that in Exodus: 65% as compared to 40%. The seventeen verses in Deuteronomy contain the ten references to divine Presence mentioned in n. 200 together with that in 5:31, while the fifty in Exodus contain twenty: the three mentioned above, plus those in 19:3 (2x), 11, 20a, 21, 22, 24; 20:20, 21, 24; 24:1, 2, 10 (2x), 11, 12 and 16.

brings the people out of the camp "*to meet God*" (19:17). Thirdly, the Exodus account has two references unique to itself. In 19:9 YHWH informs Moses, "I *am coming to you in a thick cloud*" (contrast Deut. 4:10, where the divine Presence *is* mentioned, but in terms of its localization on the mountain, and not of its journeying there). And in 19:18 the smoke on Mount Sinai is attributed to YHWH's *descent* upon it in fire (contrast Deut. 4:11 which refers to fire, darkness, cloud and gloom, but says nothing about their origin). Fourthly, Deuteronomy, on the other hand, has nine references peculiar to itself. In 4:10 the people "[stand] *before the LORD*...at Horeb" (contrast Exod. 19:17 where they merely "[take] their stand at the foot of the mountain"). In 4:12; 5:4 and 22 YHWH speaks "*out of the midst of the fire*",[203] with 5:4 intimating that such communication with the Israelites was "*face to face*" (contrast Exod. 20:1 in which God merely speaks). In 5:5 Moses stands "*between the LORD and [the people]*" (contrast Exod. 20:1 which makes no mention of such a positioning). In 5:23 the people respond to "the voice *out of the midst of the darkness*" (contrast Exod. 20:18 where they react against the largely natural phenomena accompanying the theophany). Finally, in 5:24 and 26 the people twice express surprise at having survived hearing YHWH's voice "*out of the midst of (the) fire*" (contrast Exod. 20:19 which makes no mention of their even having heard it).

It is thus clear that where the two versions deal with the same aspects of the first giving of the law, both represent YHWH as being present on the mountain. However, while Exodus includes only two unparalleled references to divine Presence (i.e. to YHWH's coming or descent), Deuteronomy includes a further nine instances of his being on the earth.

In sections occurring only in Deuteronomy

Deuteronomy contains one reference to divine Presence in a passage without any real parallel in Exodus. In Deut. 5:28-31 YHWH responds to the people's fear (5:24-27) by allowing them to return to their tents, and at the same time instructing Moses to "*stand here by me*" (5:31) so that he can receive the commandments etc. which he is to pass on to the Israelites. No such instructions are recorded in Exod. 20:22-21:1 where the

---

[203] Also from "the cloud and the thick darkness" (5:22).

divine response[204] is much less obviously related to the people's fear (20:18-20).

In sections occurring only in Exodus

Within the Exodus account the majority of divine Presence references having no parallel in the deuteronom(ist)ic version occur in sections which themselves are unique to Exodus, i.e. in 19:1-8 (2x), 10-15, 20b-25 (3x); 20:20-21 (2x); 20:22-21:1 and 24:1-18 (7x). Those in chs. 19-20 can be classified into references to his being on the mountain (19:3 [2x], 21, 22, 24; 20:21), to his descent (19:11) and to his coming (20:20, 24), while those in ch. 24 concern his being on the mountain (vv. 1, 2, 10 [2x], 11, 12 and 16).[205]

OMISSIONS FROM THE DEUTERONOM(IST)IC ACCOUNT

It should be clear from the preceding section that references to divine Presence in Exodus which are absent from Deuteronomy fall into two groups: those referring to the Deity's coming and descent on to Mount Sinai, and those to his Presence on or at the mountain. Our primary concern, however, will be to explain the absence of the *first* group, since, as has been demonstrated above, the deuteronom(ist)ic account makes ample allusion to YHWH's Presence *on or at* Horeb.[206] It will therefore be necessary to examine the contexts of Deut. 4:10-14 and 5:4-5, 22-31 to see whether they provide any indication as to why those sections of Exodus referring to YHWH's coming and descent are not included in Deuteronomy's account of the first giving of the law.

Deut. 4:10-14

It has been argued, on the basis of Deut. 4:9 and of the content of vv. 10-14, that in referring to Horeb, the writer's primary intention is to remind the Israelites that on that occasion *they personally* heard

---

[204] Exod. 20:22-26.
[205] The references to YHWH's glory (vv. 16, 17) have not been included here.
[206] Pp. 45-50, 53-66, 76-83, 88-89. Note that some of the Exod. 19-20, 24 expressions of divine Presence are used elsewhere in Deuteronomy and the Deuteronomistic History: *re* the Deity coming (19:9; 20:20, 24), cf. 1 Sam. 3:10; 4:7(?), *re* going up to him (19:3; 24:1, 12), cf. Deut. 10:1; Judg. 21:5 (2x), 8; 1 Sam. 10:3, *re* his Presence in the thick darkness (20:21), cf. Deut. 5:22 and 1 Kings 8:12, and *re* his calling out of the midst of the cloud (24:16), cf. Deut. 5:22 and all the references to divine communication out of the midst of the fire in 4:12, 15; 5:4, etc.

YHWH's declaration of his covenant.[207] This of itself is sufficient to explain the omission of all reference to the content of Exod. 19:3-8, 10-15, 20b-25, and the whole of ch. 24, since these sections are primarily concerned with Moses, either alone or with the other leaders, rather than with the people. In any case, they deal not with the declaration itself, but with events occurring either before (ch. 19) or after (ch. 24) the revelation of the covenant.

Deut. 5:4-5, 22-31

Deut. 5 consists of an address by Moses to Israel in which, having exhorted them to listen to and obey the statutes and ordinances which he is about to give them (v. 1), he points out that the Horeb covenant was made with them personally (vv. 2-5, 22) and reminds them of its content (vv. 6-21), their reaction to hearing YHWH's voice (vv. 23-27) and YHWH's response to their reaction (vv. 28-31). It is significant that of that part of the chapter consisting of narrative pertaining to the events at Horeb (i.e. vv. 2-5, 22-31: fourteen verses), nearly two-thirds is devoted to the consequences of the people's hearing the divine voice (vv. 23-31: nine verses), whether in terms of their response to it (vv. 23-27) or of YHWH's subsequent response to them (vv. 28-31).

It is proposed that the first giving of the law is mentioned in Deut. 5 primarily as a justification of Moses' demand for obedience (v. 1) toward what *he* (i.e. rather than YHWH) is about to say. This is based on the following three grounds:

The people's mandate. First, the opening verses of the narrative dealing with the events at Horeb emphasize that the original making of the covenant (whose content is described in vv. 6-21) was with Moses' *present audience*. This is indicated by the two affirmations that it was "with us", and by the accompanying denial that it was "with our fathers":

> "The LORD our God made a covenant with us in Horeb. Not
> with our fathers did the LORD make this covenant, but with
> us, who are all of us here alive this day." (vv. 2-3)

It is also implied by the use of the second person form of address in the subsequent narrative, as compared with the relevant part of the Exodus

---

passage.[208] This means that Deut. 5 represents Moses' *present audience*
as those who had personally heard YHWH's revelation of the Decalogue,
decided that they were unable to take any more (vv. 24-26), and so not
only requested Moses to listen in their stead and convey to them all that
YHWH would speak to him, but also promised to listen to and obey
whatever he passed on (v. 27). It thus appears that in this chapter Moses
is reminding the Israelites that *they themselves* originally authorized his
present claim on their obedience (v. 1b).

The divine witness. Secondly, the narrator is at some pains to stress that
the people's request to Moses to mediate YHWH's speaking to them was
witnessed by the Deity himself. Not only does Moses point out that "*the
LORD heard your words,* when you spoke to me" (v. 28a), but he also
follows it, somewhat tautologously, by a quotation of *YHWH's* statement
to that effect: "the LORD said to me, '*I have heard the words of this people,* which they have spoken to you'" (v. 28b). He then represents
YHWH as acquiescing in their entreaty by his instruction to send the
people back to their tents, while he (Moses) remains in the divine Presence to receive the commandments which he is to pass on to the Israelites
in the manner desired (vv. 30-31). Moses' claim on the people's obedience (v. 1b) is thus further supported by the reminder that YHWH himself had witnessed their request.

The use of דבר (Piel) in Deut. 5:1. Thirdly, the occurrence in v. 1 of דבר
(Piel) to refer to Moses' conveying of the statutes and ordinances to the
people is unusual. Within Deuteronomy as a whole there are numerous
instances of Moses' direct speech to the Israelites in the second person,
i.e. in which he urges them to do/keep/obey the commandments/ordi-
nances/statutes/words mediated by him. 4:1 would be typical:

> "And now, O Israel, give heed to the statutes and the ordi-
> nances which I teach you, and do them..."

---

[208] "The LORD spoke *with you* face to face" (5:4) and "These words the LORD
spoke to all *your assembly*" (5:22) [contrast "God spoke all these words (Exod.
20:1)]; "[W]hen *you* heard the voice" (5:23), and the four reminders of the people's
statements that *they* had heard it (5:24 [2x], 25, 26) [contrast "[W]hen all the people
perceived the thunderings" (Exod. 20:18)]; and "[T]he LORD heard *your* words,
when *you* spoke to me; and the LORD said to me, 'I have heard the words of *this
people,* which *they* have spoken to you'" (5:28) [contrast "[T]he LORD said to
Moses, 'Thus you shall say to the people'" (Exod. 20:22)].

Analysis of these various instances reveals that six verbs are used to express Moses' conveying of such laws *to the people*: "command" (צוה
[Piel]), "teach" (למד [Piel]), "speak" (דבר [Piel]), "declare" (נגד [Hiph.]),
"set before" (נתן לפני) and "enjoin upon" (עוד ב [Hiph.]), of which "command" (30x) is the most common, "teach" occurs four times and the
others only once or twice each. The particular combination "statutes and
ordinances" (5:1) is usually "taught" (4:1, 5, 14; 6:1), but can also be "set
before" (4:8; 11:32) or "commanded" (7:11; 8:11). However, with the
exception of 5:1, it is never "spoken".

If we now examine Deut. 5, we find that originally YHWH had spoken (דבר [Piel]) directly to the people themselves (vv. 4, 22, 24, 26), but
that they had been unable to bear it (v. 25), and so had asked Moses to
listen in their stead and then speak (דבר [Piel]) to them whatever YHWH
communicated to him (v. 27). This being the case, it is difficult to escape
the conclusion that in 5:1 the narrator has chosen דבר (Piel) in preference
to למד (Piel), נתן לפני or צוה (Piel) so as to make clear to his audience that
what Moses is about to do (i.e. *speak* statutes and ordinances in their
hearing) is no less than what they themselves had previously asked him
to do on the occasion of the first giving of the law.

Relevance to the question of divine Presence. On the basis of the above
observations,[209] it should be clear that in Deut. 5 Moses refers to the
events at Horeb in such a way as to justify his claim on the attention and
obedience of his audience. His main interest therefore lies in YHWH's
declaration of the law to the people and in their reaction to that revelation, since he (Moses) is about to do something similar himself, and it
was these two aspects of the earlier event which resulted in the people's
request that he do so. He is able to command their obedience (v. 1b) because they have asked him to, *and* in the Presence of YHWH. Thus, the
ch. 5 "account" of what happened at Horeb *begins* with YHWH speaking
to the people at the mountain (v. 4), without even the minimal prelimi-
naries recorded in the corresponding narrative in ch. 4 (i.e. those in
vv. 10-11). This overriding concern satisfactorily explains the absence of
the entire content of Exod. 19 and 24. Their various references to
YHWH's coming, descent and Presence on the mountain have all been
omitted, not because of any aversion to such notions, but because of a

---

[209] Pp. 101-103. Note that our analysis tends to undermine Mayes' (1980) literary-
critical approach to Deut. 5.

primary interest in what took place between the events which those chapters describe, i.e. YHWH's declaration of his covenant to the Israelites and their reaction to that revelation.[210]

CONCLUSION

There is a significantly higher proportion of references to divine Presence in the deuteronom(ist)ic account of the first giving of the law than there is in the Exodus one. That they occur at all in Deuteronomy shows that their author(s) had no fundamental objection to the notion either of divine Presence in general or of YHWH's localization at Horeb in particular. However, while both books represent the Deity as being present *on or at* the mountain, only Exodus refers to his coming and descent on to it. These omissions from Deuteronomy constitute a major divergence in the two accounts, but are largely explicable in terms of the contexts in which the deuteronom(ist)ic version occurs.

---

[210] Such an interest also explains the absence of the content of Exod. 20:20-21, since within the latter Moses is the principal actor, whereas in Deut. 5 the *people* occupy centre stage.

4

DEUTERONOMY 9-10

Deut. 9-10 includes an account of the incident of the Golden Calf and thus covers some of the same material as that described in Exod. 32-34. Both versions contain a number of possible references to divine Presence, and, as in the case of the first giving of the law,[1] these will be considered in groups according as they refer to the various stages of the narrative.

THE FIRST GIVING OF THE LAW

DEUT. 9:10 // EXOD. 31:18; DEUT. 10:4 // EXOD. 34:28

Both Deuteronomy and Exodus refer to the two sets of stone tables inscribed with the ten commandments. Deut. 9:10 // Exod. 31:18 refers to YHWH's giving Moses the first set of tables (i.e. before the incident of the Golden Calf), while Deut. 10:4 // Exod. 34:28b refers to his giving him the second set (i.e. after that incident):

Deut.	Exod.
"[T]he LORD gave me the two tables of stone written with the finger of God; and on them were all the words which the LORD had spoken with you...*out of the midst of the fire...*" (9:10)	[The LORD] gave to Moses...the two tables of the testimony, tables of stone, written with the finger of God. (31:18)

---

[1] See above, ch. 3.

105

Deut.	Exod.
"[H]e wrote on the tables, as at the first writing, the ten commandments which the LORD had spoken to you on the mountain *out of the midst of the fire*..." (10:4)	[H]e wrote upon the tables the words of the covenant, the ten commandments. (34:28b)

Exod. 31:18 is allocated either to P[2] or P (18a) and E (18b),[3] and Exod. 34:28b to J,[4] with some scholars assigning v. 28bβ ("the ten commandments") to a deuteronomic redactor.[5] Apart from Deut. 9:22-24 and 10:6-9, which are frequently viewed as subsequent to the basic narrative, Deut. 9:7b-10:11[6] is generally considered to be deuteronomic,[7] deuteronomistic,[8] or a mixture of both.[9,10]

Deut. 9:10; 10:4

In Deut. 9:10 and 10:4 Moses reminds his audience not only that the words inscribed on the tables were those which YHWH had conveyed to the people themselves on the occasion of the first giving of the law, but also that they were communicated "out of the midst of the fire". Such a qualification indicates, as argued earlier,[11] that YHWH himself was present within the fire and thus upon the earth. By contrast, the parallel verses in Exodus mention neither YHWH's mode of communication to the Israelites, nor even that he spoke to them, and so make no reference to the divine Presence.

---

[2] Durham 350, 353, Childs (1974) 529, 532, Michaeli (1974) 11-12.

[3] Hyatt (1971) 258, 263, 299-300, Davies (1967) 223, 227, Beer 13, 152-153, Driver (1911) 342, 346, McNeile (1908) xxxiv, 203, Holzinger (1900) XIX, 148.

[4] Scharbert 131-132, Clements (1972) 220-221, Hyatt (1971) 318-319, 326, Noth (1959) 214, Driver (1911) 364-365, 374, McNeile (1908) xxx-xxxi, xxxiv, 221, Holzinger (1900) XIX; cf. Childs (1974) 608, 615-616.

[5] Childs, McNeile; cf. Scharbert, Driver.

[6] There is some debate as to where the section begins. See below, p. 122 n. 87.

[7] Watts (1970) 181, 226-231, Noth (1967) 16-17, Wright (1953) 317, 392-398.

[8] Phillips (1973) 12, 69-74, Nicholson (1967) 29-31, de Tillesse 45-46, 56-63, 83; cf. von Rad (1964) 54-57, Smith (1918) 124, 126-138, Bertholet (1899) 30, Robinson (n.d.) 102-108.

[9] Mayes (1979) 42, 48, 194-207, Buis and Leclercq 16-17, 88-93.

[10] In addition, the occasional verse is sometimes regarded as post-deuteronomistic, but no consensus has been reached on this point.

[11] See above, pp. 60-66.

Thus, in pointing out that the writing on the two sets of tables consisted of words which YHWH had previously spoken to the people "out of the midst of the fire", Deut. 9:10 and 10:4 are locating YHWH within that fire. At these points in the narrative, therefore, and as compared with Exodus, Deuteronomy is expressing a heightened interest in divine Presence.

YHWH'S INSTRUCTION TO MOSES TO DESCEND

DEUT. 9:12 // EXOD. 32:7

Within the deuteronom(ist)ic account of the incident of the Golden Calf YHWH's instruction to Moses to descend the mountain as a result of the people's sin differs from that in Exodus in one small but significant way:

Deut.	Exod.
"[T]he LORD said to me, 'Arise, go down quickly *from here*; for your people whom you have brought from Egypt have acted corruptly...'" (9:12)	[T]he LORD said to Moses, "Go down; for your people, whom you brought up out of...Egypt, have corrupted themselves..." (32:7)

In this context the use of the expression "from here" in English implies that both speaker and addressee are present together at the same place, and thus introduces the possibility that the same might also be true of מזה in Hebrew.

Exod. 32:7-14 is usually attributed to a deuteronom(ist)ic hand,[12] as also is Deut. 9:12.[13] This raises the question as to why the same(?) author uses מזה in the one case but not in the other. Be that as it may, it will still be useful to consider the significance of the adverb in Deut. 9:12, since, if it is missing from Exod. 32:7-14, it is also likely to have been absent from its non-deuteronom(ist)ic precursor.

---

[12] Scharbert 120, Burns 161, 166-167, Hahn 113-114, 243, 260, Zenger (1978) 229-230, Childs (1974) 559-560, 567, Hyatt (1971) 300, 301, 303, 306, 307, Davies (1967) 232, Noth (1948) 33 n. 113, McNeile (1908) xxxv, xxxvii, 205-206; cf. Michaeli (1974) 272.

[13] See above, p. 106.

Actions "from here"

By human beings. Within the OT there are nine instances[14] of the single[15] use of the adverb מזה occurring on the lips of a human being and used in a spatial sense.[16] In these cases it means "from here" or "hence",[17] and can generally be shown to have some reference to the place where the speaker himself is at the moment of speaking. For example, in Gen. 37:12-17 Israel sends Joseph to Shechem to find out how his brothers are. On his arrival there he asks a man to tell him where they are pasturing their flock. The man replies: "They have gone away from here (מזה), for I heard them say, 'Let us go to Dothan'" (v. 17). This not only answers Joseph's question, but also (through the use of מזה) imparts the additional information that before the brothers set out for Dothan they were at the place where the man himself now is when giving his reply, i.e. at Shechem. That this entails a correct understanding of what מזה implies is confirmed by the earlier part of the narrative in which it is stated that the brothers did in fact go to Shechem,[18] even though they had left by the time Joseph arrived.

In the same way it can be shown that in most of the cases cited,[19] מזה is used by its speaker to make some point about the place where he is at the time. Thus when Zedekiah tells Ebed-melech, "Take three men with you *from here*" (Jer. 38:10), his use of מזה tells us what we otherwise would not know from the context, i.e. that the men in question are to be chosen from near where the king is sitting when he gives the order.

By the Deity. Apart from Deut. 9:12, there are five other OT instances of מזה occurring on the lips of the Deity. However, in four of them the immediate context contains no clear independent evidence as to the divine whereabouts at the time of speaking,[20] and in Josh. 4:3 the usage is am-

---

[14] Gen. 37:17; 42:15; 50:25; Exod. 13:3, 19; 33:15; Judg. 6:18; Jer. 38:10; Ruth 2:8.

[15] I.e. as opposed to ...מזה...מזה, which means "on one side...on the other side" (BDB 262).

[16] I.e. excluding Ps. 75:9 (EVV 8); Eccl. 6:5; 7:18; Neh. 13:4; 2 Chron. 25:9.

[17] BDB 262.

[18] "Now his brothers went to pasture their father's flock near Shechem. And Israel said to Joseph, 'Are not your brothers pasturing the flock at Shechem?'" (vv. 12-13).

[19] See above, n. 14.

[20] Exod. 11:1 (2x); 33:1 and 1 Kings 17:3. This includes Exod. 33:1 ("Depart, go up hence (מזה), you and the people"), even though within much of the Exodus portrayal of the events at Sinai YHWH is represented as being on the mountain. Certainly he is there at the end of the previous chapter ("Moses said to the people, '...I will go up to

biguous, since it is not clear whether the adverb is meant in relation to YHWH himself or to Joshua.[21]

Significance in Deut. 9:12. In none of the instances mentioned is it clear whether the Deity is present or absent from the place referred to by his use of the term מזה. Nevertheless, if its import in divine speech is the same as that in human speech, then YHWH's instruction to Moses to "go down quickly from here" tells us not only that Moses was on the mountain and that he was required to descend, but also that YHWH himself was present there with him at the time of issuing the command.

There is thus some evidence for regarding the use of מזה in Deut. 9:12 as an allusion to the divine Presence on the mountain. It has no parallel in the corresponding account in Exodus.

MOSES' FIRST INTERCESSION

DEUT. 9:18 // ---; DEUT. 9:25-26 // EXOD. 32:11

Both accounts reveal Moses as interceding for the people. In Deut. 9 this is implied by his statements, "the LORD hearkened to me that time also" (v. 19) and "I prayed for Aaron also at the same time" (v. 20), while in Exod. 32 it is stated that he "besought the LORD his God" (v. 11). However, only in the deuteronom(ist)ic version is there any reference to the prostration adopted by him during his intercession:

Deut.	Exod.
"I lay prostrate *before the LORD* as before, forty days and forty nights; I neither ate bread nor drank water...But the LORD hearkened to me that time also...and I prayed for Aaron also at the same time." (9:18-20)	____

---

the LORD...' So Moses returned to the LORD" [32:30-31]; cf. Beyerlin 27), and the מזה of 33:1 could well be construed as alluding to that fact. However, while the occasional scholar has attributed 32:30-34 and 33:1 to the same hand (J: Davies [1967] 229, 235, 237, Driver [1911] xxviii, 355-357), there is no clear consensus on this point, and as Childs (1974) has pointed out, Exod. 33:1-3 itself is "without explicit information regarding either the time or the place of the communication" (p. 587).
[21] It occurs in instructions which Joshua himself is to pass on to others: "[T]he LORD said to Joshua, 'Take twelve men...and command them, "Take twelve stones from here (מזה) out of the midst of the Jordan"'" (Josh. 4:2-3).

Deut.	Exod.
"I lay prostrate *before the LORD*...And I prayed to the LORD..." (9:25-26)	Moses besought the LORD his God, and said... (32:11)

Moreover, not only is there no reference in the Exodus account to Moses' prostration, but neither are there any instances of the expression "before the LORD" in its entire narrative of the Golden Calf incident (i.e. in chs. 32-34).[22]

Many scholars regard Exod. 32:7-14 as a deuteronom(ist)ic insertion into a narrative (ch. 32) largely composed of one or more of the old Pentateuchal sources, J and E.[23] As indicated earlier, Deut. 9:18-20 and 25-29 are generally attributed to a deuteronom(ist)ic hand.[24]

Exod. 32

As the divine Presence on the mountain is not mentioned in the Exodus account of Moses' intercession, it has to be deduced from the context. In Exod. 24, of which ch. 32 (or 31:18) is generally held to be the narrative continuation,[25] YHWH tells Moses, "Come up to me on the mountain" (v. 12). And at the end of ch. 32, on the day after the intercession, Moses first informs the people that he will "go up to the LORD" and then "return[s] to [him]" (vv. 30-31). Thus, since YHWH is represented as being on the mountain both before and after the intercession recorded in Exod. 32:11-13, it is likely that his Presence there is intended to be understood *while* Moses is interceding for the Israelites.

The act of "lying prostrate before"

Earlier views. Although no scholar has been found to comment on the significance of לפני יהוה in Deut. 9:18, 25, the application of Rabban's criteria would suggest that it does refer to the divine Presence.[26] He considers that, whenever an activity לפני יהוה is a concrete physical action[27]

---

[22] The expression does occur in Exod. 34:34, but in connection with Moses' wearing a veil on his face, a practice carried out *after* his descent from the mountain with the second set of tables.

[23] See above, p. 107 n. 12.

[24] See above, p. 106.

[25] Scharbert 100-101, Durham 347-348, Burns 160, Gispen 291, Hahn 236, Knight 160, 184, Michaeli (1974) 228, 268, 270, Clements (1972) 158, Davies (1967) 196, Noth (1959) 162, Beer 153, Driver (1911) 251, 256, 346.

[26] See below, pp. 136-138.

[27] Rabban's terminology.

understood literally,[28] then the preposition designates a *spatial* relationship between the author of the action and the one before whom it is carried out. "Lying prostrate" would appear to constitute such an action, and since no one claims to understand it in a metaphorical sense, it would appear reasonable to interpret it literally, i.e. in terms of Moses lying with his face to the ground. This means that in Deut. 9:18 and 25 the qualification לפני יהוה indicates a spatial relationship between Moses and YHWH and thus points to the divine Presence in Moses' immediate vicinity.

Usage elsewhere. Apart from the three instances in Deut. 9:18 and 25 (2x), the verb נפל (Hithp.) is found elsewhere only in Ezra 10:1, again in conjunction with לפני. There it is used to describe Ezra's "casting himself down before the house of God" and, when commented on, the prostration is generally taken to have occurred somewhere within the precincts of the temple.[29] The preposition is clearly intended in its locative sense.

Significance in Deut. 9:18, 25. First, it will be necessary to establish the whereabouts of both Moses and the Deity during the intercession[30] before we can say whether the two instances of "before the LORD" are indications of divine Presence.

---

[28] For his examples see below, p. 137 n. 29.

[29] Blenkinsopp 177, 187, 189, Holmgren 76, Williamson (1985) 149, Fensham (1982) 133, Brockington (1969) 110, Schneider 149, 152, Ryle 126.

[30] *One* intercession (contra Braulik [1986] 78-79). Although Moses' prostration is mentioned twice (i.e. in vv. 18 and 25), on two grounds it would appear to refer to only one occasion. First, if we consider the literal rendering of the Hebrew of v. 25: "So I lay prostrate before the LORD the forty days and forty nights *that I lay prostrate*", the repetition of the verb נפל (Hithp.) in the subordinate clause אשר התנפלתי ("that I lay prostrate") to qualify the reference to his doing that same thing for forty days and forty nights would seem to indicate (contra Ogden [1992] in his discussion of this *idem per idem* construction [pp. 114, 119]) that there was only *one* such period of prostration in the current crisis, and that it is to be identified with one mentioned earlier in the narrative, presumably that in v. 18. Secondly, the differences between the two sections which follow the references to that prostration (i.e. vv. 18-20 and vv. 25-29) are consistent with just one period, since the former concentrates on what Moses did and why he did it, whereas the latter gives the actual content of his prayer. The two verses thus refer to one and the same occasion: Christensen 191, Ridderbos 136, Clifford (1982) 59, 63, Craigie (1976) 196, 197, Thompson (1974) 141, 142, Watts (1970) 227, Lohfink (1963) 213, Clamer 576, Reider 101, Junker 56, Smith (1918) 131, Driver (1902) 116, Bertholet (1899) 32, Robinson (n.d.) 102, 105.

Where does Moses' intercession take place? This is complicated by
the fact that neither vv. 18-20 nor vv. 25-29 specify the location themselves, and no consistent picture emerges from their context. In vv. 15-17
Moses is represented as being at the *foot* of the mountain,[31] though he
could well have ascended it to pray, while in v. 21 his disposal of the remains of the calf in "the brook that descended out of the mountain" could
have been carried out just as much on the mountain (e.g. at the source of
the stream) as off it. Moreover, vv. 22-24 are parenthetical, and 10:1-2
contains no clear indication either of where Moses is when YHWH
speaks to him or of whether any time has elapsed between the end of
ch. 9 and the beginning of ch. 10.[32]

Nevertheless, there are two reasons for suggesting that Moses was *on*
the mountain for his intercession. First, there is a clue within vv. 18-20.
Moses comments in v. 18:

> "I lay prostrate before the LORD *as before*, forty days and
> forty nights; I neither ate bread nor drank water..."

This use of "as before" (כראשנה) leads one to expect not only that something similar had occurred on a previous occasion but also that it has already been mentioned within the present narrative.[33] In this connection
v. 9, which admittedly makes no mention of Moses' lying prostrate
(though YHWH's instruction to him in v. 12 ["Arise"] could be consistent
with his doing so),[34] refers both to the period of forty days and forty
nights and to Moses' abstaining from bread and water. It thus seems
likely that this was the occasion to which Moses is referring.[35] Since,
therefore, this earlier period of fasting is expressly stated to have been

---

[31] He comes down from the mountain, sees the calf and breaks the tables in the sight
of the people.

[32] Contra Christensen 196. Seitz describes the rather vague "At that time" (בעת ההוא)
in v. 1 as "[eine] lose anknüpfende Formel" (p. 55).

[33] Cf. Peckham 42 n. 84: "'The forty days and forty nights which I lay prostrate' refers to a definite and already-known period. Since the reason for this prostration
(9:25b) is Yahweh's threat in 9:14, this period must refer to his stay on the mountain."

[34] In Deut. 9:7b-10:11 the only times that YHWH tells Moses to "arise" are recorded
immediately after a reference to one of his two stays of forty days and forty nights on
the mountain (9:12; 10:11). Note that in Exodus, which makes no mention of Moses'
prostration, the corresponding instructions contain no such exhortation (32:7, 34 and
33:1).

[35] Cf. Cairns 105, Clamer 575, Reider 99, Driver (1902) 115, Bertholet (1899) 31.

spent *on the mountain* (בהר), it would be reasonable to presume that Moses' intercession in vv. 18 and 25 took place there also. Secondly, it is generally considered that in Deut. 10:10 the implied intercession to which YHWH responds, and which is specified as having taken place on the mountain, is that outlined in 9:25-29:[36]

> "I stayed on the mountain, as at the first time, forty days and
> forty nights, and the LORD hearkened to me that time also; the
> LORD was unwilling to destroy you."

It would therefore appear that Moses' intercession did in fact take place on the mountain.

Is YHWH present on the mountain for the intercession? In Deut. 9:12 YHWH tells Moses to go down quickly "from here", an expression which, it has been argued earlier, implies the divine Presence on the mountain prior to Moses' descent with the first set of tables.[37] In addition, in Deut. 10:1 YHWH further tells him to come up "to me" on the mountain, an instruction which, it will be argued later, represents YHWH as again being present there when Moses ascends with the second set of tables.[38] Thus, given that YHWH is present on both of these occasions,[39] it would seem reasonable to presume that he is also present for that event which intervenes between them, namely, Moses' intercession.

We are now in a position to consider the significance of Moses' prostration לפני יהוה. The two conditions enabling the qualification (לפני יהוה) of Moses' lying prostrate to be viewed as literal are thus seen to be satisfied, since both Moses and the one "before" whom he lies are present in the same place at the same time. Moreover, it is this conclusion to which the characteristics of the usage in vv. 18 and 25 point.[40] The prostration occurs at a particular place (on the mountain) and at a particular time (between the breaking of the first tables and their replacement by the sec-

---

[36] Ridderbos 140, Mayes (1979) 207, Craigie (1976) 199, 201, Peckham 4, 55, Thompson (1974) 146-147, Seitz 51-52, Watts (1970) 230, von Rad (1964) 57, Buis and Leclercq 89, Lohfink (1963) 213, Cunliffe-Jones 75, Clamer 580, Reider 106, Junker 57, Smith (1918) 138, Driver (1902) 124, Robinson (n.d.) 107-108.
[37] See above, pp. 107-109.
[38] See below, pp. 114-115.
[39] It may also be significant that it is one of these occasions, when YHWH was known to be present on the mountain, with which Moses is drawing a direct parallel in Deut. 9:18-20 ("as before").
[40] See above, p. 48.

ond), and while the latter admittedly involves an *extended* period (forty days and forty nights), the historical particularity of the action does point to its being understood in the *literal* sense.

Thus, while in the Exodus account of Moses' intercession YHWH's Presence on the mountain has to be deduced from the context, in Deuteronomy it is twice stated that Moses "lay prostrate before the LORD". In this case the qualification is intended literally, and is therefore an affirmation that YHWH was present at Horeb in close proximity to the prostrate Moses. At this juncture of the narrative it is Deuteronomy that reveals the greater interest in divine Presence.

THE GIVING OF THE SECOND SET OF LAW TABLES

The events associated with the reinstatement of the covenant are dealt with in Deut. 10:1-5 and Exod. 33:18-34:9 and 34:27-28. The Exodus account contains a large group of references to divine Presence which have no parallel in Deuteronomy, but both versions affirm YHWH's intended Presence on the mountain in relation to Moses' ascent with the second set of tables. References which the two narratives have in common will be considered first, and then an explanation offered to account for the aforementioned omissions from Deuteronomy.

DEUT. 10:1 // EXOD. 34:1-2

In Deut. 10:1-5 there is one reference to YHWH's Presence localized on the mountain for the giving of the second set of tables.[41] It is quoted below, together with the corresponding part of Exod. 34:

Deut.	Exod.
"[T]he LORD said to me, 'Hew two tables of stone like the first, and *come up to me* on the mountain'..." (10:1)	The LORD said to Moses, "Cut two tables of stone like the first...and come up...to Mount Sinai, and *present yourself there to me* on the top of the mountain." (34:1-2)

---

[41] YHWH's having spoken to the people "out of the midst of the fire" (v. 4) refers to his localization on the mountain for the giving of the *first* set of tables, and has already been dealt with (pp. 60-66).

Exod. 34:1-2, which is frequently viewed as beginning a further account of the original Sinai covenant,[42] is attributed largely to J,[43] while Deut. 10:1 is generally regarded as deuteronom(ist)ic in origin.[44]

Both Exod. 34:2 and Deut. 10:1 record YHWH as telling Moses to come up to him on the mountain:

Exod. 34:2:	ועלית...אל־הר סיני ונצבת לי שם על־ראש ההר		
Deut. 10:1:	ההרה	אלי	ועלה

The syntax and information conveyed are different in the two verses, but it is clear that they each contain the same basic idea of YHWH intending to be on the mountain and instructing Moses to ascend to him there.

Exodus and Deuteronomy each allude to the divine Presence on the mountain in their accounts of Moses' ascent with the second set of tables. Their ways of expressing that Presence are similar, and so at this point neither has a greater interest in the subject than the other.

OMISSIONS FROM DEUT. 10:1-5

It was indicated above that in Exod. 33:18-34:9 and 34:27-28 there are a number of expressions indicative of YHWH's localized Presence, but which have no parallel in Deut. 10:1-5.[45] They can be classified into three groups: references to YHWH's movement in the vicinity of the mountain,[46] references to his being present upon it,[47] and various anthropomorphisms relating to parts of the body.[48,49] It will be observed that

---

[42] כראשנים (v. 1a) and v. 1b, which together suggest that a covenant *renewal* is involved are usually assigned to subsequent redaction.

[43] Scharbert 128, Childs (1974) 607-608, 610, Clements (1972) 220, 221, Hyatt (1971) 318, 319, 322, Davies (1967) 245, Beyerlin 32, Noth (1959) 214-215, Beer 12-13, 159, Driver (1911) xxviii, 364, 365-366, McNeile (1908) xxx-xxxi, xxxiv, 216-217, Holzinger (1900) XIX.

[44] See above, p. 106.

[45] P. 114.

[46] "I will cover you...until I *have passed by*" (33:22), "[T]he LORD *descended in the cloud*" (34:5), "The LORD *passed before him*" (34:6).

[47] "[T]he LORD said, 'Behold, there is a place *by me* where you shall stand upon the rock'" (33:21), "[He] *stood with him there*" (34:5, cf. above, p. 88 n. 166), "[Moses] was there *with the LORD* forty days and forty nights" (34:28).

[48] "'But' [YHWH] said, 'you cannot see *my face*'" (33:20), "I will cover you with *my hand*" (33:22), "I will take away *my hand*, and you shall see *my back*; but *my face* shall not be seen" (33:23).

[49] *Re* Moses' request that God accompany the Israelites (34:9) see below, pp. 117-118.

most of such expressions occur in sections of Exodus[50] (i.e. 33:18-23 and 34:5-7) which *themselves* lack any parallel in Deuteronomy. This of itself would appear to rule out mere compression of the narrative as an explanation of their absence, and argue in favour of the operation of some other criterion. Before, however, that can be determined, it will be necessary to gain some understanding of the role of the two sections within the Exodus narrative as a whole.

Exod. 33:18-34:9

It is generally considered that, in its present context, the theophany described in the second section, Exod. 34:5-7, is the one promised in the first, Exod. 33:19-23,[51,52] in response to Moses' request to be shown YHWH's glory (33:18).[53] Earlier on in ch. 33 YHWH has refused to accompany the people on their way to the Promised Land on the grounds that their stubbornness would cause him to destroy them (vv. 3 and 5). Moses, however, manages to wrest from him the promise that his Pres-

---

[50] Note that two of the expressions of localized Presence found in Exod. 33:18-34:9, 34:27-28, but not in Deut. 10:1-5, occur elsewhere in Deuteronomy or the Deuteronomistic History. First, in the pre-deuteronomistic (De Vries xlvi, Jones [1984] 68, Rehm [1979] 186, Robinson [1972] 11-12, Noth [1967] 79) 1 Kings 19:11, YHWH is described as having *"passed by"* Elijah on Mount Horeb, a usage similar to that in Exod. 33:22 and 34:6. Secondly, in the deuteronom(ist)ic (see above, p. 85 n. 150) Deut. 5:31, YHWH tells Moses to "stand here *by me* (עִמָּדִי)". This is similar to Exod. 33:21; 34:5 and 34:28, which although using a variety of verbs for "standing", and in the case of 33:21, a different preposition (אֵת) to denote Moses' relationship to the Deity, all represent him as being in close proximity to YHWH on the mountain. Note that in the case of Exod. 34:5 there is some debate (referred to in Childs [1974] 603) as to whether Moses or YHWH is the subject of the verb "stood". If Moses is, then his standing "with" YHWH is paralleled by Deut. 5:31, but if YHWH is, then *his* standing is similar to that in the pre-deuteronomistic (Klein [1983] 31, Mayes [1983] 83-84, 105, McCarter [1980] 15-16, Mauchline 17, 31-32, Noth [1967] 60, Hertzberg [1965] 10-11, 32, Brockington [1962] 318, Caird 856, 860) 1 Sam. 3:10, in which "the LORD came and stood forth" (no preposition).

[51] This is stated explicitly by Burns 172, 175, Moberly 76-88, Gispen 312, Childs (1974) 612, Hyatt (1971) 317, 322-323, Cassuto 437, 439, Rylaarsdam 1075, Beer 159, McNeile (1908) 210, and Driver (1911) 367, and implied by Durham 452-455.

[52] Cf. Moberly 85 for a tabulation of the "numerous verbal and substantive links" connecting the two passages, and 82-83 for the evidence that in both cases the theophany is envisaged in two stages.

[53] Durham 452, Moberly 68, Gispen 310-311, Zenger (1978) 242, Childs (1974) 595-596, Cole 225, Clements (1972) 216, Davies (1967) 242, Cassuto 435, Noth (1959) 212, Rylaarsdam 1074-1075, Beer 159, McNeile (1908) 210, 215-216, Driver (1911) 362.

ence *will* travel with Israel (v. 17). He then asks to see the divine glory (v. 18), that is, he asks for a fuller revelation of YHWH himself, in the hope that therein will be found the solution to the problem of YHWH's going in the midst of the people without at the same time destroying them.[54] Thus Moses' request, and the theophany which results from it, is part and parcel of his (successful) attempt to secure the divine Presence with the stiff-necked Israelites on their journey to Canaan.

Deut. 10:1-5

As will be shown below, the deuteronom(ist)ic account of the incident of the Golden Calf betrays little interest in the journey to the land.[55] This means that the question as to how a holy God might accompany a sinful people on their travels simply does not arise. Consequently, Moses' request to be shown YHWH's "glory", and the whole nexus of localized Presence expressions which appear within the Exodus narrative as a result,[56] are basically irrelevant at this juncture. It is this, rather than any aversion to the notion of divine Presence as such, which explains the absence of such expressions from Deuteronomy, since, as has already been pointed out, Deut. 10:1-5 does indicate that YHWH was on the mountain for the giving of the second set of tables.[57]

THE IMPENDING JOURNEY TO CANAAN

--- // EXOD. 33:1-6, 12-16; 34:9

In Exod. 33 and 34 there is a further group of references to divine Presence without parallel in Deut. 9:7b-10:11. These occur in 33:1-6, 12-16, and 34:9, and relate to the Deity accompanying the Israelites on their journey to Canaan. They can be subdivided as follows: instances of YHWH going (up) *among/in the midst of* (בקרב) the people,[58] references to his *Presence* (פנים),[59,60] and one instance of his going *with* (עם) them.[61]

---

[54] Moberly 75-76.

[55] Pp. 126-127.

[56] See above, p. 115 nn. 46-48.

[57] See above, pp. 114-115.

[58] "Go up to a land flowing with milk and honey; but I *will not go up among you*, lest I consume you" (33:3), "[I]f...I *should go up among you*, I would consume you" (33:5), "[L]et the Lord...*go in the midst of us*" (34:9).

[59] "[YHWH] said, '*My presence* will go with you, and I will give you rest.' And [Moses] said to him, 'If *thy presence* will not go with me, do not carry us up from

However, it is unlikely that such expressions have been omitted from Deut. 9-10 on account of their notion of divine Presence, since they are all attested in deuteronom(ist)ic contexts elsewhere. The idea of YHWH being among/in the midst of the Israelites occurs in Deut. 1:42;[62] 6:15;[63] 7:21;[64] 23:15 (EVV 14)[65] and Josh. 3:10,[66] of his פנים accompanying them on a journey in Deut. 4:37,[67] and of his going with them in Deut. 20:4[68] and 31:6.[69,70] Rather, the reason for their non-inclusion at *this* point is to be sought in the particular context in which the deuteronom(ist)ic account occurs. This will be considered in the final section of the chapter.[71]

---

here'" (33:14-15). Note that the phrases "with you" and "with me" in vv. 14 and 15 (RSV) do not occur in the Hebrew.

[60] While many scholars regard the divine פנים in this context as equivalent to YHWH himself (Simian-Yofre 636, Fretheim [1984] 63, 97, Terrien [1978] 96 n. 11, 140, Mann 157, Brueggemann [1976] 681, Reindl 63-65, 223, 225-226, 304 n. 614, Clements [1965] 26-27, Schnutenhaus 19, Johnson [1947] 159, Phythian-Adams [1934] 38 n. 5, Nötscher 47-48, Dhorme [1921] 391), there are also those who view it as in some sense distinct from him (Vriezen [1970] 210, Lindblom 100 n. 16, Barr 35-36, Eichrodt [1935] 13, Gulin 26-27, Morgenstern [1918] 126, Baudissin 198-199).

[61] "[H]ow shall it be known that I have found favour in thy sight, I and thy people? Is it not in *thy going with us*, so that we are distinct" (33:16).

[62] See above, p. 13 n. 52.

[63] D: Clifford (1982) 2-3, 31, Phillips (1973) 3, 12, Nicholson (1967) 29, Noth (1967) 16, von Rad (1964) 7-8, Buis and Leclercq 16, 74, de Tillesse 55-56, 74-75; Dtr: Mayes (1979) 45-46, 175.

[64] D: Clifford (1982) 2-3, 31, Mayes (1979) 48, 187, Rose 127, Phillips (1973) 3, 12, Nicholson (1967) 22, 36, Noth (1967) 16, von Rad (1964) 7-8, Buis and Leclercq 16, 74, de Tillesse 74-75; pre-Dtr: Preuß (1982) 49.

[65] D: Clifford (1982) 2-3, 31, Mayes (1979) 48, 318, Phillips (1973) 3, 12, 82, Nicholson (1967) 22, 32, 36, Noth (1967) 16, von Rad (1964) 7-8, Buis and Leclercq 16, 98, de Tillesse 74-75; D+Dtr: Preuß (1982) 57.

[66] Dtr: Butler xxi, Boling and Wright 170, Miller and Tucker 34, Noth (1971) 9, Soggin 43-44, Bright 543.

[67] See above, p. 56 n. 43.

[68] D: Clifford (1982) 2-3, 31, Noth (1967) 16, Buis and Leclercq 16, 98; Dtr: Mayes (1979) 291-292, Phillips (1973) 3, 12, Nicholson (1967) 31, 36; D or Dtr: Preuß (1982) 55.

[69] Dtr: Butler 6, 12, Clifford (1982) 1-2, 28, 31, 160, Nelson 76, Mayes (1979) 42, 372, Nicholson (1967) 27, 31, 36, 108, Buis and Leclercq 17, 188, de Tillesse 32.

[70] Note that several of such instances occur in the context of Holy War; see above, p. 24 n. 42.

[71] See below, pp. 121-127.

THE TENT OF MEETING

--- // EXOD. 33:7-11

Finally, Exod. 33:7-11 describes YHWH's practice of communicating with Moses in the tent of meeting far off from the camp, and in so doing mentions the pillar of cloud descending[72] and YHWH speaking to Moses face to face,[73] neither of which occurs in Deut. 9:7b-10:11. Nevertheless, while, as has already been pointed out, there are no deuteronom(ist)ic instances of divine descent,[74] speaking face to face is predicated of YHWH in Deut. 5:4[75] (cf. 34:10).[76]

OVERALL COMPARISON OF THE DEUTERONOMY AND EXODUS ACCOUNTS

Before comparing the two versions,[77] it will again be useful, as in the case of the first giving of the law, to point out some of the obvious differences between them. First, the Exodus account consists of third-person narrative, while that in Deuteronomy is presented as an address by Moses to the people, and so is written in the first and second persons. Secondly, the Exodus account is three times as long as the one in Deuteronomy (75 verses as opposed to 25), the following sections being without parallel in the latter: 32:1-6, 21-24, 25-29,[78] 30-34; 33:1-6, 7-11, 12-16, 18-23 and 34:5-9.

---

[72] "When Moses entered the tent, the pillar of cloud would descend and stand at the door of the tent" (33:9). The descent of the cloud is generally taken to imply the descent of the Deity; see above, p. 77 n. 129.

[73] "[T]he LORD used to speak to Moses *face to face*, as a man speaks to his friend" (33:11).

[74] See above, pp. 52-53.

[75] See above, pp. 76-78.

[76] Generally regarded as deuteronomistic (Preuß [1982] 61, Phillips [1973] 229, 231, Watts [1970] 296, Nicholson [1967] 27, 31, 36, 108, von Rad [1964] 7, 150, Buis and Leclercq 214-215), though some scholars see it as post-deuteronomistic (Clifford [1982] 3, 175, 184, Mayes [1979] 47, 413-414, Noth [1967] 213).

[77] If the legal material and account of Moses' practice after his final descent are excluded from Exod. 32-34, and the various parentheses from Deut. 9:7b-10:11, then the Exodus account consists of 32:1-34:10 and 34:27-33, while that in Deuteronomy includes 9:9-21, 25-29 and 10:1-5, 10-11.

[78] This may well be alluded to in Deut. 10:8-9.

THE FREQUENCY OF DIVINE PRESENCE REFERENCES

In sections common to Deuteronomy and Exodus

First, a comparison of those sections which Deuteronomy and Exodus have in common[79] reveals there to be over two and a half times the incidence of divine Presence expressions in the deuteronom(ist)ic account as there are in the Exodus one: while 62%[80] of the verses in Deuteronomy contain such a reference, only 24%[81] of those in Exodus do so. Secondly, both versions refer to YHWH localized on Horeb/Sinai for the giving of the second set of tables: in Deuteronomy he tells Moses, "*come up to me on the mountain*" (10:1), and in Exodus, "*present yourself there to me*" (34:2). Thirdly, the Exodus account has only one reference unique to itself. 34:28 indicates that Moses did in fact enter the divine Presence following YHWH's instruction in 34:2: "he was there *with the LORD*" (contrast Deut. 10:4).[82] Fourthly, and in contrast, Deuteronomy has four references peculiar to itself. In 9:10 Moses describes the first tables as having on them "all the words which the LORD had spoken…*out of the midst of the fire*" (and similarly in 10:4), whereas Exod. 31:18 is silent as to their content, and Exod. 34:28b refers merely to their being inscribed with "the words of the covenant, the ten commandments". In 9:12, and as a result of the people's sin, YHWH instructs Moses, "go down quickly *from here*", while in Exod. 32:7 he tells him merely to "[g]o down". And finally, in 9:25 Moses prays to YHWH while lying "prostrate *before the LORD*", whereas in Exod. 32:11 he merely "beseeches" him. It should thus be clear that, in this case also, where the two versions deal with the same aspects of the same incident, it is the deuteronom(ist)ic one which contains the greater number of allusions to divine Presence.

In sections occurring only in Exodus

Within the Exodus account, the majority of references to divine Presence which have no parallel in the deuteronom(ist)ic one occur in sec-

---

[79] Deut. 9:10 // Exod. 31:18; Deut. 9:12 // Exod. 32:7; Deut. 9:25-26a // Exod. 32:11a; Deut. 10:1-4, 10a // Exod. 34:1-4, 27-28.

[80] The eight verses concerned contain five references to divine Presence: in 9:10, 12, 25 and 10:1, 4 .

[81] The eight and a half verses concerned contain two references to divine Presence: in 34:2, 28.

[82] Note, however, that Moses' proximity to the divine Presence on that occasion *is* affirmed in Deuteronomy, though in a different literary context: "I lay prostrate *before the LORD*" (9:18). See above, pp. 110-114.

tions which themselves are unique to Exodus, i.e. in 32:30-34 (2x); 33:1-23 (14x) and 34:5-9 (4x). They refer to YHWH being on the mountain (32:30, 31; 33:21; 34:5), accompanying the Israelites on their way to Canaan (33:3, 5, 14, 15, 16; 34:9), descending (33:9; 34:5) and passing in close proximity to Moses (33:22; 34:6). There are also a number of anthropomorphisms (33:11, 20, 22, 23 [3x]).

OMISSIONS FROM THE DEUTERONOM(IST)IC ACCOUNT

It has already been noted that the theophany in Exod. 34 is both promised (33:19-23) and takes place (34:5-7) in connection with Moses' (successful) attempt to secure the Presence of YHWH on the journey to Canaan.[83] This means that most of the references to divine Presence which are absent from Deuteronomy[84] occur in sections related to that journey, whether directly (33:1-6, 12-16; 34:9) or indirectly (33:19-23; 34:5-7). In view of this, our primary concern will be to explain the absence of such sections from the deuteronom(ist)ic account, in order that the concomitant absence of their various references to divine Presence might be understood. To this end we will consider first the narrators' intention in dealing with the incident (i.e. of the Golden Calf),[85] and then the role of the journey in each account.

The purpose of each account

Exodus. The writer of the Exodus account provides us with no clear indication as to his aim in recounting the episode of the Golden Calf. The immediate context is of no help, since although the surrounding chapters (i.e. 25-31 and 35-40) are concerned with the issue of divine Presence, in that they deal with the construction of the dwelling in which YHWH is to accompany his people on their journeyings, they are generally attributed to P, and thus considered to have been added *after* the completion of chs. 32-34. Neither is any light shed on the matter by ch. 24, of which chs. 32-34 are held to be its original continuation,[86] nor by the beginning of the account itself, since without explanation it launches straight into a description of what was happening at the foot of the mountain in Moses' absence.

---

[83] See above, pp. 116-117.
[84] Sixteen of the twenty listed in the previous paragraph.
[85] In so far as it can be gleaned from either contextual or internal considerations.
[86] See above, p. 110 n. 25.

Deuteronomy. Although Deut. 9:7b-10:11[87] is frequently considered to have been inserted[88] into its present setting,[89] the redactor's intention in so doing may be sought in the preceding verses (9:1-7a), since it can reasonably be assumed that its inclusion there was regarded as contextually appropriate.

In 9:1-7a, therefore, the writer is envisaging a future time when the Israelites have entered the land and are attributing YHWH's bringing them in to their "righteousness" or "uprightness of heart" (vv. 4-6). Before that happens, however, he wishes to disabuse them of such illusions. He does this in two ways: first, by giving them the *actual* reasons for YHWH's driving out the original inhabitants, i.e. the wickedness of the latter (vv. 4 and 5) and the promise to the fathers (v. 5), and secondly, by pointing out the absurdity of such thinking on the part of people with their characteristics and past record:

> "[Y]ou are a stubborn people (עַם־קְשֵׁה־עֹרֶף). Remember and do
> not forget how you provoked the LORD your God to wrath
> (הִקְצַפְתָּ אֶת־יְהוָה אֱלֹהֶיךָ) in the wilderness..." (vv. 6-7a)

When, therefore, it is noticed that the stubbornness is referred to not only in v. 6 but also in vv. 13 (עַם־קְשֵׁה־עֹרֶף) and 27 (קְשִׁי הָעָם הַזֶּה), and that the Israelites' provoking of YHWH to wrath (קצף [Hiph.]) introduces both the Golden Calf incident itself (הִקְצַפְתֶּם אֶת־יְהוָה [v. 8]) and the further instances of rebellion in vv. 22-24 (מַקְצִפִים הֱיִיתֶם אֶת־יְהוָה),[90] it is difficult to avoid the conclusion that Deut. 9:7b-10:11 has been placed in its present position precisely because of its suitability for invalidating any future

---

[87] Whether the inserted section is regarded as beginning with 9:7a (Von Rad [1964] 54-55, though see 7), 9:7b (Hahn 246, 264, Phillips [1973] 12, 69, Noth [1967] 17, de Tillesse 45, 56, 83, Bertholet [1899] 30; cf. Davies [1962a] 275), 9:8 (Preuß [1982] 49, though see 102) or 9:9 (Braulik [1986] 74, Mayes [1979] 42, 195; cf. Steuernagel [1900] 33, Robinson [n.d.] 103) makes little difference to the argument which follows.

[88] Hahn 246, 258, 259, Mayes (1979) 42, Phillips (1973) 12, 69, Nicholson (1967) 30-31, von Rad (1964) 7, Buis and Leclercq 17, Bertholet (1899) 30. Note, however, that Braulik (1986) considers 9:1-8 to have been added secondarily (p. 74).

[89] On the basis of such criteria as the change in form of address (note, however, that the singular ends at יָצָאת [9:7b] and recommences with אֱלֹהֶיךָ [10:9b]), the historical nature of its content, and "formgeschichtlichen Merkmale" (Von Rad [1964] 54).

[90] Neither of these instances of קצף (Hiph.) is paralleled in Exod. 32-34. YHWH's wrath *is* mentioned (in 32:10, 11), but in a different context and using a different idiom, that of his anger burning hot (חָרָה אַף).

claims which the people might have about their own intrinsic merit being
the reason for their occupation of the land.

This verdict is strikingly reinforced by a comparison of Deut. 9:7b-
10:11 with Exod. 32-34, when it is found that in the deuteronom(ist)ic
account, and consistently with 9:6-7a, there is a marked concern to emphasize the *sinfulness* of the people. This is apparent in a number of
places, but particularly in those parts of the narrative where Moses is represented as commenting on what occurred at Horeb.[91] In Deuteronomy,
when he first sees the calf he observes that the people have "sinned
against the LORD" and "turned aside...from the way which [he] had
commanded [them]" (9:16), whereas in Exodus the narrator states merely
that his "anger burned hot" (32:19). Secondly, while both accounts point
out either explicitly (Deut. 9:25) or implicitly (Exod. 32:12) that Moses'
intercession is motivated by YHWH's intended killing of the people, it is
only in Deuteronomy that the reason for the divine anger is given: "because of all the sin which you had committed, in doing what was evil in
the sight of the LORD" (9:18). Thirdly, while both versions provide
similar descriptions of Moses' destruction of the calf, in Deuteronomy he
refers to it as a "sinful thing" (9:21). No such value judgement is expressed in Exod. 32:20. And finally, only the Deuteronomy version of
Moses' intercession (9:26-29) betrays any *explicit* awareness that
YHWH's desire to kill the Israelites has arisen as a direct consequence of
what they have done: "do not regard the stubbornness of this people, or
their wickedness, or their sin" (9:27, contrast Exod. 32:11-13).[92,93] It

---

[91] Cf. Polzin's distinction between Deut. 1-3, in which Moses mainly *reports* the
past, and Deut. 4, in which he *analyses* it with a view to its significance for present
and future action (p. 40). Hahn considers that Deut. 9:25-29 contains "eine starke
theologische Reflexion" (p. 245).

[92] Exod. 32:11-13 (with possible supplementation from elsewhere) and Deut. 9:26-29
are generally considered to be parallel: Balentine (1989) 599, Braulik (1986) 80,
Ridderbos 136, Hahn 239, 245, Mayes (1979) 202, Peckham 42, Corvin 223, 265,
Seitz 52-54, Rennes 58, de Tillesse 45 n. 3, Cunliffe-Jones 73, Clamer 576, Junker
56, Robinson (n.d.) 105. Contrast Driver (1902) 116.

[93] Rather, two features of the Exodus intercession indicate that almost the opposite
may be the case. First, the two questions which Moses addresses to YHWH represent
him as apparently not understanding the reason for the divine anger: "O LORD, *why*
(למה) does thy wrath burn hot against thy people?" (32:11, contrast Deut. 9:26 and
29), and "*Why* (למה) should the Egyptians say, 'With evil intent did he bring them
forth, to slay...and...consume them'?" (32:12, contrast Deut. 9:28). Cf. Balentine
(1989) 607: "[V]v 11-14 leave...the clear impression that from Moses' perspective

should therefore be clear from these four sets of observations that in the deuteronom(ist)ic portrayal of the incident of the Golden Calf the *highlighting* of the sin involved is of primary concern.

There is, however, a second emphasis which is also present in Deut. 9:7b-10:11. Echoing the reference to the Israelite provocation referred to in the context (v. 7a), Moses introduces the deuteronom(ist)ic account by reminding the people that at Horeb YHWH's anger was so intense that he was ready to destroy them (v. 8). In this case also such a theme is given much greater prominence in Deuteronomy, i.e. in 9:14, 19, 20, 25 (שמד [Hiph.]); 9:26; 10:10 (שחת [Hiph.]) and 9:28 (מת [Hiph.]) than it is in Exodus, i.e. in 32:10, 12 (כלה [Piel])[94] and 32:12 (הרג). Towards the beginning of the narrative YHWH's threat to destroy the people is revealed to Moses as the consequence of their disobedience (9:14 // Exod. 32:10). Later, Moses gives it as his main motive for interceding both for them (9:19, 25) and for Aaron (9:20). In the prayer itself it is the first, and essentially the only, thing for which he prays (9:26, see also 9:28 // Exod. 32:12). And finally, its successful averting is mentioned by him at the end of the section (10:10). It should therefore be clear that within the deuteronom(ist)ic account of the incident of the Golden Calf, YHWH's threatened destruction of the people plays a key role.

Thus, within the deuteronom(ist)ic account of the Golden Calf there are two emphases, both of which can be related to the immediate context. One concerns the stubbornness referred to in 9:6, and relates to the people's sinfulness. The other highlights dramatically the *extent* of the provocation referred to in 9:7a, and relates to the divine destruction threatened as a result of Israelite disobedience. This clear relationship be-

---

God's announced intentions are both *incomprehensible* [our italics] and unacceptable". And secondly, instead of YHWH's wrath being viewed as his justifiable reaction to the people's sin, it is presented as "evil", both by Moses in his petition and by the narrator in noting its successful outcome: "Why should the Egyptians say, 'With *evil* (ברעה) intent did he bring them forth...'? Turn from thy fierce wrath, and repent of this *evil* (הרעה) against thy people" (32:12) and "[T]he LORD repented of the *evil* (הרעה) which he thought to do to his people" (32:14). Note that the deuteronom(ist)ic account imagines the Egyptians attributing YHWH's killing of the Israelites to his hatred of them (9:28). It contains, however, no parallels to the other Exod. 32 instances of רעה whether in Moses' plea (v. 12) or in the narrator's report of its success (v. 14).

[94] Excluding 33:3, 5, in which the divine "consumption" of the Israelites will only occur if YHWH accompanies them on their journey.

tween interpolation and context makes it difficult to avoid the conclusion that 9:7b-10:11 was placed immediately after 9:1-7a precisely because of its suitability for illustrating the points made in vv. 6-7a. If this be granted,[95] then the redactor's purpose in referring to the Golden Calf is not to provide an alternative version of the incident. Rather, it is to tell the story in such a way as to disabuse the Israelites of any future illusions they might entertain about YHWH having given them the land on the basis of merit. Thus, in pursuance of this aim he first emphasizes the people's sinfulness which, as was shown above, is highlighted in the deuteronom(ist)ic account.[96] And secondly, as a way of indicating the enormity of what they had done, he introduces (v. 8) and then emphasizes the idea of the *Israelites'* courting of the divine destruction decreed for the inhabitants of the land (9:3). That any "righteousness" on their part could have stimulated the divine gift of land to them is thus shown to be absurd, since YHWH is about to take it from those whom he intends to destroy (שמד [Hiph.], v. 3) because of their wickedness (רשעה, vv. 4 and 5) in order to give it to the Israelites whom he nearly destroyed (שמד [Hiph.], vv. 14, 19 and 25) on account of *theirs* (רשע, v. 27).

The role of the journey

Exodus. It has already been noted that Exod. 33:1-23 and 34:5-9 contain a number of allusions to divine Presence which, one way or another, are connected with the journey to Canaan.[97] This is particularly true of the references to YHWH being "among" (בקרב) or "with" (עם) either Moses or the people, or to his Presence (פנים), since most of them occur in conjunction with a verb of *motion*, either "to go up" (עלה), as in 33:3 and 5, or "to go" (הלך), as in 33:14, 15, 16 and 34:9.[98] It must also be pointed out that these are not the only indications of an interest in Israel's future wanderings. The calf itself is seen by the people as pertinent to the journey ahead,[99] YHWH several times tells Moses to set out for the Prom-

---

95 Even if it is *not*, the two emphases clearly illustrate the two points made about the Israelites at the beginning of the insertion itself, i.e. in vv. 7b-8.

96 I.e. relative to that in Exodus. See pp. 123-124.

97 See above, pp. 116-117.

98 Apart from 33:21 (את) and 34:5 (עם), both of which refer to the theophany (see above, p. 115 n. 47), there are no other instances of YHWH merely *being* in close proximity to the Israelites.

99 "[M]ake us gods, who *shall go before us*" (32:1, 23).

ised Land,[100] and the narrator refers to the Israelites stripping themselves of their ornaments "from Mount Horeb onward (מהר הורב)".[101] All such indications, however, are consistent with the standpoint of the narrative, in that the people are still at the foot of Mount Sinai, and the journey to Canaan lies in the future.

Thus, in line with the perspective of his account, the author of Exod. 32-34 both refers to the journey ahead (i.e. in 32:1, 23, 34 and 33:1, 3, 6, 12) and, when describing the consequences of the people's sin, deals not only with YHWH's threat of destruction but also with that of denying them his Presence on their travels.

Deuteronomy. The absence from Deut. 9:7b-10:11 of all mention of the second consequence of the people's sin, i.e. YHWH's threat to withdraw his Presence from the journey, cannot be attributed to an aversion to the notion of such accompaniment, since it is referred to earlier on in the deuteronomistic[102] 1:32-33 ("[T]he LORD your God, who went before you [ההלך לפניכם][103] in the way...in fire by night...and in the cloud by day") and 2:7b ("[T]hese forty years the LORD your God has been with you [עמך]").[104] It *is*, however, consistent with the total lack of interest shown in the journey as such until the very end of the account, i.e. in 10:11, where it is introduced after the giving of the second set of tables.[105] The latter is portrayed as a repetition of the giving of the first set,[106] and this suggests that the author regards it as a return to the situa-

---

[100] "[G]o, *lead the people to the place of which I have spoken to you*" (32:34, and similarly in 33:1, 3 and 12).

[101] 33:6.

[102] See above, p. 28 n. 58.

[103] Contrast Exod. 32:34 and 33:2, which speak merely of an *angel* going "before" (לפני) the people.

[104] This is a nominal sentence. The journey is implied, however, since v. 7a refers to the people's "*going* (לכתך) through this great wilderness". Cf. Exod. 33:16 (עם).

[105] It *is* mentioned in 10:6-7, and possibly implied in 10:8-9, i.e. by the reference to the Levites carrying (לשאת) the ark, but, as was pointed out earlier (p. 106), these sections are frequently viewed as *subsequent* to the basic narrative.

[106] First, almost identical wording is used in both Deut. 9:10 and 10:4 to describe what was written on the tables (כל־הדברים אשר דבר יהוה עמכם בהר מתוך האש ביום הקהל // עשרת הדברים אשר דבר יהוה אליכם בהר מתוך האש ביום הקהל); cf. the inclusion in 10:4 of the expression "as at the first writing". Secondly, both Deut. 9:11 and 10:4 record, though the latter is briefer, that YHWH gave Moses the tables. Thirdly, identical wording is used in both Deut. 9:15 and 10:5 to refer to Moses' descent from Horeb (ואפן וארד מן־ההר).

tion prior to YHWH's discovery of the people's sin, and thus as a reinstatement of the covenant. That he makes no reference to the journey
until *after* this resumption of the status quo, implies that he considers it
to have no bearing on what he wants to say about the Golden Calf incident as a whole. Secondly, and as in the case of the Exodus account, the
standpoint of the narrative is relevant, since the episode is presented as
part of an address (by Moses) to an audience who at the moment of
telling are themselves on the verge of the Promised Land, the journey being substantially over. Thirdly, of the two consequences of the people's
sin referred to in Exod. 32-34, only the threat of divine destruction is
specified as resulting from the divine anger.[107] That to withdraw
YHWH's accompanying Presence is not so portrayed. If this is significant,[108] it would appear that in referring to the threat of destruction but
not to that of the withdrawal of the divine Presence, the author of Deut.
9:7b-10:11 has chosen to highlight that consequence of God's response
which most clearly reflects his having been "provoked to wrath" (9:7a).

The absence from Deut. 9:7b-10:11 of all reference to YHWH's *accompanying* Presence[109] is primarily due to the journey's irrelevance to
the point its author wishes to make. Not only is it virtually over, i.e. from
the standpoint of the narrative, but YHWH's threat to withdraw from it is
unrelated to the divine anger whose extent the author wishes to emphasize.

---

[107] In 32:10 YHWH requests Moses to let him alone "that my wrath may burn hot
against [the people] and I may consume them", and in vv. 11-12 Moses responds
with the questions: "[W]hy does thy wrath burn hot against thy people...Why should
the Egyptians say, 'With evil intent did he bring them forth, to slay them in the mountains, and to consume them from the face of the earth?'".

[108] It could be argued that chs. 33-34 *presuppose* that the threat to withdraw
YHWH's accompanying Presence has arisen as a result of the divine anger. However,
in view of the effect on the people if YHWH remains among them (cf. 33:3, 5) such
an intention may well be a consequence of the divine mercy instead. Cf. Mann 157:
"The sending of the divine messenger here simply means that Yahweh himself is not
fully present--and this self-imposed distance is as much *gracious* [our italics] as it is
punitive, for it prevents the destruction of a sinful people by a wrathful God".

[109] I.e. as found in Exod. 33:3, 5, 14, 15, 16 and 34:9, in addition to those dependent
on them in 33:21, 22, 23 and 34:5 and 6; cf. above, pp. 116-117.

CONCLUSION

In bringing up the episode of the Golden Calf, the author of Deut. 9:7b-10:11 is not primarily concerned with presenting an alternative account to that in Exodus, but with illustrating the people's "stubbornness" and "provocation of YHWH to wrath" referred to in those verses (9:6-7a) following which he has chosen to place his own reflections on the subject. To this end he confines himself to the main aspects of the incident, outlining the nature of the sin (but without going into details), its immediate consequence involving the divine anger, i.e. YHWH's threatened destruction of the people, Moses' successful attempt to avert the divine judgement and, finally, the renewal of the status quo. His telling of the story well serves to quash any future Israelite notion that YHWH has given them the land on the basis of merit, since he tells it in such a way as to emphasize both their sinfulness, i.e. relative to the Exodus account, and its immediate consequence, the threat of divine destruction, which, according to the context, is the very fate determined for the present inhabitants of the land as a result of *their* wickedness. In this account all the action takes place on or at the foot of Horeb, and so all its references to divine Presence involve the mountain. Thus YHWH is present there for the first giving of the law (9:10 and 10:4), prior to Moses' first descent (9:12), during his intercession (9:18 and 25), and for his return with the second set of tables (10:1). The net result is that, where comparisons can be made, there are *more* allusions to divine Presence in Deut. 9:7b-10:11 than there are in Exod. 32-34.

Within the Exodus account most of the additional references to YHWH's Presence, i.e. those in ch. 33 and the beginning of ch. 34, are connected either directly or indirectly with the journey to the land, an event which is regarded as still in the future. The narrator is thus interested not only in the immediate effects of the people's sin but also in that consequence of it which entails the possible withdrawal of YHWH's Presence from them on the journey ahead. As far as the deuteronom(ist)ic account is concerned, however, the journey is essentially over, and so its narrator has no interest either in that particular feature of the incident, or in the related question as to whether YHWH is still prepared to accompany the people on their travels. Rather, his concern is primarily with those aspects which best serve to illustrate the people's behaviour referred to in the verses immediately preceding his account, i.e. their sinfulness and provocation of YHWH to wrath.

Thus, the author of Deut. 9:7b-10:11 has omitted the references to divine Presence, not because of a distaste for the notion in general, since his account *does* represent YHWH as being localized in the earthly sphere (i.e. on the mountain) and, in any case, he himself uses a number of the omitted expressions (particularly בקרב) elsewhere. Neither has he omitted them because of an aversion to the notion of YHWH's accompanying Presence in particular, since he himself refers to it in Deut. 1:33 and 2:7. Rather, he has done so because of their essential irrelevance to the context in which he has chosen to place his own reflections about that particular event from Israel's past.

5

לפני יהוה IN DEUTERONOMY 12-26:
GENERAL CHARACTERISTICS

The expression לפני יהוה ("before the LORD") occurs twenty-five times in Deuteronomy. Sixteen of these are found within chs. 12-26, the main legal section of the book.[1] However, whereas its frequent occurrences in P are, when commented on,[2] generally taken to refer either to the proximate Presence of God[3] or simply to the sanctuary,[4] those in Deut. 12-26

---

[1] In 12:7, 12, 18 (2x); 14:23, 26; 15:20; 16:11; 18:7; 19:17; 24:4, 13; 26:5, 10 (2x), 13.

[2] Note the absence of comment on any of its fifty-nine occurrences in Leviticus by Snaith, Heinisch (1935) or Kennedy.

[3] Simian-Yofre 651-653: "Im räumlich-dynamischen Sinn führt *lipnê* die Person oder Sache ein, in deren Gegenwart eine Bewegung zum Abschluß kommt...Der häufigste Gebrauch von *lipnê JHWH*...in räumlich-statischem und dynamischem Sinn findet sich in kultischem Kontext. P lokalisiert *lipnê JHWH*", Fowler 387: "[E]very occurrence [of *lipnê* YHWH in Leviticus] refers to the divine presence in the Tabernacle", Sollamo 23: "I Prästskriften, särskilt i lagtexter, är *lifne Jahve* ett slags kultisk *terminus technicus*, som...betyder...överhuvudtaget 'på den plats där Jahve är närvarande'", Haran 26: "[T]he formula 'before the Lord'...stems from the basic conception of the temple as a divine dwelling-place", van der Woude (1976) 458: "[S]ehr häufig...ist die Wendung, vor allem in den Gesetzespartien von P, als kultischer terminus technicus. Sie meint in diesen Fällen...'im Heiligtum' oder 'beim Heiligtum', gelegentlich auch 'vor der Lade', also 'vor' der Stelle, wo Jahwe gegenwärtig ist", Schmitt 225: "Sachlich besagt diese Wendung [*lipnê jhwh*], daß Jahwe im Heiligtum präsent gedacht wird" (cf. p. 227), Weinfeld (1972a) 192: "All these acts [in Israelite Priestly theology] are performed 'before the Lord (לפני יהוה)', that is, in his presence", Reindl 220: "Nach der priesterlichen Gesetzgebung und Erzählung ist alles, was sich im heiligen Zelt oder seinem näheren Umkreis befindet, 'vor Jahwe'...[die erwähnten

have elicited a more mixed response. They designate the Presence of YHWH,[5] they are equivalent to "at the sanctuary/central shrine" (or similar),[6] or they mean something much less definite.[7] Three kinds of interpretation are thus on offer, though it must be said that little has been written to justify any of them. By way of contrast, therefore, this and the succeeding chapter will examine in some detail those instances of the expression which occur in Deut. 12-26 in order to determine whether adequate grounds can be adduced for affirming that they do in fact refer to the proximate Presence of God.

EARLIER VIEWS

A number of discussions of the significance of the phrase לפני יהוה as it is used in the OT have appeared in print. They can be found in dic-

---

Stellen] sind ein Zeugnis für den Glauben an die Gegenwart Gottes selbst an dem Ort, den sie bezeichnen", Koch 31 n. 1: "[Die] Aussage 'vor Jahwe' [voraussetzt]... eine ständige Gegenwart Jahwes bei Kulthandlungen", von Rad (1947) 27: "[I]nnerhalb der Priesterschrift [finden sich] Spuren einer Anschauung, die Jahwe als gegenwärtig und am Kultort wohnend voraussetzt. Innerhalb der einzelnen Ritualien findet sich überaus häufig der Hinweis, daß Kulthandlungen 'vor Jahwe' vollzogen werden", Westphal 131: "'Vor Jahwe' heißt soviel wie 'in der Nähe der Gottheit' 'in der Sphäre des Heiligen'", BDB 817: "spec. of acts done with a solemn sense of [YHWH's] presence, often...at a sanctuary...and constantly in P"; cf. Janowski (1982), who understands the expression to refer to the divine Presence, but "ohne eine spezifische Aussage über den Modus (ständig *oder* zeitweise) der Gegenwart Jahwes im Heiligtum zu implizieren" (300 n. 155). See also Wenham (1979) 16, Porter 23, and Bertholet (1901) 5, 12, in their commentaries on Leviticus.

[4] Kornfeld 14, Noth (1962) 12-13, 152, cf. 28, 29, 103-104.

[5] See above, p. 10 n. 43. Cf. also Tournay 60-61, Terrien (1978) 396 with 407 n. 32, Craigie (1976) 217, 218, 233, 322, Thompson (1974) 168, 197, Cazelles (1966): most instances rendered "en présence de Yahvé", Dus 193, Wright (1953) 412, Cunliffe-Jones 144. Note that neither Terrien nor Wright considers what consequences such an interpretation might have for "Name Theology".

[6] Clifford (1982) 77, 105, Reider 122, 188, 240, Driver (1902) 143 (though see his comments on 26:13, where "before Jehovah" and "at the central sanctuary" appear to be distinguished). Note that it is not generally stated whether the sanctuary in question is the place where YHWH is to be found, and so this interpretation tends to rob the expression of any connection with divine Presence.

[7] Reindl 28-29: "jede *Äußerung des religiösen Lebens*", Nötscher 103: "[Sie erlangen] eine Art kausaler Bedeutung". Cf. Cairns on Deut. 14:26: "The licence to buy 'whatever you desire' does not remove the occasion from the sphere of the sacred; the celebration is 'before Yahweh'" (p. 145), L'Hour on Deut. 19:17: "[L]'expression לפני יהוה exprime seulement le caractère sacral de la procédure" (p. 19).

tionary entries,[8] survey articles[9] and major studies on the divine פנים[10] and dwelling-place.[11] However, before considering the various instances of the expression in Deut. 12-26 it will be useful to review the general approaches adopted in several of such discussions:[12]

F. NÖTSCHER

In the chapter of his monograph *Das Angesicht Gottes schauen* entitled "Vor Jahwe", Nötscher distinguishes two main uses of the phrase: spatial (räumlich) and causal (kausal).[13] They will be dealt with in turn:

Spatial

Nötscher's discussion of the spatial usage of לפני יהוה proceeds on the assumption that it is YHWH's *Name* that dwells in the temple. There is no personal dwelling of the Deity there, only a symbolic Presence dependent on the presence of the ark.[14] From the examples which he quotes, with their frequent use of appropriate adverbs or adverbial phrases to indicate location, it is clear that actions carried out לפני יהוה in his spatial sense are those which occur within the sphere of the sanctuary in the vicinity of either the ark, the door of the tent of meeting or the altar

---

[8] *TWAT* 6, 652-655, *THAT* 2, 457-459, BDB 817.

[9] Fowler, Sollamo, Rabban.

[10] Reindl 24-36, Nötscher ch. 4.

[11] Westphal 128-142.

[12] Excluding Westphal, who is primarily interested in YHWH's dwelling-place rather than his פנים. He makes no attempt to classify the various uses of לפני יהוה, but concentrates on those instances which form part of the vocabulary of the cult. He argues that, like the layout of the building, such terminology can only be understood on the assumption that YHWH dwells in the most holy place of the temple (p. 128). He suggests that the occasional supplementing of לפני יהוה by other expressions such as פתח אהל מועד shows that it means more than, for example, "at the door of the tent of meeting". In fact, in contrast to such phrases, which show only the external practice, it reveals the real meaning and original significance of the sacred action concerned, i.e. that it takes place in the vicinity of the Deity (p. 131). Interestingly, he includes several of the Deut. 12-26 references to eating and rejoicing לפני יהוה (12:12, 18b; 14:23, 26; 15:20) in his discussion, without distinguishing them from the large number of Priestly instances which he cites. However, in a subsequent section on the views of the Deuteronomists (pp. 186-194) he affirms that their stress on YHWH's Name dwelling in the temple *excludes* the thought that YHWH himself could be found there (p. 194).

[13] Pp. 98, 102.

[14] "Es ist dies…kein 'leibhaftiges Wohnen im Tempel'…sondern eine symbolische Gegenwart, bedingt durch die Anwesenheit der Lade" (p. 99).

of burnt offering. He argues that in such contexts the phrase is an expression of proximity to the *ark*.[15]

Causal

By contrast, his causal usage of לפני יהוה has no necessary connection with the sanctuary, but often exceeds its bounds and encompasses anything that somehow has YHWH as its basis or aim.[16] In this case, the majority of his examples contain no adverbs or adverbial phrases indicating location.

Literal

In addition to the spatial and causal usages of לפני יהוה, Nötscher also recognizes a literal (buchstäblich) sense, but solely with the verb "to stand" (עמד), and then only in the case of Gen. 18:22 and perhaps also ("etwa noch") Deut. 4:10. He regards it as referring to YHWH conceived of as vividly present through the theophany.[17]

Comment

Nötscher's analysis is unsatisfactory in general, and on several counts. First, it is by no means clear what is to be understood by his assertion of "eine symbolische Gegenwart, bedingt durch die Anwesenheit der Lade" (i.e. within the temple). On the one hand he denies that YHWH dwells there in person,[18] and on the other he refers to his (invisible) Presence over the ark,[19] in the latter case twice implying a *permanent* association with that particular object.[20] Secondly, in his discussion of the significance of the spatial usage of לפני יהוה, surprisingly he appears not to distinguish between its occurrences in contexts relating to the temple and in

---

[15] "Wo immer ein Opfer im Tempel oder im Wüstenheiligtum stattfindet, geschieht es 'vor Jahwe' deswegen, weil es näher oder entfernter vor der Lade stattfindet" (p. 102).

[16] "Dieser Begriff geht...oft über die Sphäre des Heiligtums hinaus und...er alles umschließt, was Jahwe irgendwie zum Grund oder zum Ziel hat" (p. 103).

[17] "Wo ihr buchstäblicher Sinn erhalten ist, bezieht sie sich auf den durch die Theophanie lebendig gegenwärtig gedachten Jahwe...kultisch auf die unsichtbare Gegenwart Jahwes im Heiligtum" (p. 87).

[18] "Es heißt niemals, daß Jahwe im Tempel wohne, sondern immer nur: sein Name" (p. 99 n. 1). See also above, p. 133 n. 14.

[19] Pp. 20, 31, 36-37, 48 n. 3, 59, 87, 95, 99, 100.

[20] He refers both to "das *Wohnen* Gottes über der Lade" (p. 95), and to the Shewbread as "*ständig* vor dem Angesicht Jahwes liegende, der über der Lade zugegen ist" (p. 100) [our italics].

those relating to the tabernacle. He argues, as mentioned above, by denying YHWH's personal dwelling in the *temple*, and concludes that לפני יהוה
indicates proximity to the ark.[21] Now, it is clear from the references to
YHWH's Name being in the temple that some sort of case can be made
out for denying that YHWH himself dwelt there, and thus that לפני יהוה in
contexts relating to the temple does indicate proximity to the ark. However, in Nötscher's subsequent discussion of this spatial usage he quotes
extensively from contexts referring to the *tabernacle*. In so doing he apparently fails to consider the possibility that YHWH might be represented as dwelling there personally,[22] and thus that the majority of the sig-

---

[21] P. 131.

[22] Exod. 25:8; 29:45-46. There has been much discussion as to whether the tabernacle was the place of YHWH's permanent Presence (*Wohnungsort*) or only of his
occasional visits (*Begegnungsort*). Those regarding it primarily as a dwelling-place
include: Mettinger 96: "The P-materials…emphasize that God is present in his Tabernacle", Brueggemann (1976) 681: "[The] tradition of the tabernacle…moves closer to
affirming that Yahweh is actually there, not simply that he meets there with his people", Schmitt 227: "Die wesentlichen Elemente des *šākan/miškān*, der Vorstellung
des '*lipnê jhwh*' und des *ʿānān-kābôd*-Komplexes, verbunden mit der in Ex 29,42f.
auftretenden Betonung des ausschließlichen Kultortes, laufen auf die Annahme einer
dauernden Präsenz Jahwes im Heiligtum hinaus", Weinfeld (1972a) 191 n. 2: "The
passages which refer to the tabernacle as a place of meeting…do not prove that P
conceived it as serving this purpose only…The tabernacle did serve as a meeting-
place…but otherwise it was the Deity's permanent place of habitation", Fretheim
(1968b) 319: "[In] the Priestly writing…the presence of Yahweh is never associated
with any particular place…the only place mentioned by P is 'above the mercy-seat
that was upon the ark of the testimony, from between the two cherubim'…This points
up one of the most important things about the sanctuary in P: it was portable. Thus,
while the tent was the dwelling place of Yahweh, it did not confine him to a definite
place; it moved about", de Vaux (1966) 448: "Ce sanctuaire n'est pas, pour P, le lieu
de théophanies transitoires…il est le siège d'une présence permanente", Clements
(1965) 114-115: "[The tabernacle] is the shrine…in which Yahweh's glory, and thus
Yahweh's very presence, will come to take up its abode in the midst of Israel…for
Yahweh to be the God of Israel means that he dwells in their midst", Davies (1962c)
499: "a dwelling place for the tabernacling presence of Yahweh", Lindblom 92: "[I]t
was believed that [Yahweh] was present in the tent-shrine in the desert…'The tent of
meeting' in the wilderness was also called משכן, i.e. the dwelling-place of Yahweh in
the midst of his people", Rost (1938) 37: "Das dem Wohnzelt nachgestaltete Heiligtum…wird Wohnung Jahwes", Morgenstern (1911) 148: "[The tabernacle] was to be
Jahwe's eternal abode, in which the *kᵉbhod Jahwe* was ever to be present, to dwell".
Others view it mainly as a meeting place: Görg (1967) 60, Kuschke 87-88, 103-104,
Noth (1948) 265-266, von Rad (1931) 492. Note, however, that even though such
scholars regard the dwelling-place idea as having been superseded, two of them, in
marked contrast to Nötscher, nevertheless see לפני יהוה as evidence for YHWH's per-

nificantly large number of instances of לפני יהוה in such contexts[23] could well indicate proximity to YHWH himself rather than to the ark. Clearly in this case the expression would have to be placed in his *literal* category, and his view of all its instances occurring in the context of a sanctuary as referring to the ark, would have to be rejected. Thirdly, it is by no means clear why, if the writers really did mean proximity to the ark, they did not use ארון instead of יהוה, particularly as there would be ample precedent for such usage in the OT. Several activities are described elsewhere as taking place "before the ark",[24] and the extensive use of the divine Name as a circumlocution for it would seem to be unlikely. Nötscher's analysis is also unsatisfactory as regards the thirteen Deut. 12-26 instances of לפני יהוה which he discusses,[25] since he assigns most of them to his causal category. The majority, however, are specified, by either an adverb or adverbial phrase, as occurring at the "chosen place", and thus presumably within the sphere of the sanctuary there. On the basis of Nötscher's own criteria, one would have expected them to be placed in his *spatial* rather than his causal category.[26]

N. RABBAN

Rabban, in an article devoted to a consideration of לפני יהוה itself[27] recognizes two broad uses of the term: concrete (קונקרטי) and abstract (מופשט):[28]

---

manent Presence within the tabernacle: Kuschke 103: "[I]n der Lagerordnung der P-Erzählung…stießen [wir]…den Begriff [משכן] und alle mit ihm verbundenen Vorstellungen vom Wohnen Jahwes am Kultort, die Lade und das kultische Handeln 'vor Jahwe'", von Rad (1931) 477-478: "[D]ie Vorstellung, daß Jahwe in dem Zelt wohnt, ist bei P wohl zu belegen. Wir finden…einen überaus häufigen Gebrauch der Phrase [לפני יהוה] in kultischem Sinn" (note that the point still stands despite his subsequent qualification in [1958] 238 n. 109). See Janowski (1982) for a discussion of some recent views (pp. 295-303).

[23] Over sixty in the three large blocks of material which deal with the tabernacle, i.e. Exod. 25-31, 35-40 and the whole of Leviticus (apart from the Holiness Code [17-26]).

[24] Exod. 40:5; Josh. 4:5; 6:4, 6, 7, 13; 7:6; 1 Sam. 5:3, 4; 2 Sam. 6:4; 1 Kings 3:15; 8:5; 1 Chron. 15:24; 16:4, 6, 37 (2x); 2 Chron. 5:6.

[25] 12:7, 12, 18 (2x); 14:23, 26; 15:20; 16:11; 18:7; 24:4; 26:5, 10, 13 (pp. 85-87, 98-119).

[26] See above, pp. 133-134.

[27] "לפני ה'", *Tarbiẓ* 23 (1952) 1-8.

[28] P. 7; cf. p. 6.

Concrete

Within this category Rabban considers that לפני יהוה can express prox-imity either to the Deity or to the ark. If the activity carried out לפני יהוה is a concrete physical action[29] (פעולה קונקרטית-גופנית) understood liter-ally,[30] then the preposition designates a spatial relationship between the author(s) of the action and the one before whom it is carried out. Thus, in Gen. 18:22 Abraham's standing לפני יהוה is a real (i.e. literal) standing, and so לפני signifies his physical proximity to the divine Presence.[31] On the other hand, by appealing to its usage in connection with the taber-nacle, Rabban argues that the expression can also be equivalent to "be-fore the ark". In these contexts, however, it is not indicative of the divine Presence since YHWH does not reside above the ark permanently, but only on those occasions when he "meets" there with Moses.[32] Never-theless, because of the real link between the two, the ark can be seen as a symbol of that Presence, and is treated as if YHWH did actually reside over it.[33]

Rabban distinguishes between the two uses in the following way. If cultic activities לפני יהוה are accompanied by a description of the concrete location near the ark ("at the door of the tent of meeting" etc.) they are linked to the ark, but if they are not so described they are linked to the Presence.[34]

Abstract

In this use of the expression, that which is predicated as being לפני יהוה is abstract[35] and does not entail a spatial proximity to the Deity. The

---

[29] Such as "standing", "casting down", "bowing down", "going out" (pp. 6-7).

[30] Rabban also envisages instances of a concrete physical action being understood in a descriptive-symbolic (ציורי-סמלי) sense. In 1 Kings 1:2, for example, Abishag's standing לפני David is not to be taken literally, but as referring to a range of actions associated not with a literal standing, but rather (presumably) with nursing. In this case, just as there is no real standing, so there is no prominent spatial relationship in-volved, since the standing לפני encapsulates a variety of relationships between Abi-shag and the king (pp. 6-7). Curiously, Rabban gives no instances of לפני יהוה used in this way.

[31] P. 7.

[32] (p. 4). "לא מצינו בתורה שהשכינה שורה על הכפורת אף בשעה שאינה נועדת עם משה"

[33] Pp. 3-4.

[34] "לגבי פעולות פולחניות מסוימות, שכל עצמן זיקה לשכינה, נוקט הכתוב את התיאור 'לפני ה'' (p. 3). בלבד, בלי לציין את המקום הקונקרטי הקרוב לארון (כנון 'פתח אהל מועד' וכדומה).

[35] E.g. "remembrance", "judgement", "atonement", "clean" (p. 7).

phrase could be rendered "in YHWH's eyes"[36] and indicates how he regards particular people or their actions.

Comment

Rabban's understanding of לפני יהוה in the context of the tabernacle material, i.e. as indicating proximity to the ark, is similar to Nötscher's and is equally dependent on whether that particular sanctuary is regarded primarily as a meeting- or a dwelling-place. However, his discussion marks an advance on that of Nötscher in that he hints at criteria by which some of the uses of the phrase might be distinguished. First, he raises the possibility of understanding concrete physical actions carried out לפני יהוה in one of two ways: either literally, in which case they refer to only one activity, or symbolically, in which case they include a variety of actions not associated with the literal meaning, but for which there may be evidence in the immediate context. And secondly, he observes that usage in the sense of "in YHWH's eyes" is characterized by the abstract nature of that which is predicated as being לפני יהוה.

J. REINDL

In his study *Das Angesicht Gottes im Sprachgebrauch des Alten Testaments*, Reindl isolates *three* main uses of the phrase: local (lokal), an "expression of the religious life" (Äußerung des religiösen Lebens) and metaphorical (metaphorisch):[37]

Local

Reindl distinguishes two categories of local usage. לפני יהוה either has a literal (wörtlich) local sense, which appears only in reports of divine appearances, visions or metaphorical descriptions,[38] or it is a technical term for any event which happens in the cult. In the latter case the decisive factor is not proximity to the ark, but the sphere of the cult.[39] This

---

[36] "בעיני ה'" (p. 7).
[37] Pp. 25, 29, 31.
[38] "[D]er wörtliche, lokale Sinn der Präposition [auftritt] nur in Berichten von Gotteserscheinungen, Visionen oder metaphorischen Schilderungen" (p. 32).
[39] "[Es] ist...nicht schwierig, in לפני י' einen *terminus technicus des priesterlichen Sprachgebrauchs* zu erkennen...einen formelhaften Ausdruck *für jedes Geschehen, das sich im kultischen Bereich vollzieht*...Das entscheidende Moment für die Anwendung der Formel ist nicht die Nähe zur Lade, sondern die Sphäre des Kultes" (pp. 26-27).

usage occurs predominantly in P.[40] Moreover, in further contrast to Nötscher and Rabban, Reindl considers that God is not only present in the sanctuary, but is also known to be so from the local use of לפני יהוה in contexts which refer to it.[41] During a cultic act Israel experiences the proximity of its God,[42] and so it would appear that both of his local usages can refer to YHWH's Presence on the earth.

An "expression of the religious life"

In this case the phrase is no longer confined to the cultic sphere, but is used to indicate the religious nature of an inner attitude[43] or of certain conduct or behaviour.[44] It may be, but is not necessarily, used with reference to a sanctuary. According to Reindl, such usage occurs only rarely in P, but is very common in the deuteronomistic writings and Psalms.[45]

Metaphorical

Here, Reindl identifies two main uses, in which לפני יהוה can mean either "in YHWH's opinion"[46] or "according to YHWH's will".[47] He considers this usage to be rarer than the other two, but distributed throughout most of the OT traditions.[45]

Comment

Reindl's classification of לפני יהוה is an improvement on those of Nötscher and Rabban in its isolation of three (as opposed to two) main

---

[40] P. 33.

[41] "Das Heiligtum ist…auch durch die reale Gegenwart Gottes ausgezeichnet. Das läßt sich an den Stellen erkennen, an denen der Terminus ל לפני im strengen Sinn lokal gebraucht wird, während der so bezeichnete Ort durch den Kontext gleichzeitig als das Heiligtum ausgewiesen wird" (p. 220).

[42] "Bei allen kultischen Handlungen erfährt Israel die Nähe seines Gottes" (p. 27). See also pp. 221-222.

[43] Reindl considers, for example, that the rejoicing "before YHWH" found in Deuteronomy is "ein Ausdruck einer inneren religiösen Haltung" (p. 29), and that Josiah's weeping "before YHWH" is "Ausdruck der religiösen Haltung, die ihn beseelt" (p. 30).

[44] "Der Kultterminus [i.e. לפני יהוה]…wird zur Kennzeichnung des religiösen Tuns oder Verhaltens überhaupt angewendet" (p. 32).

[45] P. 34.

[46] "לפני kann nämlich…auch gebraucht werden, um festzustellen, daß ein Sachverhalt 'in den Augen' [= im Urteil (p. 33f.)] einer Person…erscheint. Dies wird nun sehr häufig von Jahwe gesagt" (p. 31).

[47] "Wie das Urteil, so ist auch der Ratschluß Jahwes mit ל לפני ausgedrückt" (p. 31). See also pp. 33-34.

uses of the phrase.[48] However, it is unsatisfactory in its treatment of the occurrences of לפני יהוה in Deut. 12-26. As indicated above, Reindl emphasizes that the *sine qua non* for the local usage of the expression is activity within *the sphere of the cult*,[49] while at the same time pointing out that all his cited examples have their localization either in or near a sanctuary.[50] In the case of his "expression of the religious life" usage, however, he mentions no essential feature, though the majority of instances referred to (praying, fasting, pouring out one's heart, etc.) involve expressions of personal piety capable of being carried out by the individual Israelite without either priestly mediation or spatial restriction. He points out that such instances are not confined to the cultic sphere,[51] though they do sometimes occur in connection with a sanctuary, and provides a number of examples illustrating the absence of any necessary connection with either. In his view, it is possible to carry out an activity like "humbling oneself before YHWH" both at and away from a sanctuary, the presence of the latter constituting no vital pre-condition which must be satisfied before the action לפני יהוה can take place. That being the case, it is strange that he regards (without justifying his classification) all but one[52] of the Deut. 12-26 instances which he discusses[53] as "expressions of the religious life", since the majority take place in the context of the cult,[54] and, apart from 12:12, 18b, the use of לפני יהוה is expressly limited to those activities occurring at the "chosen place".[55] Such limitation is particularly striking in the case of *eating* לפני יהוה,[56] and would appear to be

---

[48] Cf. Reindl's own estimate of Nötscher's classification: "Vor allem ist der letztere Ausdruck [eines 'kausalen' 'vor Jahwe'] zu ungenau, um den verschiedenen Differenzierungen des לפני י gerecht zu werden" (p. 245 n. 51).

[49] P. 136.

[50] "Alle hier aufgeführten Stellen haben eine Lokalisierung im Heiligtum oder doch die Beschreibung eines kultischen Vorganges im Bereich des Heiligtums im Blick, wenn sie die Worte לפני י gebrauchen' (p. 27). See also p. 221.

[51] "Der Ausdruck לפני י bleibt...keineswegs auf den eigentlichen kultischen Bereich beschränkt" (p. 28).

[52] 24:4, which he considers to be metaphorical (p. 31).

[53] I.e. the various instances of eating and rejoicing לפני יהוה.

[54] 12:7, 18a; 14:23, 26; 15:20; 16:11.

[55] See below, p. 146.

[56] Note the repeated use of שם in 12:5-7 to insist that the Israelites eat לפני יהוה only at the "chosen place": "you shall seek the place which the LORD...will choose...*thither* (שמה) you shall go, and *thither* (שמה) you shall bring your burnt offerings...and *there* (שם) you shall eat before the LORD", and the prohibitions against eating tithes etc. away from the "chosen place", explicitly in 12:17-18: "You may not eat within your

inconsistent with Reindl's own view of the phrase as an "expression of the religious life" and thus as involving no necessary connection with either the cult or a sanctuary. It thus seems that, as with Nötscher, so also with Reindl, the criteria which he established should have resulted in a classification of the occurrences in Deut. 12-26, at least as regards eating לפני יהוה, as *local*, and therefore as referring to the Presence of God.

R. SOLLAMO

Sollamo, also in a survey article dealing with לפני יהוה itself,[57] examines its usage in the different literary layers of the OT, but without attempting any kind of systematic classification or providing any criteria in support of her various interpretations. She regards its occurrences in the Priestly Code and all but three[58] of those in Deuteronomy as referring to the divine Presence at the cult-place.[59]

M.D. FOWLER

In an article primarily devoted to determining whether the occurrence of לפני יהוה is evidence *per se* for the existence of a permanent sanctuary,[60] Fowler identifies *four* distinct uses of the expression.[61] First, it can mean "in the sight (estimation) of" YHWH. Secondly, it can refer to the divine omnipresence, especially in the Psalms (e.g. the rejoicing לפני יהוה of the sea, field and trees in Ps. 96:11-13). Thirdly, it can have "a heightened metaphorical sense" which expresses the direct and personal communication between God and man (e.g. Exod. 6:12, 30). Finally, he suggests that most instances of the phrase occur in contexts where a sanctuary of sorts is clearly in mind, and in such cases the idiom does seem to refer to the localized Presence of YHWH. Again, there is no mention of any criteria employed to distinguish the various uses, though in connection with several instances of the expression in 1 Kings 8 and 9,

---

towns the tithe etc....but you shall eat them before the LORD...in the place which the LORD...will choose", and implicitly in 14:24-26 in the instructions to those who live far from the "chosen place".
[57] "Den bibliska formeln 'Inför Herren/Inför Gud", *SEÅ* 50 (1985) 21-32.
[58] 6:25; 24:4, 13 (p. 26).
[59] Pp. 23, 26.
[60] "The Meaning of *lipnê* YHWH in the Old Testament", *ZAW* 99 (1987) 384-390.
[61] See his conclusion (p. 390).

he does cite some independent evidence for YHWH's Presence in the
temple, i.e. from the immediate context.[62]

OVERALL COMMENT

Examination of all five discussions reveals a paucity of criteria to
which appeal might be made in order to distinguish between the various
OT uses of לפני יהוה. It is clear, however, that the establishment of such
criteria will be vital if any scholarly consensus is to arise as to the significance of the expression in particular cases. To this end our own
analysis will suggest ways of identifying the two uses most obviously
present in Deut. 12-26.

CHARACTERISTICS OF לפני יהוה IN DEUT 12-26

RELATION TO PLACE

Two distinct uses of לפני יהוה can be detected in the legal section of
Deuteronomy. They will be discussed in turn:

Irrelevant

Two instances of לפני יהוה (24:4, 13) form part of the following sequence: the verb היה, either implicitly (v. 4) or explicitly (v. 13), an abstract noun,[63] תועבה (v. 4) or צדקה (v. 13), and the phrase לפני יהוה. In
each case, the combination of noun plus לפני יהוה refers back to an act
mentioned earlier in the text: the remarriage of a man to his ex-wife following the termination of her second marriage (v. 4), or the restoration to
a pauper of a cloak taken as security for a loan (v. 13). Neither context
gives any indication (e.g. by the use of an appropriate adverbial phrase)
that the לפני יהוה applies only to a specific locality. The most natural
understanding of the phrase in both v. 4[64] and v. 13[65] is therefore "in
YHWH's estimation" or "as far as YHWH is concerned".

---

[62] [T]he Temple was filled by a cloud (1K 8:10), that cloud which, in the stories of
the desert, was the sign of Yahweh's presence in the Tent of Reunion" (p. 388).
[63] Cf. Rabban's second broad use of the term לפני יהוה (above, pp. 137-138).
[64] Simian-Yofre 654: "[L]ipnê JHWH kann auch den Gesichtspunkt JHWHs und sein
Urteil über Situationen oder Personen ausdrücken (Dtn 24,4)", Sollamo 26: "I...Dtn
24:4. 13...uppträder [Gud] som den högste domaren och väger människornas gär-
ningar", van der Woude (1976) 459: "[L]ifnē Jhwh [meint] 'in den Augen, nach dem
Urteil, nach Ansicht Jahwes' (Dtn 24,4)", Thompson (1974) 244: "[T]o take her back
would be an abomination to Yahweh", Reindl 31: "לפני י" beschreibt...das Urteil, das

Explicit

In ten instances (12:7, 18a; 14:23, 26; 15:20; 16:11; 18:7; 26:5, 10 [2x]) it is indicated that an activity is to take place not only לפני יהוה, but also at "the place which YHWH...will choose". Seven specify the site by inserting the adverbial phrase [יהוה] המקום אשר יבחר either before (26:5, 10 [2x], cf. v. 2) or after (12:18a; 14:23; 15:20; 16:11) the occurrence of לפני יהוה. The other three do so by the use of the adverb שם ("there"),[66] which in each case refers back to an earlier mention of the "chosen place" (12:7, cf. vv. 5-6; 14:26, cf. v. 25; 18:7, cf. v. 6).

Implicit

In the remaining four cases (12:12, 18b; 19:17; 26:13) the activity carried out לפני יהוה is qualified neither by an adverbial phrase ("at the place which...") or adverb ("there"), nor by any features suggesting a more general applicability. However, although superficially there are no clear indications whether such activities were intended to take place at a particular locality or over a wide area, closer examination of the immediate contexts suggests that possibly three of the four were meant to occur at the "chosen place".

Deut. 12:12. Since the exhortation to "rejoice before YHWH" falls between two references to the necessity of carrying out certain cultic activities at the "chosen place" (vv. 11 and 13-14), it is reasonable to presume that such rejoicing is intended to occur there as well. This would mean that שמה ("thither", v. 11), which refers back to the "chosen place" men-

---

Gott über einen Menschen oder eine Sache fällt...Er findet sich...mit folgenden Urteilsaussagen: Dtn 24,4", Watts (1970) 265: "The reason given is...in terms of what is abominable to the Lord", Cazelles (1966) 99-100: "[I]l y a là une abomination aux yeux de Yahvé" (own translation), Nötscher 110 n. 4: "[לפני] bedeutet 'nach dem Urteil'; vgl. Dt. 24,4", BDB 817: "*in the sight* (estimation) *of*...Dt 24⁴...v¹³", Driver (1902) 272: "a variation of the usual expression 'Jehovah's abomination'", Steuernagel (1900) 88: "[E]in solches Weib [sei] unrein geworden und Jahve es verabscheue."

[65] Sollamo 26: *idem*, Thompson (1974) 247: "Such consideration...would...result in blessing to the creditor, whose generosity was right...in God's eyes", Watts (1970) 265-266: "[T]he creditor will be rewarded by...the accounting of this act as righteousness by the Lord", Cazelles (1966) 101: "[C]e sera une bonne action aux yeux de Yahvé" (own translation), Davies (1962a) 279: "Such behaviour is right conduct acceptable to God", Cunliffe-Jones 137: "This kind of activity will stand to a person's credit with God", BDB 817: *idem*.

[66] Tournay sees the use of this adverb in close proximity to an occurrence of the divine Name (שם) as evidence of a play on words (p. 78).

tioned earlier in the verse, specifies not only the site to which the Israelites must bring all that YHWH commands them, but also the one at
which they must "rejoice before [him]" (v. 12). This interpretation is the
one most generally accepted.[67]

Deut. 12:18b. This second injunction to "rejoice before YHWH" is located between two commands relating to care for the Levite. In v. 18a
the Israelites are encouraged to share with him the eating of their tithes,
firstlings and offerings at the "chosen place", and in v. 19 they are
warned against forsaking him. Driver has suggested that v. 19 is repeating in more general terms what is commanded specifically in v. 18a.[68] If
this is the case, then both v. 18a and v. 19 are concerned with the Israelites' behaviour at the "chosen place", and so their "rejoicing before
YHWH" (v. 18b) can be presumed to occur there as well.[69] The focus of
that rejoicing, the rather comprehensive-sounding "in all that you undertake" (בכל משלח ידך), is thus likely to be the fruit of their labour, a part of
which (the tithes, etc.) they and others are commanded to eat at the "chosen place" (vv. 17-18a).[70]

Deut. 19:17. The demand that both parties to a dispute involving a malicious witness "appear before the LORD, before the priests and the judges
who are in office in those days" is generally considered to refer to "the
central sanctuary".[71] Usually one of two reasons is implied. Sometimes
the similarities between 19:15-21 and 17:8-13 appear to form the basis
for the deduction. Cases requiring decision between different kinds of
homicide, legal right or assault - "any case within your towns which is

[67] Thompson (1974) 169, Phillips (1973) 87, Rennes 70, Clamer 593, Junker 63,
Smith (1918) 167, BDB 970, Driver (1902) 144, Keil 452.
[68] (1902) 147, see also Keil 453.
[69] So Sollamo 26, Thompson (1974) 171, Watts (1970) 239, BDB 970, Driver (1902)
144 (on v. 12), Steuernagel (1900) 46.
[70] Similar to the rejoicing "in all that you undertake" of v. 7. There the בכל משלח ידכם
must refer back to the various offerings listed in v. 6, since it is qualified by "in
which the LORD...has blessed you" (אשר ברכך יהוה).
[71] Except by Davies (1962a), who regards it as referring to *local* sanctuaries (p. 278)
and von Rad (1964), who relates it to "die junge Institution eines staatlich organisier-
ten Richterstandes" in Deut. 16:18 (p. 92). L'Hour 18-19 considers that, prior to the
later (deuteronomic) addition of the reference to priests and judges, which in the
present form of the text points to the settling of the affair at the central sanctuary, the
reference to appearing לפני יהוה merely expressed the sacral nature of a procedure
which was intended to take place in the towns. Cf. Mayes (1979) 290, Smith (1918)
242.

too difficult for you" - are to be dealt with at "the place which the LORD...will choose" (17:8-13). Those involving a malicious witness (another difficult situation) require a similarly constituted judiciary,[72] and so are tried at the same place.[73] Alternatively, the use of לפני יהוה in 19:17 is regarded as of itself pointing to the central sanctuary.[74] For our purposes, however, the latter reason is unsatisfactory, since we are looking for *independent* evidence for the identity of any site(s) to which the expression may refer.

Deut. 26:13. Following the distribution of the triennial tithe (presumably in the *towns*, cf. v. 12 and 14:28-29) to the Levite, sojourner, etc., the Israelite is expected to make a declaration לפני יהוה. Most scholars, frequently on the basis of the presence of לפני יהוה itself, consider this declaration to take place at the central sanctuary.[75] Others locate it in the

---

[72] Priests and judges in 19:17, Levitical priests and judge in 17:9.

[73] Carmichael (1974) 115: "An...affinity between xvii and xix is that the difficult legal case in xvii and the case of the false witness in xix have each to be taken to the central tribunal, to the priests and judge(s) who practice in those days", Phillips (1973) 132: "[B]*efore the priests and the judges*: the case has proved too difficult for the local judiciary, who have referred it to the central appeal court in Jerusalem (cp. on 17:8-13)", Buis and Leclercq 142: "S'il ne se présente qu'un témoin à charge, on se trouve devant l'un de ces cas 'trop difficiles' pour un tribunal local (17,8); l'affaire doit donc être déférée au tribunal suprême [cf. p. 131 on 17:8-13], aux prêtres ou aux juges laïcs", Steuernagel (1900) 73: "לפני י"י, erklärt durch das folgende לפני הכהנים, also sie sollen nach Jerusalem gehen, wo die schwierigen Fälle nach 17:8ff. entschieden werden sollen."

[74] Clifford (1982) 105: "The phrase 'before the Lord' usually means in Deuteronomy 'in the central shrine'", Craigie (1976) 270: "there they would stand before the Lord (v. 17), a symbolic manner of referring to the sanctuary (see 17:8)", Watts (1970) 256: "he and the accused should *appear before the Lord*. This probably means the [central (p. 238)] sanctuary where God's presence is invoked", Wright (1953) 454: "all parties of the dispute shall be taken before the supreme court at the central sanctuary (before the LORD), an institution already referred to in 17:8-13", Clamer 639: "La comparution devant Yahweh implique que l'affaire doit être portée au sanctuaire central", Hölscher (1922) 206: "Die Streitenden sollen לפני יהוה treten, d.h. im Sinne des Gesetzgebers natürlich in Jerusalem", Robinson (n.d.): 154 "The case is referred to the court at Jerusalem (xvii. 9) as 'before Yahweh' (cf. xii. 7) implies". Others regard 19:15-21 as referring to the central sanctuary, but their reason(s) for doing so are not clear: Patrick 125, Ridderbos 212, Thompson (1974) 217, Cunliffe-Jones 118, Reider 188, Driver (1902) 235-236.

[75] Cairns 224, McConville (1984) 72, Ridderbos 245, Clifford (1982) 137, Mayes (1979) 336, Milgrom 108 n. 404, Thompson (1974) 257, Phillips (1973) 175, Buis and Leclercq 167, Davies (1962a) 280, Wright (1953) 486, Cazelles (1948) 54,

settlements, at either a local sanctuary or in the Israelite's home,[76] the main reasons advanced against the majority view being the instructions in v. 12 (Watts [1970]), and the absence of all reference to a pilgrimage to the central sanctuary (Von Rad [1964]). However, neither reason is adequate to establish the point. In the first case, v. 12 indicates *when* (כי), rather than where, the "saying before YHWH" (v. 13) is to take place, and in the second case, if the use of לפני יהוה *were* to imply the "chosen place", then it would not be necessary to refer to a journey there. For all that, the context contains insufficient information to permit a definite decision one way or the other.

Summary

Of the sixteen instances of לפני יהוה in Deut. 12-26, thirteen are used to qualify activities which occur at the "chosen place". That locality is specified for 12:7, 18a; 14:23, 26; 15:20; 16:11; 18:7; 26:5 and 10 (2x), and can be deduced for 12:12, 18b and 19:17. Of the remaining three occurrences, two are used in the metaphorical sense of "in YHWH's estimation" (24:4, 13) and one (26:13), though considered by many scholars (frequently on the basis of לפני יהוה itself) to refer to the central sanctuary, has insufficient information in its immediate context to permit a definite identification to be made. Nevertheless, it is important to note that the *only* instances of לפני יהוה which are qualified by an adverbial phrase specifying a locality are those which refer to activities occurring at the "chosen place".

LAWS GOVERNING EATING

As already implied, there are in the deuteronomic law corpus no instances of לפני יהוה being applied to an activity taking place "within [the] towns".[77] However, of the thirteen associated with the "chosen place", five are concerned with the same activity, namely *eating*, and thus consti-

---

Reider 240, Smith (1918) 296, Driver (1902) 290, Steuernagel (1900) 95, Robinson (n.d.) 188.
[76] Alternatives: Craigie (1976) 323: "in the home", von Rad (1964) 115: "an einem Heiligtum", Clamer 677: "L'expression *devant Yahweh* s'entend...au sens qu'elle a dans d'autres endroits: Gen., xxvii, 7; Ex., vi, 12, 30, partout Yahweh entend notre prière". Cf. Bertholet (1899) 81: "Es fragt sich, ob man sich wegen לפני יהוה die folgenden Worte am Heiligtum oder im Hause des Einzelnen (vgl. Gen 27 7) gesprochen zu denken hat."
[77] See the previous paragraph.

tute a group of texts which can usefully be compared with the corresponding legislation relating to eating "within [the] towns". As will be shown below, the comparison serves to emphasize further the connection between being present at the "chosen place" and acting לפני יהוה.

Certain items are allowed to be eaten "within [the] towns", but in contrast to what happens at the "chosen place", their consumption is nowhere described as being לפני יהוה: flesh from animals killed in a noncultic context (12:15, 20-21, contrast 12:6-7), triennial tithes given to Levites, sojourners, etc. (14:28-29; 26:12, contrast 12:18a), and animals with a blemish (15:22, contrast 15:20).

Other items are prohibited from being consumed in the settlements. This is particularly the case with the tithe, for which there are two sets of legislation depending on how far the individual lives from the "chosen place". For the Israelite living in its vicinity the eating of the tithe[78] is not allowed "within [the] towns" (12:17), but must be carried out at the "chosen place" (12:18). For the one living at a distance the same prohibition operates, though it is implied rather than stated (14:22-26). In this case, however, the Israelite is expected to sell the tithe in his home town, take the money thus obtained to the "chosen place" and there use it to buy and then eat the same kind of fare (oxen, sheep, wine) that he had tithed originally. That eating of the actual tithe "within [the] towns" is forbidden in favour of the consumption of purchased substitutes at the "chosen place" points to the special character of the latter site. In both cases (12:17-18; 14:22-26) it is only the eating at the "chosen place" which is described as being לפני יהוה.

There is thus a contrast between eating "within [the] towns" and eating at the "chosen place" in that what is prohibited in the former is commanded at the latter. The fact that only consumption at the latter is qualified by the use of לפני יהוה, is further confirmation of a close link between that expression and the "chosen place".

THE CHOICE OF לפני IN RELATION TO YHWH

It has already been noted that, with the exception of its occurrences in 24:4, 13 ("in YHWH's estimation") and 26:13 (location unspecified),[79]

---

[78] Or of firstlings and various other offerings.

[79] Though, as a number of scholars have suggested, it may in fact be the "chosen place". See above, p. 145 n. 75.

the expression לפני יהוה appears in Deut.12-26 solely in connection with
the "chosen place".[80] There are no instances of an activity occurring לפני
יהוה "within [the] towns". This specificity in usage is further indicated by
an investigation of the prepositions immediately preceding the divine
Name in those sections which refer to the "chosen place": 12:5-14, 18-
19, 26-27; 14:22-26/27; 15:19-21; 16:1-17; 17:1 (by implication),[81] 8-13;
18:1-8; 19:15-21(?); 26:1-11. As will be shown below, although in most
cases the preposition chosen to follow any given verb is that generally
used elsewhere in the OT, in five of the thirteen instances לפני is used
instead of the preposition most commonly associated with the particular
verb concerned.

Activities carried out with explicit reference to YHWH will be examined under two main headings:

Activities governed by other prepositions
לפני *never used outside Deut. 12-26.* Within the sections referring to the
"chosen place" there are nine exhortations to carry out an activity in relation to YHWH, in each of which the preposition immediately preceding
the divine Name is the one most commonly used after the verb or noun
in question:

> "[T]o the place which the LORD...will choose...you shall
> bring...all your votive offerings which you vow *to* (ל) the
> LORD." (12:11)

> "All the firstling males that are born of your herd and flock
> you shall consecrate *to* (ל) the LORD...you shall do no work
> with the firstling of your herd...You shall eat it...at the place
> which the LORD will choose." (15:19-20)

> "[K]eep the passover *to* (ל) the LORD...And you shall offer
> the passover sacrifice *to* (ל) the LORD...at the place which the
> LORD will choose..." (16:1-2)

> "[Y]ou shall boil [the passover sacrifice]...at the place which
> the LORD...will choose...For six days you shall eat unleav-
> ened bread; and on the seventh day there shall be a solemn as-
> sembly *to* (ל) the LORD..." (16:7-8)

---

[80] See above, p. 146.
[81] Cf. 12:5-6, 11, 26-27.

"[Y]ou shall keep the feast of weeks *to* (ל) the LORD...and you shall rejoice...at the place which the LORD...will choose..." (16:10-11)

"For seven days you shall keep the feast *to* (ל) the LORD...at the place which the LORD will choose..." (16:15)

"Three times a year all your males shall appear[82] *before* (את־פני) the LORD...at the place which he will choose...They shall not appear *before* (את־פני) the LORD empty-handed..." (16:16)

Examination of the usage elsewhere in the OT (Table 5.1)[83] shows that when God/YHWH is the indirect object of any of the named activities, the preposition ל is almost invariably used: נדר (to vow), קדש (Hiph., to consecrate), עשה פסח (to keep the passover) and חגג (to keep a feast).[84] Similarly, ראה (Niph., to appear) occurs with either את־פני or פני.[85] There are no clear instances of any of these words being used with לפני.[86] It therefore appears that, in Hebrew, vows and feasts, for example, are made and kept "to" rather than "before" God. Since, therefore, the use of the prepositions in Deut. 12:11; 15:19; 16:1, 2, 8, 10, 15, 16 is consistent with that found in the rest of the OT, it is not any aversion to the use of לפני that has dictated the choice of preposition in these verses.

---

[82] A number of scholars consider that the verb was originally Qal but was vocalised as a Niphal to avoid the suggestion that the Israelites could actually see the divine face: Mayes (1979) 261, Reindl 147-149, Buis and Leclercq 126, Nötscher 92-93, Westphal 128 n. 1, Driver (1902) 198-199, Bertholet (1899) 52.

[83] See below, p. 150.

[84] The same applies to the nouns נדר (vow), פסח (passover) and חג (feast).

[85] לפני *is* used in Dan. 1:13, but the indirect object is human.

[86] There is a possible exception in 1 Kings 8:65 where ויעש...את־החג occurs in association with לפני יהוה. Apart from Lev. 23:34, in which "seven days" also intervenes between חג and ליהוה, the usual preposition (ל) follows *directly* after חגג, חג or the noun to which the construct of the latter is attached (cf. Exod. 5:1; 12:14; 13:6; 23:14; 32:5; Lev. 23:6, 41; Num. 29:12). In 1 Kings 8:65, however, the את־החג is separated from the לפני יהוה by "and all Israel with him, a great assembly, from the entrance of Hamath to the Brook of Egypt". It is thus possible that the verse is to be understood as expressing that "Solomon held the feast", i.e. without an indirect object (as in the parallel 2 Chron. 7:8, but also in 1 Kings 12:32; Ezra 3:4; 6:22; Neh. 8:18; 2 Chron. 7:9; 30:13, 21; 35:17), and that the somewhat distant לפני יהוה qualifies instead the "great assembly" (cf. Gen. 10:9, in which the same expression also refers to a phrase placed in apposition to an earlier subject: "Like Nimrod a mighty hunter before the LORD"). In other words, Solomon is recorded merely as holding a feast, and not as holding one לפני יהוה.

Out of the Midst of the Fire

Table 5.1: Prepositions used in relation to the Deity

Activity in Deut. 12-26ᵃ		Governing prepositionᵇ	
Hebrew	English	Deut. 12-26ᶜ	Elsewhere

לפני never used outside Deut. 12-26

Hebrew	English	Deut. 12-26	Elsewhere
נדר	vow	ל (1)ᵈ	ל (11)
(Hiph.) קדש	consecrate	ל (1)	ל (10)
עשה פסח	keep the passover	ל (1)	ל (7)
זבח פסח	offer the passover sacrifice	ל (1)	
עצרת	be a solemn assembly	ל (1(	
עשה חג	keep the feast	ל (1)	
(חגג) חג	keep the feast	ל (1)	ל (5)
(Niph.) ראה	appear	את־פני / פני (2)	את־פניᵉ (5) / פני (4)

לפני occasionally used outside Deut. 12-26

Hebrew	English	Deut. 12-26	Elsewhere
זבח	sacrifice	ל (2)	ל (37) / לפני (4)
(Hiph.) נגד	declare	ל (1)	אל (1) / ל (1) / לפני (1) / על (1)

לפני in Deut. 12-26 as the prevalent OT preposition

Hebrew	English	Deut. 12-26	Elsewhere
אכל	eat	לפני (5)	לפני (3)
עמד	stand	לפני (2)	לפני (29) / על (3) / את־פני (1) / בין...בין (1) / ממעל ל (1) / על־ימין (1)
(Hiph.) נוח	set down		לפני (4)

לפני in Deut. 12-26 instead of the prevalent OT preposition

Hebrew	English	Deut. 12-26	Elsewhere
שמח	rejoice	לפני (3)	ב (12) / לפני (3)
אמר	say	לפני (2)	אל (26) / ל (10) / לפני (1) / על (1)
(Hithp.) שחה	worship	לפני (1)	ל (23) / לפני (5)

ᵃ Carried out at the "chosen place".

ᵇ Used in relation to the Deity, but excluding gods other than YHWH.

ᶜ All the instances within Deut. 12-26 are cited in the discussion on pp. 148-152.

ᵈ The number of occurrences are shown in parentheses.

ᵉ Where applicable, the prepositions most commonly employed in relation to the Deity are listed in descending order of frequency.

לפני *occasionally used outside Deut. 12-26.* The sections referring to the "chosen place" contain three instances of activities which elsewhere in the OT may be carried out לפני יהוה, but which here (as in the previous paragraph) are combined with the preposition that is more normally used with the verb. Deut. 15:21 and 17:1 refer to sacrificing ליהוה, and 26:3 refers to declaring "to" (ל) him. In the case of sacrifice this prepositional usage would definitely appear to be significant, since, while it is *usually* carried out "to" YHWH (ליהוה), there are four OT instances of it occurring "before" (לפני) him. These, together with the only instance of declaring לפני יהוה, will therefore be considered below, with a view to ascertaining their possible significance for Deut. 15:21; 17:1 and 26:3:

The four instances of sacrificing (זבח) "before" YHWH (Lev. 9:4; 1 Sam. 11:15; 1 Kings 8:62; 2 Chron. 7:4) raise the question as to why the same preposition might not also have been used in Deut. 15:21 and 17:1, particularly in view of its thirteen other occurrences (in combination with YHWH) within ch. 12-26, in relation to the "chosen place". Two observations may help to provide an answer. First, the two instances in Deuteronomy are both *negative*, and involve prohibitions against sacrifice.[87] Secondly, while the use of either preposition would indicate that the sacrifice was to be in some sense for the benefit of YHWH, only לפני, understood spatially, could convey that it must also be in close proximity to him.[88] This being the case, it seems reasonable to presume that in Deut. 15:21 and 17:1 ל was used in preference to לפני to avoid the possible implication that, whereas it was forbidden to sacrifice blemished livestock לפני יהוה, it was permissible to sacrifice them to him elsewhere, since that would not be in the divine Presence.

The OT contains very few instances of declaring (נגד [Hiph.]) in combination with a preposition and followed by the Deity as its indirect object. Aside from Deut. 26:3, it occurs once each with אל (Exod. 19:9), ל (Is. 41:22), לפני (Ps. 142:3 [EVV 2]) and על (Job 36:33). Clearly none of these prepositions can meaningfully be said to be applied to YHWH more commonly than any other, though that in Deut. 26:3 (ל) is the one most frequently used when declaring to a *human* being (>250 occur-

---

[87] In contrast to the four non-deuteronomic instances, which are all *positive* and refer to the people either sacrificing to YHWH (1 Sam. 11:15, 1 Kings 8:62 and 2 Chron. 7:4) or being commanded to do so (Lev. 9:4).

[88] Regardless of whether it means "in his Presence" or "in front of him".

rences). However, since לפני is used in Ps. 142:3 it could well have been an option in Deut. 26:3.

Thus, in only one of the twelve instances involving an activity governed by a preposition other than לפני (i.e. 26:3), does the latter appear to have been a possible alternative to the preposition actually used. In the remainder of cases the choice (whether of ל or את־פני) was dictated by conventional Hebrew usage rather than by an aversion to לפני itself.

Activities governed by לפני

*לפני as the prevalent OT preposition.*Within the sections dealing with the "chosen place" there are references to eating (Deut. 12:7, 18a; 14:23, 26; 15:20), standing (18:7; 19:17) and setting down (26:10) לפני יהוה. In each case לפני is the preposition most frequently associated with the particular activity when it is carried out in relation to the Deity (Table 5.1). It is the only preposition used with אכל (to eat) and נוח (Hiph., to set down), and is the main one occurring with עמד (to stand).

לפני instead of the prevalent OT preposition. There are five other instances of an activity being carried out לפני יהוה at the "chosen place". They involve rejoicing (12:12, 18b; 16:11), making response (26:5) and worshipping (26:10). All three verbs occur elsewhere with לפני, but, in relation to YHWH, שמח (to rejoice) is more commonly followed by ב (especially in the Psalms), אמר (to say) by אל or ל, and שחה (Hithp., to worship) by ל. This use of לפני יהוה within Deut. 12-26 is particularly striking in the case of אמר. There are only three instances of אמר לפני יהוה in the whole of the OT, and yet two of them are in Deut. 26 (in vv. 5 and 13).[89]

Summary

The usage of prepositions immediately preceding the Name of God in those sections of Deut. 12-26 which refer to the "chosen place" is generally consistent with that observed elsewhere in the OT. This applies in almost all (eleven out of twelve) of the instances where לפני is *not* used, the majority (eight out of thirteen) of those where it *is*, and may help to explain the paucity of references to לפני יהוה in 15:19-23 and especially 16:1-17. However, one feature stands out regarding the usage of לפני יהוה as it occurs in relation to the "chosen place". There are five instances of the divine Name in combination with לפני rather than with the preposi-

---

[89] Note that there is insufficient evidence to determine whether Deut. 26:13 refers to the "chosen place". See above, pp. 145-146.

tions most commonly associated with the verbs in question.[90] Here it can be assumed that the writer was faced with a choice[91] and deliberately opted for לפני in preference to the more usual alternatives. This is in contrast to the other eight instances of לפני יהוה (i.e. those involving אכל, עמד, and נוח [Hiph.]), about which it could be argued that, given that the writer wanted to specify the activity as taking place in relation to YHWH, he had little say in the matter.[92] These additional five instances increase significantly (from eight to thirteen) the incidence of the expression לפני יהוה within ch. 12-26. This reveals, as far as the use of prepositions in relation to the Deity is concerned, a general compliance with Hebrew syntax where little or no choice is involved, but a definite favouring of לפני when there are alternatives from which to choose.

Such a clear bias towards using the preposition לפני (i.e. in preference to possible alternatives) with the divine Name when referring to the "chosen place", together with the previously noted restriction of the resulting expression to that particular site, whenever one is specified,[93] suggests a deliberate intention on the part of the writer to bring the phrase לפני יהוה and the "chosen place" into close association with each other.

THE INTERPRETATION OF לפני יהוה IN DEUT. 12-26

Having established some of the characteristics of לפני יהוה as it occurs in Deut. 12-26 we shall now consider three of the possible interpretations of the expression.

"LINGUISTIC FOSSIL"?

How far Mettinger wishes to draw the palaeontological parallel when he raises the possibility that the usage of לפני יהוה in Deut. 12-26 might

---

[90] 12:12, 18b; 16:11; 26:5, 10.

[91] Within Deut. 12-26 all three verbs occur at least once in conjunction with the prepositions most commonly associated with them: שמח ב [12:7, 18; 16:14; 26:11], אמר אל [15:16; 18:17; 20:3; 21:20; 22:16; 26:3], אמר ל [17:11, 16], שחה ל (Hithp.) [17:3]. Although in none of these instances does the activity take place in relation to YHWH, (17:3 refers to the worship of *other* gods), the choice would appear to have been a real one.

[92] Note that with עמד, where alternatives *do* exist, they are all (at least sometimes) used to denote divine Presence.

[93] See above, p. 146.

be "a sort of linguistic fossil" is not clear.[94] If by that he is referring to terminology which once was prevalent, but no longer is, then support for such a view vis-à-vis the majority of its occurrences would appear to be lacking. With the exception of עמד לפני יהוה[95] there is little evidence for the major use elsewhere of לפני יהוה for *any* of the activities so qualified in Deut. 12-26.[96] Furthermore, Mettinger's suggestion that within these chapters לפני יהוה might bear "no semantic cargo of importance" would seem to be intrinsically unlikely. Neither the strong links with the "chosen place", nor the selection of לפני in apparent preference to other more usual prepositions would seem to be consistent with the expression's being devoid of significant content. In addition, it needs to be asked why the writer included/retained the phrase at all, when most of the same activities at the chosen place are referred to without the use of it,[97] and when the text would make perfect sense even if it were omitted altogether.

CIRCUMLOCUTION FOR "AT THE SANCTUARY"?

It was indicated above that the instances of לפני יהוה in Deut. 12-26 have, where discussed,[98] sometimes been interpreted as equivalent to "at the sanctuary/central shrine" (or similar).[99] It was also noted that little justification has been offered for such a view. However, despite the difficulty, in the present case, of establishing whether the expression refers to a place or to the Deity who might be present at that place, the following observations would seem to weigh against the former understanding of the phrase.

First, within Deut. 12-26 there are three instances of לפני יהוה אלהיך standing in close proximity to a reference to the "chosen place". In

---

[94] See above, p. 10. Note that Schmitt refers to "[die] oft kultisch erstarrten Formel *lipnê jhwh*" (p. 215, cf. p. 221).

[95] Twenty-nine instances, albeit with a variety of meanings: Gen. 18:22; Lev. 9:5; Deut. 4:10; 10:8; 29:14 (EVV 15); 1 Sam. 6:20; 1 Kings 17:1; 18:15; 19:11; 22:21; 2 Kings 3:14; 5:16; Is. 66:22; Jer. 7:10; 15:1, 19; 18:20; 35:19; 49:19; 50:44; Ezek. 22:30; 44:15; Ps. 76:8 (EVV 7); 106:23; Ezra 9:15; 2 Chron. 18:20; 20:9, 13; 29:11.

[96] The ratios of occurrences in Deut. 12-26 relative to those in the OT as a whole are as follows: eat: 5/8, rejoice: 3/6, say: 2/3, set down: 1/5, worship: 1/6. See ch. 6.

[97] Cf. to eat (12:27; 16:3, 7, 8; 18:8), rejoice (12:7; 14:26; 16:14; 26:11), stand (17:12; 18:5), say (17:11), set down (26:4).

[98] Excluding 24:4, 13.

[99] P. 132.

12:18a the two expressions are separated by תאכלנו, in 15:20 by תאכלנו
שנה בשנה, while in 14:23 they are *in juxtaposition*. This being the case, it
is difficult to think of לפני יהוה being a circumlocution for "at the chosen
place" when it occurs with the very expression that it is supposed to replace.

Secondly, elsewhere in the OT occurrences of לפני יהוה directly adjacent to adverbial phrases referring to a sanctuary[100] seem to involve a
similar distinction between the two sets of expressions. While in such
cases the two are clearly related, it would seem that carrying out an activity לפני יהוה is to be distinguished from carrying it out merely at a
place of worship.[101] This is not to deny the possible absence of such a
distinction *within Deut. 12-26*, but to suggest that since the literal sense
is the one most naturally understood, any departure from it will need to
be demonstrated.

Thirdly, while it is possible to envisage לפני יהוה coming to *imply* "at
the sanctuary" or "at the chosen place" (e.g. in Deut. 19:17),[102] because
that was where YHWH was to be found, it is difficult to conceive of the
personal reference (i.e. to the Deity) becoming redundant to the extent
that the expression is used merely to refer to a physical structure or city.
Even in its metaphorical instances there is still a personal referent: it is
YHWH whom Elijah and Elisha are serving when they claim to stand
"before" him,[103] and *YHWH* whose opinion is expressed about the remarriage and the restoration of the cloak when such actions are referred to
as, respectively, an abomination or righteousness "before" him.[104]

Finally, if, as advocates of Name Theology affirm, the Deuteronomic
writings are concerned to emphasize the transcendence of YHWH, it
would have been unwise of them to use (or retain) as a circumlocution
for "at the sanctuary/chosen place" an expression which is more naturally

---

[100] הקדש (Exod. 28:35), פתח אהל מועד (Exod. 29:11, 42; Lev. 4:4; 14:11, 23; 15:14;
16:7; Josh. 19:51), אהל העדת (Num. 17:22 [EVV 7]), בית (Jer. 7:10; 34:15; 2 Chron.
6:24).
[101] Cf. Westphal 131: "Derartige Ergänzungen des לפני יהוה durch פתח אהל מועד oder
מזבח bezeugen, daß ersterer Ausdruck mehr besagt als die übrigen". Contrast Noth
(1962), who sees לפני יהוה simply as a reference to the holy place (pp. 12-13), and
thus regards such juxtaposition (e.g. in Lev. 4:4; 16:7) as evidence of redactional activity (pp. 28, 103-104).
[102] See above, pp. 144-145.
[103] 1 Kings 17:1; 18:15; 2 Kings 3:14; 5:16.
[104] Deut. 24:4, 13.

understood as referring to the proximate Presence of God (and thus as implying the very opposite of what Name Theology represents). The question is raised as to why, if the writers really did wish to avoid such a misunderstanding, they chose to use this misleading expression when they could have referred explicitly to a place of worship.

Thus, the close proximity, whether within or outside Deut. 12-26, of לפני יהוה to adverbial expressions referring to a sanctuary or the "chosen place", the inadvisability of using an expression whose literal sense is the opposite of what the Deuteronomic circle are supposed to have believed, and the lack of precedent for the apparent redundancy of the personal reference to YHWH suggest the need for caution before the two sets of expressions are equated.

DIVINE PRESENCE

For two reasons it is proposed that the significance of לפני יהוה in Deut. 12-26 should be determined independently of the references to either the divine Name at the "chosen place" (12:5, 11, etc.) or to YHWH himself in heaven (26:15). First, the current variety of opinion among scholars as to the significance of the divine Name in such contexts[105] means that its presence provides no reliable basis for interpreting לפני יהוה. Secondly, the fact that YHWH is portrayed as dwelling in heaven (26:15) in no way precludes the possibility of his also being present at the "chosen place", since, as has been shown earlier, there are instances within the OT (e.g. Deut. 4:36 and a number of Psalms) where he is represented as being in two locations at once.[106]

The need for criteria

One feature which has emerged from an examination of the views of those scholars who have dealt with לפני יהוה is the paucity of discussion as to the criteria employed to distinguish the different interpretations of the phrase.[107] Reasons are rarely given, and the expression generally appears to be interpreted *intuitively*. It will therefore be useful, prior to our own discussion of its various occurrences in Deut. 12-26, to outline the criteria which we consider to be relevant, particularly as regards identification of the *literal* use of the phrase.

---

[105] See above, pp. 5 n. 22, 7 n. 30 and 8 nn. 33-35.
[106] See above, pp. 68-70.
[107] See above, pp. 132-142.

The characteristics of a context in which an activity is carried out "before" YHWH in this sense (i.e. in proximity to the Deity conceived of as localized in the immediate vicinity of the one carrying out the action) are likely to be similar to those of one in which the same activity is carried out "before" (in front of/in the presence of) a *human* being. They would include any features pointing to the historical particularity of the action (e.g. reference to the time and/or place), and/or providing independent evidence for the spatial proximity of the parties concerned (e.g. the addressing of remarks by one to the other, and/or the carrying out of any other actions which *necessitate* that the two parties are proximate, together with the use of additional expressions indicative of physical nearness).

Deut. 24:4, 13

First, the writer clearly envisages specific occasions when a particular remarriage might occur, or a particular cloak be restored to its owner. However, the use of abstract nouns ("abomination", "righteousness") to describe the quality of those acts implies a time*less* divine value judgement beyond and above such particular occasions. Secondly, neither instance refers to a specific locality (apart from the very general reference to "the land" in v. 4) at which the value judgement is to be applied. The one is an "abomination" and the other "righteousness" לפני (i.e. "in the estimation of") YHWH regardless of when or where such acts are carried out. The reference here is to YHWH's opinion, rather than his Presence, and so, as argued above, it represents a metaphorical usage of the expression לפני יהוה.[108]

Deut. 12:7, 12, 18; 14:23, 26; 15:20; 16:11; 18:7; 19:17; 26:5, 10

The majority of activities described in these verses as taking place לפני יהוה are characterized by two important features. First, their *location* is stipulated. They are to be carried out at the "chosen place".[109] And secondly, although their timing is never mentioned explicitly, it is clear that in most cases[110] the writer has *particular occasions* in mind. 14:23, for

---

[108] P. 142.
[109] Explicitly in most cases, arguably in the rest (12:12, 18b; 19:17). See above, pp. 143-146.
[110] Except for 18:7, where the use of the participle העמדים indicates a more continuous state of affairs.

example, envisages the various specific times that the Israelites will take their tithes and firstlings to the "chosen place" and eat them there. The historical particularity implied by these two aspects of time[111] and place suggests a *literal* understanding of such activities לפני יהוה, and thus their occurrence in the divine Presence.[112]

This interpretation of לפני יהוה is able to account for two other features of its usage outlined above.[113] The fact that the "chosen place" is the only location at which activities are specified as occurring לפני יהוה is intelligible particularly if the Deity is in some sense localized there. It explains why the expression is not used to qualify similar activities carried out "within [the] towns", and it characterizes the "chosen place" as the only site at which activities *could* be carried out "before" YHWH, since it was only there that his Presence was to be found. It also explains the apparent preference for the preposition לפני in those cases where non-locational alternatives (שמח ב, ל/אל אמר ל, שחה [Hithp.]) were available. If YHWH were indeed present at the "chosen place", then לפני, with its strong locative associations, would be ideal for expressing the thought that the eating, rejoicing, etc., were to be in immediate proximity to him.

CONCLUSION

Examination of the general characteristics of the phrase לפני יהוה as it occurs in Deut. 12-26 suggests that, with the exception of the two in ch. 24, the majority of occurrences are to be understood in the literal sense. Activities qualified by the expression are intended to take place in

---

[111] In all these instances (apart from 18:7), the narrator is referring to activities which are presented as occurring in the *future*. This means that the information given about the activities taking place לפני יהוה is less detailed than might otherwise have been the case had the narrator been referring to events which had already taken place. Thus, many of the features which we have argued characterize an activity "before" someone in the literal sense are inevitably absent from the immediate context.

[112] A conclusion to which Reindl's own observations ought to have led him, since specification of place seems to be an important, though not essential, characteristic of his local usage of לפני יהוה. The presence of this aspect in many of the Deut. 12-26 instances, coupled with the fact that the majority refer to an event taking place in the cultic area (another of his important criteria) should have caused him either to classify them as local, and thus as references to divine Presence, or at least to explain why he did not do so: "Bei allen kultischen Handlungen erfährt Israel die Nähe seines Gottes" (p. 27).

[113] Pp. 146, 152-153.

the immediate vicinity of the Deity. They therefore provide evidence for a belief in his localized Presence at the "chosen place".

6

לפני יהוה IN DEUTERONOMY 12-26: INDIVIDUAL INSTANCES

The various activities predicated as occurring לפני יהוה at the "chosen place" will be discussed in turn. Each section will entail first an evaluation of earlier views, secondly an examination of the other OT occurrences of the activity before both the Deity and human beings,[1] and finally a presentation of our own position.

EATING BEFORE

EARLIER VIEWS

As indicated above, Nötscher regards eating (אכל) לפני יהוה as a causal (and therefore non-spatial) concept.[2] This conclusion is based on three passages, namely Ezek. 44:3; Lev. 23:40 and 1 Kings 8:65. From these he infers that such an activity (which he regards as a sacrificial meal) was not restricted to the area round the altar or before the dwelling of YHWH.[3] Accordingly, eating לפני יהוה falls outside his spatial category,

---

[1] A precedent for considering such material can be found in the discussions of eating לפני יהוה by Reindl (p. 29), Nötscher (pp. 103-104), and Westphal (p. 131), who, although not dealing with the data in precisely the same way as here, assume a common OT understanding of the idiom. In addition, Nötscher draws parallels with the equivalent activity in relation to a (human) king (pp. 85-87).

[2] P. 136.

[3] "[D]as Opfermahl ist gewiß an den Raum um den Altar oder vor 'der Wohnung Jahwes'...nicht gebunden" (pp. 103-104).

since it lacks the *sine qua non* of taking place in the immediate vicinity of the ark. His support for this conclusion is based on two observations. First, in commenting on Ezek. 44:3, he points out that only the prince may sit down in the East Gate to consume the sacrificial meal.[4] And secondly, with regard to Lev. 23:40 and 1 Kings 8:65, both of which refer to seven-day feasts, he remarks that this was a time during which one certainly did not always stay in the temple [*sic*].[5] These observations imply on the one hand that the Israelites ate, and on the other that they feasted (at least for some of the time) לפני יהוה *away from the sanctuary concerned*, and thus that the carrying out of such activities was not restricted to the immediate vicinity of the ark. However, it must be said that Nötscher appears to have missed the point of Ezek. 44:3, which is not that only the prince may eat לפני יהוה within the building, and thus that everyone else must do so outside, but that only he can eat *in the East Gate*. Nowhere in Ezekiel is it stipulated that the people cannot eat elsewhere within the Temple, or that eating away from the building would itself be described as לפני יהוה. Further, the fact that the rejoicing and eating in Lev. 23:40 and 1 Kings 8:65 are described as לפני יהוה in no way implies that other activities necessitated by the length of the festivities and in all probability taking place away from the temple (e.g. sleeping), would also have been so described. Clearly Nötscher has not established a convincing case against לפני יהוה having a close connection with the two sanctuaries concerned. His grounds for denying the spatial nature of the usage, particularly in view of the insistence in Deut. 12-26 on eating לפני יהוה *at the "chosen place"*, are thus seen to be inadequate.

Reindl classifies eating לפני יהוה as an "expression of the religious life" in general,[6] but neither gives a reason for doing so nor offers any indication as to how he understands such an activity in particular. He points out that the five instances in Deuteronomy and two[7] of the other three in the OT all involve the consumption of sacrificial meals, and that all take place at a specified locality. However, despite this satisfying of

---

[4] "[I]m ezechielischen Tempel darf ja nur noch der Fürst im Osttor sich niederlassen, um das Opfermahl zu verzehren" (pp. 103-104).

[5] "Jedes Opferfest ist ein Fest vor Jahwe...auch wenn es 7 Tage dauert...eine Zeit, während der man sich gewiß nicht immer im Tempel aufhielt" (p. 104).

[6] Pp. 28-29.

[7] Exod. 18:12 ("zweifellos eben dort, wo [Jetro] das Opfer dargebracht hat" [p. 29]) and Ezek. 44:3.

his own criteria for the *local* usage of the term[8] and thus for understanding the activity as occurring in proximity to the divine Presence, he fails to explain why he regards it as merely an "expression of the religious life".

USAGE ELSEWHERE

Eating before human beings

Within the OT there are three references to an individual eating לפני another human being. In two cases, 2 Sam. 11:13 and 1 Kings 1:25, the natural inference to be drawn is that the eating is done in the presence of the person concerned, i.e. David and Adonijah respectively. In the third passage, 2 Kings 25:29 // Jer. 52:33, because of the time-scale ("every day of his life") and the unusual nature of the relationship between the two parties involved (captor-captive), there is some debate as to whether Jehoiachin's eating לפני the king of Babylon did involve his dining regularly in the royal presence.[9]

Eating before the Deity

Two of the three non-deuteronomic instances of a human being eating לפני the Deity occur in proximity to the latter. In Exod. 18:12 Jethro's eating לפני האלהים takes place at Sinai (v. 5). Many commentators assign the two verses to E,[10] and since, according to this source, God dwells on the

---

[8] See above, p. 138 n. 39. In the case of 1 Chron. 29:22 he even mentions the *cultic* nature of the activity: "Mindestens an dieser Stelle ist also in ר לפני keine Ortsangabe zu sehen, sondern ein Ausdruck für den kultischen Charakter der Zeremonie" (p. 29).

[9] See, for example, Cogan and Tadmor 328-329, who see v. 30 as possibly explicating v. 29 (לפניו being interpreted as "by [the king's] favour and ארחה ["allowance"] as food), and so implying that they did *not* eat together; cf. Zenger (1968) 26 n. 75, Šanda (1912) 395. With regard to the interpretation of ארחה, however, Cogan and Tadmor also describe it as being of "unknown etymology", and suggest that it could equally refer to "an additional allowance of personal items, e.g. oil used for cosmetic purposes"; cf. the interpretations of Rehm (1982) 246 ("Lebensunterhalt") and Ketter 326 ("Ehrensold"). In addition, the description of Jehoiachin's "allowance" (וארחתו) as a *continual* one (ארחת תמיד), following the reference to his eating before Amel-Marduk *continually* (תמיד), strongly implies the introduction of a *further* aspect of the Babylonian king's generosity, i.e. rather than a mere amplification of what is said in v. 29. It thus appears that the case for denying Jehoiachin's proximity to his captor when he ate לפני him falls short of proof; cf. Reindl 21-22.

[10] Knight 125, Clements (1972) 107, Hyatt (1971) 186, Fritz 13, Davies (1967) 147, Noth (1959) 117, Beer 12, 93, Driver (1911) xxvi, 161, McNeile (1908) xxiv, 105-106.

mountain,[11] it can reasonably be assumed that such eating takes place in the divine Presence.[12] In Ezek. 44:3 the stipulation that only the prince may sit in the East Gate to eat bread לפני יהוה is preceded by an indication that once again YHWH has taken up residence in the temple (v. 2). Here also it may be presumed that the prince's eating לפני יהוה occurs in the vicinity of the Deity.[13] The third instance (1 Chron. 29:22) contains no independent evidence of divine Presence, but is reminiscent of the references to eating לפני יהוה in Deut. 12-26 in that David's prayer (vv. 10-19) mentions the projected building of a house "for [YHWH's] holy name" (v. 16).

SIGNIFICANCE IN DEUT. 12:7, 18a; 14:23, 26; 15:20

The only interpretation of eating לפני someone for which a clear OT precedent exists, is that in terms of the spatial proximity of the parties involved. This applies in four of the examples outside Deuteronomy, and regardless of whether the one before whom the eating takes place is human or divine. On the assumption of a common OT idiom it would appear that the instances of eating לפני יהוה in Deut. 12-26 could well refer to the proximate Presence of the Deity.

Such a conclusion is in no way affected by Nötscher's alternative (causal) understandings of the phrase. His suggestion, that to eat לפני יהוה means to hold a meal involving sacrificial meat or in YHWH's honour,[14] may well relate to what is involved. Certainly such eating usually takes place both in the specific context of sacrifice (except for Ezek. 44:3), and so is likely to involve the consumption of sacrificial food, and also in contexts which imply that the meal is in YHWH's honour.[15] However, it is clear from the independent indications of divine Presence in the contexts of Exod. 18:12 and Ezek. 44:3 that neither of these suggestions exhausts the meaning of the phrase. There is no reason why eating לפני יהוה

---

[11] See above, p. 3.

[12] Durham 245, Gispen 175, Nicholson (1974) 87, Cole 139, Davies (1942) 16.

[13] Cf. the Priestly usage in which, if it be granted that YHWH does reside in the tabernacle (see above, p. 135 n. 22), actions taking place at some distance from the divine Presence (e.g. "at the door of the tent of meeting") are still described as occurring לפני יהוה: Exod. 29:11, 42; Lev. 4:4, etc.

[14] P. 104, followed by Braulik (1983) 50 n. 194.

[15] In Exod. 18:12 for YHWH's deliverance of the Israelites from the Egyptians, in Deut. 12-26 for his goodness in supplying them with food, and in 1 Chron. 29:22 for his provision of material for the building of the temple (cf. vv. 11-12, 14, 16).

should not involve both eating sacrificial food (or in YHWH's honour) *and* eating in his Presence. In addition, Nötscher's further suggestion that to eat לפני יהוה means to be YHWH's guest, in the same way that to eat before a king means to be his guest,[16] serves only to argue *for* divine Presence rather than against it. Guests at meals are normally in close proximity to their (human) hosts (cf. above on 2 Sam. 11:13 and 1 Kings 1:25).[17]

The above-mentioned evidence, that the one "before" whom eating takes place is in close proximity to the eater,[18] is consistent with the general characteristics of the term לפני יהוה as it is used in Deut. 12-26.[19] We conclude that, within those chapters, eating לפני יהוה describes an activity carried out in the divine Presence.

REJOICING BEFORE

EARLIER VIEWS

Beyond categorizing rejoicing (שמח) לפני יהוה as a causal activity Nötscher has no specific comments to make as to its meaning.[20] Reindl, however, points out that, although in Deuteronomy it is closely associated with the sacrificial meal, there are instances of rejoicing לפני יהוה unconnected with such eating, i.e. in Lev. 23:40 and Is. 9:2 (EVV 3). From this observation he deduces that it can mean neither an act in the immediate area of the sanctuary, nor an actual cultic act, but rather an expression of an inner religious attitude.[21] There is, however, no obvious

---

[16] See above, p. 164 n. 14.

[17] P. 163.

[18] In addition, it is noticeable that eating לפני is used only in connection with royalty or the Deity. Other prepositions are employed when the parties concerned are on a more equal footing. For example, את is used of both Joseph's brothers and the Egyptians dining with Joseph (Gen. 43:16, 32 [2x]), while עם is used of Aaron and the elders eating with Jethro (Exod. 18:12), Samuel with Saul (1 Sam. 9:19), Job's daughters with their brothers (Job 1:4) and Job's brothers and sisters with Job (Job 42:11). It may therefore be that eating לפני (i.e. as opposed to את or עם) not only indicates spatial proximity but also expresses deference to persons of higher rank. Cf. the conclusions reached by Klein (1979) about the Targumic use of קדם (p. 507).

[19] See above, pp. 142-159.

[20] P. 104.

[21] "Eng verbunden mit dem Opfermahl ist…der Aufruf zur 'Freude vor Jahwe' (Dtn 12,12. 18; 16,11; 27,7), eine Formulierung, die auch ohne die Beziehung zum Opfermahl vorkommt (Lev 23,40 beim Laubhüttenfest, Jes 9,2 und…). Damit kann nun weder eine Handlung im unmittelbaren Bereich des Heiligtums, noch ein eigentlicher

reason why rejoicing לפני יהוה should have to be inextricably linked to a sacrificial meal before it could refer to an act in the immediate area of a sanctuary. Reindl's metaphorical interpretation would thus appear to be without adequate foundation.

USAGE ELSEWHERE

Little light can be thrown on the significance of rejoicing לפני יהוה by an examination of the instances of rejoicing "before" someone outside Deut. 12-26. There are no examples of rejoicing לפני a human being, and of those relating to the Deity (Lev. 23:40; Deut. 27:7 and Is. 9:2 [EVV 3]) none provides any independent indication of his whereabouts.

SIGNIFICANCE IN DEUT. 12:12, 18b; 16:11

The main objection to a *metaphorical* understanding of the activity lies in the choice of preposition. Had the writer wanted Israel's rejoicing in relation to YHWH to be understood in some kind of figurative sense, it would have been preferable to use the preposition ב. Not only is it the one most commonly used to denote such rejoicing,[22] but also it carries no implication of a spatial relationship between the worshipper and God. It would no doubt be possible to rejoice ביהוה at the same time as being in close proximity to him, but the expression does not imply such proximity *of itself*. To rejoice ביהוה must be regarded as having a solely metaphorical sense.[23]

In Deut. 12:12, 18b; 16:11, however, the writer has used לפני rather than ב, employing a preposition which, in addition to whatever other (metaphorical) meanings it might introduce, clearly involves the possibility of Israel's rejoicing being understood in the *spatial* sense of "in YHWH's presence" or "in front of YHWH" (i.e. in close proximity to him). It would appear, however, to be more than a possibility, since the three instances of rejoicing לפני יהוה are either stated (Deut. 16:11) or implied (Deut. 12:12, 18b) as having to take place at a particular location,[24] a circumstance consistent with a spatial interpretation of the expression and in sharp contrast to the twelve OT instances of rejoicing

---

kultischer Akt gemeint sein, sondern vielmehr ein Ausdruck einer inneren religiösen Haltung" (p. 29). Cf. Braulik (1981) 353.

[22] See above, pp. 150 (Table 5.1) and 152.

[23] Cf. BDB 970: to "rejoice religiously".

[24] The "chosen place".

בַיהוה,[25] of which only one (Ps. 66:6) indicates the site.[26] It is difficult to avoid the conclusion that לפני has been chosen in preference to ב precisely because of the added dimension which it contributes to the activity of rejoicing in relation to YHWH, i.e. that of being understood in a literal as opposed to a purely metaphorical sense.

A figurative understanding of the injunction to rejoice לפני יהוה[27] would appear to be unlikely in view of the strong spatial connotations of its preposition. Thus, although none of the OT contexts in which such rejoicing is mentioned contains any independent evidence of the Presence of YHWH, we favour a literal interpretation of the preposition, and so see the Deut. 12-26 exhortations to rejoice לפני יהוה as referring to the divine Presence at the "chosen place".

STANDING BEFORE IN A CULTIC CONTEXT

EARLIER VIEWS

According to Westphal, to stand (עמד) לפני יהוה can mean the same as to hold the office of priest.[28] He detects this usage in Deut.10:8; 18:5 (LXX) and 18:7, and sees the additional information about blessing (10:8) and/or ministering 10:8; 18:5, 7) as serving to explain more precisely the nature of the standing לפני יהוה.[29] He also states that the same expression in 2 Chron. 29:11 is subsequently more closely defined as ministering to YHWH and acting as his ministers.[30] It is thus clear, particularly in the light of his statement of the Deuteronomists' conception of the divine Name dwelling at the sanctuary,[31] that Westphal views the standing לפני יהוה in Deut. 18:7 in a solely metaphorical sense.

As the heading "Stehen vor dem König und vor Gott" suggests, Nötscher's discussion deals primarily with kings rather than with human

---

[25] Joel 2:23; Ps. 32:11; 33:21; 40:17 (EVV 16); 63:12 (EVV 11); 64:11 (EVV 10); 66:6; 70:5 (EVV 4); 85:7 (EVV 6); 97:12; 104:34; 149:2.
[26] "[T]here (שם)", by the sea/river through which men passed on foot.
[27] E.g. Reindl's "Ausdruck einer inneren religiösen Haltung" (p. 29).
[28] "'Das Priesteramt bekleiden' wird ausgedrückt durch 'vor Jahwe stehen' עמד לפני יהוה" (p. 134).
[29] "Durch שרת und ברך wird עמד לפני יהוה näher erklärt" (p. 134).
[30] "Nach 2 Chr 29, 11 hat Jahwe Priester und Leviten...ausersehen לעמד לפניו, das wird dann näher bezeichnet als לשרתו, bzw. משרתים לו להיות" (p. 135).
[31] See above, p. 133 n. 12.

beings in general.[32] He does, however, refer to the Levites' standing לִפְנֵי
Aaron (Num. 3:6 [עָמַד (Hiph.)]) and standing לִפְנֵי the people (Ezek.
44:11), but interprets the former in terms of service and the latter in
terms of being at the people's disposal.[33] As far as standing לִפְנֵי יהוה is
concerned, his view is by no means clear. On the one hand, he appears to
distinguish the priests' [*sic*] standing לִפְנֵי יהוה in Deut. 10:8; 18:7 and 2
Chron. 29:11 both from the quite literal ("ganz buchstäblich") sense
analogous to the secular "have an audience with", and from the purely
spiritual sense ("ein rein geistiges Verhältnis") referring to the prophets'
service of YHWH, which involves no spatial reference (1 Kings 17:1;
18:15; 2 Kings 3:14; 5:16; Jer. 15:19). On the other hand, in his sum-
ming up he asserts that the literal sense (i.e. the one referring to divine
Presence) is to be understood when the expression occurs in the context
either of a theophany or of *behaviour at a sanctuary*.[34] He gives no examples of the latter, but it would seem reasonable to suppose that Deut.
18:7 would fall into such a category in view of its reference to the Levites' standing לִפְנֵי יהוה "*there*" (שָׁם), i.e. at the "chosen place" (v. 6).

Reindl deals with only one connotation of standing "before" someone,
namely that of being in their service. He finds it in references to standing
before either royalty[35] or YHWH,[36] though in the latter case only in
I Kings 17:1; 18:15; 2 Kings 3:14; 5:16, and Jer. 35:19. As far as the four
OT instances of *Levites'* standing לִפְנֵי יהוה are concerned, he makes no
comment beyond pointing out that Deut. 10:8 and 18:7 illustrate typical
deuteronomic phraseology belonging to the cult,[37] and that the meaning
of 2 Chron. 29:11 differs from that of 1 Kings 17:1, etc.[38] However, in
the light of his identification of the two deuteronomic instances as cultic,

---

[32] Pp. 85-87.
[33] "Die Leviten stehen…'vor', d. i. dienen Aaron (Nu. 3,6; vgl. 8,13) und 'vor dem
Volke', d. i. sie sind zu dessen Verfügung (Ez. 44,11)" (p. 86).
[34] "Wo ihr buchstäblicher Sinn erhalten ist, bezieht sie sich…kultisch auf die unsichtbare Gegenwart Jahwes im Heiligtum, die durch die Lade symbolisiert wird"
(p. 87).
[35] Pp. 20, 246 n. 60.
[36] Pp. 34, 246 n. 60.
[37] "Eigene Formulierungen hat das Dtn…mit לפני ' durch Verbindung mit bestimm-
ten Verben gebildet; sie gehören zwar vielfach ebenfalls dem kultischen Bereich an"
(p. 232). See also p. 306 n. 633.
[38] "2 Chr 29,11 hat wohl einen anderen Sinn" (p. 246 n. 60). Unfortunately, he omits
to say what it *does* mean.

and particularly in view of their reference to *Levites* who *minister* either
to YHWH or *in his name*, one would have expected him to assign them to
his local (divine Presence) rather than to his "expression of the religious
life" category.[39]

USAGE ELSEWHERE

Deut. 18:7 links standing לפני יהוה with ministering (שרת).[40] This
raises the question as to whether the activity represents a literal "standing
before",[41] during which, for the purpose of "ministering in his name", the
Levites stand in the Presence of the Deity, or whether it is essentially
only another way of referring to that ministering[42] and so represents a
metaphorical "standing before", entailing (like 1 Kings 17:1, etc.) no necessary connotations of divine Presence.

Standing before human beings

Within the OT there are three instances of Levites standing לפני other
human beings in the context of ministry. In Num. 3:6 YHWH instructs
Moses to "set[43] [the tribe of Levi] לפני Aaron...that they may minister to
him". In Num. 16:9 Moses reminds Korah and all his company ["you
sons of Levi"] that God has separated them "to stand לפני the congregation to minister to them". And in Ezek. 44:11 YHWH appoints the
Levites to "stand לפני the people, to serve them". However, in none of the
three cases is there any clear indication as to whether the standing is literal or metaphorical.

Standing before the Deity

In addition to Deut. 18:7 there are three other references to Levites
standing לפני יהוה in close association with some form of ministering:
Deut. 10:8; Ezek. 44:15 and 2 Chron. 29:11. Four points can be made.
First, of the two activities predicated of these Levites in relation to

---

[39] See above, pp. 138-139.
[40] "[T]hen he may minister in the name of the LORD his God, like all his fellow-
Levites who stand there before the LORD".
[41] Cf. Hoffmann 335: "העומדים, sowie in v. 5 לעמוד, lehrt, dass der Priesterdienst ste-
hend verrichtet werden müsse. Die Wiederholung hier zeigt...dass der sitzend ver-
richtete Dienst פסול (untauglich) ist".
[42] Cf. Mayes (1979) 206, Amsler 331, Thompson (1974) 146, Clamer 579, Reider
105, Smith (1918) 136, Driver (1902) 123 (all on 10:8).
[43] עמד (Hiph.).

YHWH, i.e. "standing before" or "ministering", only the latter occurs on its own (in Deut. 21:5; Jer. 33:22; Ezek. 40:46; 43:19; 44:16; 1 Chron. 15:2 and 2 Chron. 29:11bβ?). There are no OT instances of Levites standing before YHWH (in the sense of being in his service) without an accompanying reference to ministering. This suggests that in these contexts the notion of the Levitical service of the Deity is expressed by means of שרת rather than עמד לפני. Secondly, that in these verses a *literal* interpretation of the standing (and thus of the "standing before") is possible is implied by Deut. 17:12 and 18:5, in which עמד is linked to שרת but without the preposition. In such contexts the Levites' standing is likely to be literal[44] since there is no obvious reason why עמד should be rendered "remain" (or similar), and the metaphorical interpretations under consideration arise only when it is followed by לפני. Thirdly, if, as has been suggested, עמד לפני יהוה *is* synonymous with "to minister/wait upon/serve",[45] then the subsequent references to ministering to YHWH in Deut. 10:8 and 2 Chron. 29:11bα would appear to be redundant. Fourthly, in two of the three instances outside Deut. 12-26, there are independent indications within their immediate contexts that YHWH was believed to be present. Ezek. 44:15 itself prescribes that "the Levitical priests...shall *come near* to [YHWH] to minister to [him]",[46] while 2 Chron. 29:6, which, like v. 11, is part of Hezekiah's sermon (vv. 5-11) and generally regarded as coming from the same hand,[47] refers to the temple as "the *habitation* (משכן) of the LORD". In these cases there is thus a high probability that the standing לפני יהוה is intended to be understood as an allusion to the divine Presence localized in the vicinity of the Levites.

---

[44] Contrast 1 Kings 8:11 // 2 Chron. 5:14, which refers to the priests' inability to "stand to minister" because of the cloud; here עמד may be used in the sense of "remain" rather than "stand" in the literal sense; cf. BDB 764.

[45] See above, p. 169 n. 42.

[46] Cf. the reference in v. 2 to YHWH's entry into the temple.

[47] Dillard 234, Williamson (1982) 351, 352, Michaeli (1967) 230, Welch (1939) 102, Curtis and Madsen 463.

DEUT. 18:7

The context

Vv. 3-5 concern the Levitical priests (v. 1) who live at the "chosen place",[48] and deal with their responsibilities and payment. They are to "stand and minister in the name of the LORD" (v. 5), and in return are to be given the shoulder, cheeks and stomach of the sacrifice (v. 3) and various first fruits (v. 4). Vv. 6-8, on the other hand, are about Levites who live in the towns but who wish to go to the "chosen place". These verses protect such Levites against possible discrimination by insisting that they have the same responsibility ("ministering in the name of the LORD" [v. 7])[49] and the same payment ("equal portions to eat" [v. 8]) as their centralized brethren.[50]

The significance of standing before the LORD

It was suggested above that the standing in v. 5 ("the LORD...has chosen him...to stand and minister in [his] name") is a *literal* standing.[51] Thus, given that vv. 6-8 are granting to the urban Levites the same right to minister as their brethren at the "chosen place", it would seem reasonable to presume that the standing in v. 7 is intended to be understood in the same way. This means that the entire expression העמדים...לפני יהוה should be viewed in its *local* sense, since if its standing is literal, it is difficult to conceive how the לפני יהוה which qualifies such standing could be taken other than in *its* literal sense of proximity to the Deity.[52]

A consideration of the immediate context therefore suggests that in Deut. 18:7 the Levites' standing is intended to be understood literally, and thus that העמדים...לפני יהוה refers to their being in the localized Presence of YHWH. This interpretation is consistent with OT usage elsewhere, since the alternative (i.e. that of the Levites' divine service) is always expressed less ambiguously by the use of the verb שרת, and there are two instances of such standing לפני יהוה occurring in proximity to the Deity.

---

[48] Implied by the reference to sacrifice (v. 3), which, on the basis of 12:5-6, 11, 26-27; 15:19-21; 16:2, 5-6, can only be offered there.
[49] Westphal 134: "Nach D darf noch jeder auswärtige Levit in Jerusalem denselben Dienst verrichten, wie die in Jerusalem ansässigen Leviten".
[50] That vv. 6-8 intend to make this point seems clear from the fact that the Levites' function is identical in the two sections, and is mentioned nowhere else in the OT.
[51] P. 170.
[52] Cf. Rabban 6-7.

STANDING BEFORE IN A JUDICIAL CONTEXT

EARLIER VIEWS

Westphal, in a discussion of the difficult legal cases which are decided לפני יהוה by the priest, attributes the validity of the decision to the proximity of the Deity who dwells at the holy place where the case is tried, and who is able to exert a direct influence on the priest concerned.[53] This may not apply to Deut. 19:17, however, since he considers that it seems to portray YHWH as speaking through the priests.[54] Nötscher makes no comment on the verse, but Reindl categorizes its injunction to stand (עמד) לפני יהוה as local,[55] though not in his literal sense.[56] This means that he regards it as belonging to the cultic arena[57] and so represents an allusion to the divine Presence.[58]

USAGE ELSEWHERE

Standing before human beings

Within the OT there are five references to an individual standing לפני other human beings in a judicial context. In Num. 35:12 and Josh. 20:6, 9 an Israelite who has killed someone unwittingly is expected to stand לפני the congregation "for judgment" (למשפט). In Num. 27:2 the daughters of Zelophehad stand לפני Moses, and their case in respect of their father's inheritance is described as a משפט (v. 5). Finally, the same term is applied to the resolution (1 Kings 3:28) of the dispute between the two prostitutes standing לפני Solomon (v. 16). In all five cases it is clear that the people concerned are in close proximity to those "before" whom they stand.

---

[53] "Was...die Richtigkeit der priesterlichen Entscheidung garantiert, ist die heilige Stätte, an der das Verfahren stattfindet, die Nähe der Gottheit, die hier wohnt und unter deren unmittelbar inspirierender Wirkung der Priester steht" (p. 141).
[54] "Der Gedanke, daß Jahwe durch den Mund seiner Priester redet, scheint in Dt 19,17 לפני יהוה לפני הכהנים durchzuschimmern" (p. 141).
[55] P. 306 n. 633.
[56] His "wörtliche, lokale Sinn" is mentioned on p. 32 and the texts illustrating it on p. 245 n. 50.
[57] "Lokale Bedeutung liegt...der Verwendung von י לפני im kultischen Bereich zugrunde" (p. 32).
[58] See above, p. 139 n. 42.

Standing before the Deity

Apart from Deut. 19:17 there are no other OT instances of a human being *standing* לפני the Deity in a judicial context. There are, however, two references to human beings presenting a case "before" him. First, in Num. 27:5 Moses brings the case of Zelophehad's daughters לפני יהוה, and although in their comments on the verse no recent scholars specifically relate this to divine Presence, the mention in v. 2 of the tent of meeting may well provide adequate grounds for doing so.[59] Secondly, in Job 23:4 when Job imagines laying his case [לפני אלהים], he clearly anticipates entering the divine Presence, since he refers to "finding him" and "coming to his seat" (v. 3). It is thus possible that both[60] instances of someone being לפני the Deity in a judicial context employ the preposition in its local sense of "in the presence of".[61]

DEUT. 19:17

The integrity of the present text

A number of scholars consider that the present text has been expanded from a shorter original, either "before the LORD" or "before the judges who are in office in those days".[62] Aside from appeals to perceived overcrowding,[63] or the presence of the double לפני,[64] neither of which has called forth comment in the case of the three other OT instances of the same construction (Exod. 14:2; 30:6; Num. 3:38; see be-

---

[59] See above, p. 135 n. 22.

[60] Job's presentation of a case לפני יהוה is also *implied* in Job 13:13-18. His confidence that no godless man will come לפני God (v. 16) is often related to a literal appearing in the divine Presence (Hartley 223, Habel 227, 229-230, 349, Rowley 123, Horst 202, Terrien [1954] 1006). Convinced of *his own* innocence, Job refers both to the case (משפט) which he has prepared, and to his certainty of vindication (v. 18), and so implies that he envisages coming לפני the Deity (i.e. into his Presence) and successfully defending the case against him.

[61] Hartley 336, 338-339, Habel 347-348, Reichert 122, Terrien (1954) 1080-1081, Hölscher (1952) 61, Strahan 206-207.

[62] Seitz 114, Hölscher (1922) 205 n. 3, Puukko 233 n. 3, 251, Bertholet (1899) 62; cf. Smith (1918) 242. This excludes those who consider Deut. 19:17 to be the result of additions which were either deuteronom(ist)ic (L'Hour 18 n. 1, Steuernagel [1900] 73) or were added to bring it into line with deuteronomic legislation elsewhere (Mayes [1979] 289-290), and who thus see its present prescription as in some sense reflecting deuteronom(ist)ic thought.

[63] Hölscher (1922) 205 n. 3; cf. Smith (1918), who regards the construction as "awkward" (p. 242).

[64] L'Hour 18, Bertholet (1899) 62.

low),[65] the main arguments put forward to support the two positions are as follows. First, in favour of an original "before YHWH",[66] Hölscher, for example, not only claims that one does *not* "stand before" priests or judges (but only before the Deity or king),[67] but also that any cross-examination by priests and judges would be inappropriate, since what is really required here is the judgement of God.[68] However, his implication that "to stand before" is a technical term used only in relation to God or the king ignores its additional application to a variety of types of people including both a priest (Num. 27:21) and the congregation in the context of judgement (Num. 35:12; Josh. 20:6, 9).[69] Moreover, despite the claim that initially the law prescribed only a consultation of the Deity, his proposed "original" text contains no clear intimation of any such approach.[70] Neither reason is thus adequate ground for postulating a shorter original. Secondly, arguing in favour of an original "before the judges", Bertholet queries the existence of a court made up of priests and secular judges *together*.[71] However, there are those who regard the court attributed to Jehoshaphat's reform (2 Chron. 19:8) as providing an example of one composed of both sacred (Levites and priests) and secular members (heads of families),[72] and, despite the scepticism of some,[73] a substantial body of

---

[65] Pp. 175-176. On Exodus see the commentaries by Scharbert, Durham, Burns, Zenger, Knight, Childs, Michaeli, Clements, Hyatt, Davies, Noth, Rylaarsdam, Beer, Heinisch, Driver, McNeile, Holzinger (the latter makes no comment on overcrowding [or similar] but does see a contradiction in 30:6 between the ark being both before the veil and before the mercy seat [p. 44]); cf. Michaeli [1974] 263, McNeile [1908] 195-196). On Numbers see those by Budd, Sturdy, de Vaulx, Snaith, Noth, Greenstone, Heinisch, Binns, McNeile, Gray, Holzinger, Dillmann, Kennedy.

[66] This view normally also requires the elimination of the reference to the judges' inquiring (v. 18a), the original text being regarded as: "both parties...shall stand before the LORD, and if the witness is a false witness...".

[67] "עמד לפני פ'" gebraucht man, wenn man vor die Gottheit oder etwa auch vor den König tritt, aber nicht vor die Priester oder Richter" (p. 205 n. 3).

[68] "[D]ie Untersuchung der Richter hier, wo es sich um das Gottesurteil handelt, nicht mehr am Platze ist" (p. 205 n. 3); cf. Mayes (1979) 290, Seitz 114, L'Hour 18.

[69] Cf. Welch (1924) 169-170.

[70] See above, n. 66. Inquiries addressed to the Deity are usually expressed by דרש (את־)יהוה, there being no OT precedents for understanding עמד לפני יהוה *of itself* in this way.

[71] "Die Existenz eines aus Priestern und [weltlichen] Richtern gemischten Gerichtes ist sehr fraglich" (p. 62).

[72] Usually in their comments on Deut. 17:8-13: Ridderbos 196, Thompson (1974) 203, Phillips (1973) 119, Weinfeld (1972a) 164, Buis and Leclercq 131, Wright

scholarly opinion does regard the Chronicler as having preserved an historically reliable account of Jehoshaphat's reform (2 Chron. 19:4-11).[74] There would thus appear to be no adequate grounds for impugning the integrity of Deut. 19:17 in its present form.

Synonymous apposition?

Among those scholars who either accept the text as it stands or who consider that, although added later, לפני יהוה in some sense represents deuteronom(ist)ic (i.e. rather than subsequent) thinking, the majority who comment on the expression[75] regard it as equivalent to "at the central sanctuary".[76] Others, however, have suggested that לפני יהוה is explained by some or all of the subsequent "before the priests and the judges",[77] and so render it necessary to investigate whether or not the two phrases *are* in apposition in this sense.

There are three other instances of the kind of syntactical apposition exhibited by Deut. 19:17, i.e. of לפני...לפני, in which the second לפני is *not* preceded by a connective.[78] Of these Num. 3:38 exhibits the kind of synonymous apposition which Seitz and Steuernagel claim exists in Deut. 19:17.[77] Its reference to Moses and Aaron and his sons having to camp "before the tabernacle on the east, before the tent of meeting toward the sunrise" clearly denotes two ways of saying the same thing. In Exod. 14:2, on the other hand, the Israelites are told to camp "in front of Pi-ha-hiroth...in front of Baal-zephon". In this case the names are not synonymous, but refer to two different places. Taken together the two phrases act like the coordinates of a point by specifying more closely the

---

(1953) 440-441, Cunliffe-Jones 107, Clamer 623, Reider 169, Driver (1902) 208, Robinson (n.d.) 144.

[73] Coggins 217-218, Ackroyd (1973) 146, Benzinger 104, Wellhausen 196-197.

[74] Dillard 148, Williamson (1982) 289, Whitelam 190, 205, Macholz 321, 330, 336 (apart from the reference to Levites [v. 8], which he regards as a "chronistische Erweiterung" [p. 322 n. 13]), Phillips (1970) 22-23, Myers (1965b) 108, Knierim 162-164, de Vaux (1958) 237-238, Albright 82.

[75] Clifford (1982) 105, Mayes (1979) 290, Craigie (1976) 270, Wright (1953) 454, Clamer 639.

[76] For a discussion of this interpretation see above, pp. 154-156.

[77] Seitz 114: "Die Erwähnung der Priester ist dann eine sachlich richtige Erklärung zu לפני יהוה; denn die Gottesbefragung ging so vor sich, daß man ein Heiligtum aufsuchte und sich von den Priestern den göttlichen Entscheid erteilen ließ", Steuernagel (1900) 73: "לפני י"י, erklärt durch das folgende לפני הכהנים".

[78] Exod. 14:2; 30:6; Num. 3:38.

location of the camp. The same can be said of Exod. 30:6, in which the golden altar is to be put "before the veil that is by the ark of the testimony, before the mercy seat that is over the testimony".[79] The veil and the mercy seat are distinct items of tabernacle furniture. Thus, Exod. 14:2 and 30:6 both involve phrases which are in syntactical apposition, but are not synonymous. These examples show, therefore, that the two halves of the syntactically apposite construction לפני...לפני *may* be synonymous, as in Num. 3:38, but that they can also have distinct referents, as in Exod. 14:2 and 30:6, even while fulfilling complementary functions in a text.[80]

The significance of standing before the LORD

On the basis of the following it would appear that there is a case for seeing לפני יהוה in Deut. 19:17 in terms of divine Presence. First, such parallels as there are offer support for the idea of syntactical apposition which is not synonymous. Secondly, the standing לפני the priests and judges involves physical proximity to them. The judges have to "inquire (דרש) diligently", and since there is no specific reference to YHWH in this connection,[81] such queries will probably be addressed to the two parties involved in the case. That they *are* the addressees in the inquiry gains further support from the use of the adverb היטב ("diligently"), which elsewhere is found in connection with דרש only in Deut. 13:15 (EVV 14) and 17:4, is not used of any inquiring directed to the Deity, and only occurs when the responsibility for making a decision with potentially extreme consequences[82] lies solely in the hands of humans, i.e. when there is no question of direct assistance from God.[83] Since, therefore, the inquiry is directed to the two parties involved in the dispute, it is clear that their standing לפני the priests and judges will indeed involve

---

[79] Cf. McNeile (1908) 196: "*before the propitiatory...*may be an explanation of the preceding clause, defining the position of the altar more exactly - in front of the veil, in such a position that it was in front of (in a line with) the propitiatory".

[80] There is a kind of synonymous apposition in Ps. 97:5 and 114:7 in connection with the Deity. However, the construction [here מלפני...מלפני] stems from the poetic parallelism, and so is not strictly relevant.

[81] See above, p. 174.

[82] The total destruction of a city and its inhabitants (13:16-17 [EVV 15-16]), a stoning (17:5-7) or the *lex talionis* (19:19-21).

[83] Certainly there is no hint of YHWH being consulted in Deut. 13:13-19 (EVV 12-18) or 17:2-7.

their physical proximity to them. Thirdly, examination of the other OT instances of לפני...לפני[84] suggests that the two prepositions are used in the same sense in each case. In none of the three is the second לפני in the pair used in a different way from the first. It would thus seem reasonable to presume that the author of Deut. 19:17 intended to convey that just as the standing is in proximity to the priests and judges, so also it is in proximity to the Deity, and so represents a further allusion to his Presence. Finally, this is consistent with the only interpretation of standing לפני someone in a judicial context for which a clear OT precedent exists. There are five instances of the expression outside Deuteronomy, and, though involving standing לפני *humans*, they all entail the proximity of the parties concerned. In addition, while there are no other such instances of *standing* לפני the Deity, there are two examples of a man being "before" him to present a case (משפט), and in at least one of these both he and the plaintiff are proximate.

The pericope (Deut. 19:16-21) thus deals with a particular example of a "case within your towns which is too difficult for you" (17:8), in this instance one involving a malicious witness. As prescribed in 17:8-13, the two parties to the dispute are to go to the "chosen place",[85] where the judges are to conduct the investigation in the presence of the priests. YHWH himself is not consulted regarding the truth or otherwise of the witness's accusation.[86] Rather, the reference to standing "before" him is there for the dual purpose of indicating the location of the inquiry and emphasizing the seriousness of the charge on account of the trial's taking place in the Presence of God himself.

Usage elsewhere in the OT suggests that the double לפני construction in Deut. 19:17 is capable of supporting an interpretation of standing לפני יהוה in terms of being in the divine Presence. Such a view is consistent with other instances both of standing "before" humans and of being "before" the Deity in a judicial context.

---

[84] See above, pp. 175-176.

[85] In view of the apparent restriction of the use of the phrase לפני יהוה to the "chosen place", i.e. in Deut. 12-26, it is likely that the instance in 19:17 is intended to be understood as alluding to that locality.

[86] *Contra* Sheriffs 63, Seitz 114, Buis and Leclercq 142, L'Hour 18, Hölscher (1922) 205 n. 3.

SAYING BEFORE

EARLIER VIEWS

Nötscher regards the saying (אמר [Piel]) לפני יהוה in Deut. 26:5, 13 as
one example of a broader activity, that of *praying* לפני יהוה,[87] which, on
two counts, he categorizes as causal. First, examination of parallel verses
suggests that to pray "before" YHWH is often no different from to pray
"to" him,[88] and secondly, although such prayer frequently occurs in the
temple or sanctuary, it is not restricted to them.[89] However, two observations should be made in response. First, several instances of prayer לפני
יהוה which Nötscher regards as possibly freed from a temple connection
contain some reference to the *Presence* of YHWH,[90] and so may imply
that such praying was intended to take place in proximity to that Presence. They can hardly be used, therefore, to justify a *causal* interpretation of prayer לפני יהוה in the temple or sanctuary, especially as the contexts of most of Nötscher's examples contain either reference or allusion
to the ark of the covenant.[91] Secondly, it is not possible simply to sub-
sume saying לפני יהוה under the general category of prayer. By definition,
the latter is always directed to the Deity, regardless of whether it is "to"
or "before" him, whereas, as will be shown below, *saying* לפני יהוה may
well be addressed to someone else.[92] It will therefore be preferable to
consider saying לפני יהוה as a category on its own.

---

[87] "[D]as Gebet 'vor Jahwe'...ist zunächst ein Gebet im Tempel, im Heiligtum; dort
'redet' man vor Gott Dt. 26,5.10.13" (p. 104).

[88] "'Vor Jahwe beten' ist oft nicht mehr als 'zu (ל bezw. אל) Jahwe beten': 1. Sa. 1,3
verglichen mit V. 19; 2. Sa. 7,27 mit 1. Chr. 17,25; 1. Kö. 8,33 mit 2. Chr. 6,24
(לפניך־אליך)" (p. 105).

[89] "An manchen Psalmstellen...ist es zum mindesten zweifelhaft, ob noch an den
sichtbaren Tempel als Gebetsstätte gedacht, oder ob das Gebet 'vor Jahwe' vom Tempel losgelöst ist...Es ist ein Gebet und Lobgesang an Jahwe, ob im Tempel oder fern
von ihm, ist nebensächlich" (p. 105).

[90] In Ps. 95:6, the exhortation to "kneel before the LORD, our Maker" follows on
from an earlier invitation to "come into his *presence* (פניו)" (v. 2), while YHWH's
coming is given as the reason (כי בא) why "the trees...[will] sing for joy before the
LORD" (Ps. 96:12-13 // 1 Chron. 16:33), the worshippers should "make a joyful
noise before the King, the LORD" (Ps. 98:6) and the hills should "sing for joy together before the LORD" (Ps. 98:9).

[91] 1 Kings 8:22, 54 (cf. v. 21); 2 Chron. 6:12 (cf. vv. 11, 41); 2 Kings 19:14-15 (cf.
v. 15); Is. 37:14 (cf. v. 16); 2 Sam. 7:18 (cf. v. 2); 1 Chron. 17:16 (cf. v. 1), etc. It
will be observed that several of Nötscher's examples of prayer "before" YHWH do
not even mention לפני.

[92] Pp. 180-187.

Reindl makes no mention of Deut. 26:5 or 13, though he does regard the speaking (דבר [Piel], אמר) לפני יהוה of Exod. 6:12, 30 as examples of his literal, local sense.[93] However, in view of the clear cultic contexts in which Deut. 26:5 and 13 occur, it would seem reasonable to presume that he would allocate them to his *local* category,[94] and thus see the occurrences of לפני יהוה as referring to the divine Presence.[95]

USAGE ELSEWHERE

Saying/speaking before humans

Within the OT there are six instances of saying (אמר) "before" human beings.[96] There are also three instances of speaking (דבר [Piel]) "before" them,[97] and in view of the similarity in meaning between the two verbs, the discussion will be broadened to include דבר (Piel) as well.

Examination of these nine occurrences reveals two distinct uses of the preposition such that remarks said/spoken לפני a human being can be addressed either to that person or to *someone else*. Examples of the first usage can be found in 1 Sam. 20:1; Eccl. 5:5 (EVV 6) and Neh. 3:34 (EVV 4:2), of the second in 1 Kings 3:22, and of both together in Num. 36:1. In 1 Sam. 20:1 David's saying (אמר) לפני Jonathan is most naturally understood as being addressed to *him*, since no one else is recorded as being present during their conversation (vv. 1-11). In Eccl. 5:5 (EVV 6) the worshipper is advised against saying (אמר) לפני the messenger that the unfulfilled vow which he made at the temple was a mistake, an excuse generally regarded as being proffered to the *messenger* (whether priest or other emissary sent from the temple to exact payment of the vow).[98] In Esth. 8:3 Esther's speaking (דבר [Piel]) לפני the king is clearly directed to *him*, since she falls at his feet and beseeches him with tears. And in Neh. 3:34 (EVV 4:2) Sanballat's saying (אמר) לפני his brethren and the Samaritan army is most naturally understood as being addressed to *them* (i.e. rather than to the Jews), since there is no indication that his sarcasm was delivered within earshot of the Jerusalem wall. In contrast, the two pros-

---

[93] See above, p. 172 n. 56.
[94] See above, p. 172 n. 57.
[95] See above, p. 139 n. 42.
[96] 1 Sam. 20:1; Ezek. 28:9; Eccl. 5:5 (EVV 6); Esth. 1:16; Neh. 3:34; 6:19.
[97] Num. 36:1; 1 Kings 3:22; Esth. 8:3.
[98] Whybray (1989) 96, Crenshaw 117, Ogden (1987) 79, Loader 59, Eaton 100, Lohfink (1980) 41, Barucq 103, Leupold (1952) 121.

titutes arguing over the fate of the living child (1 Kings 3:22) speak (דבר [Piel]) לפני Solomon, but address *each other* since both describe the dead child as "yours" (בנך):

> But the other woman said, "No, the living child is mine, and the dead child is *yours*." The first said, "No, the dead child is *yours*, and the living child is mine." Thus they spoke before the king.

Finally, both uses appear to be present in Num. 36:1. The Gileadites speak (דבר [Piel]) לפני Moses and לפני the leaders, but from their references to "my lord" (v. 2) and from the fact that it is *Moses* who responds (v. 5) it is likely that such speaking לפני the leaders is addressed primarily to him rather than to them.

There are thus two distinct uses of saying/speaking לפני humans: A says/speaks לפני B, and in so doing addresses B; A says/speaks לפני B, and in so doing addresses C. The following two points can be made. First, a reference to someone saying/speaking לפני another is no guarantee *of itself* that the latter is being addressed. And secondly, while in both usages the speaker is clearly in proximity to those humans לפני whom he says/speaks, it should be noted that the second usage arises as a direct consequence of the *local* use of the preposition. The two prostitutes are able to address each other לפני Solomon precisely because they are proximate to him. Their speaking לפני him is a speaking *in his presence*.

Saying/speaking before the Deity

There are three instances of saying/speaking לפני יהוה outside Deut. 26, namely Exod. 6:30 (אמר), and Exod. 6:12; Judg. 11:11 (דבר [Piel]). None contains any independent indications of divine Presence in its context, but, taken together, they provide evidence for the same dual usage of the preposition לפני as that observed above with regard to humans. In Exod. 6:12, 30 Moses speaks/says לפני יהוה in response to YHWH's commands to him in the preceding verses (11, 29), and in the absence of any positive indication that his remarks are directed elsewhere, such speaking/saying is most naturally understood as being addressed to *YHWH*. In the case of Judg. 11:11, however, it is possible that the other usage of speaking לפני יהוה is intended. A number of scholars see its reference to Jephthah "[speaking] all his words before the LORD" as indicating the reaffirmation at Mizpah by both Jephthah *and* the elders of the vows which they had previously made at Tob (in vv. 9f.),[99] though this time, and in keeping with v. 10, with YHWH as witness to the agreement.[100] Certainly it is clear from the second person form of address used in vv. 9f. that Jephthah's part of the agreement (v. 9) is addressed to the elders, and that theirs (v. 10) is addressed to him, with neither party speaking to the Deity. Thus if the above reading of v. 11 is correct, it would appear that in reaffirming at Mizpah what he had previously said at Tob, Jephthah's speaking לפני יהוה is addressed not to him, but to *the elders*, and so constitutes an example of speaking לפני the Deity parallel to that in 1 Kings 3:22, where the prostitutes speak לפני Solomon, but in fact address each other.[101] The significance of this will be taken up when we come to consider Deut. 26:5, 13.

DEUT. 26:5, 13

It is intended to argue that the above two uses of saying/speaking לפני someone[102] are also represented in Deut. 26, the first by v. 13, and the second by v. 5. The two instances will be dealt with separately.

Deut. 26:5

Many commentators regard vv. 5-10a as a prayer,[103] and so addressed to God. However, on several grounds it would seem likely that the bulk of the section is directed elsewhere, and that YHWH himself is not addressed until v. 10:

---

[99] Webb 53: "A more solemn, ceremonial ratification of the terms already agreed between Jephthah and the elders is indicated in 11c...where 'his words' refers back to 9b-d via 'your word' in 10c, and where 'before Yahweh' is in fulfilment of 10b, 'let Yahweh be witness between us'", Martin (1975) 138: "[T]he whole transaction is ratified *in the presence of the LORD* at the sanctuary at Mizpah. *the LORD* is *witness* to the agreement", Cundall 142: "The compact between Jephthah and the elders was sealed in a solemn ceremony...at...Mizpah...Yahweh...was invoked as the witness to this agreement (10, 11)"; cf. Sheriffs 58-59.

[100] "The LORD will be (יהוה) witness between us".

[101] This distinction between the two uses of לפני is implied by Ridderbos in his comments on Deut. 26:13: "The prescribed declaration...is...not something that is merely pronounced before the Lord, it is also addressed directly to Him" (p. 245).

[102] P. 180.

[103] Corvin 121, 204, 205, 212, 261, 268, Weinfeld (1972a) 32-33, 213, Lohfink (1971) 22, Hyatt (1970) 153, 164, von Rad (1938) 3 (see, however, the denials in his commentary 113 and *TAT* 1 127), Reider 238, Junker 105, Smith (1918) 292, Steuernagel (1900) 93-94; cf. Thompson (1968) 58, Fohrer (1965) 129.

The mode of referring to YHWH. Within the Deuteronomistic History
speech addressed to YHWH can be identified in one or more of the following ways: first, by the narrator specifying that YHWH is being addressed,[104] secondly, by representation of the speech as a response to
something said by YHWH,[105] and thirdly, by the speaker naming
YHWH in the vocative,[106] usually, when such is the principal clue to the
identity of the addressee, in his opening words.[107] Moreover, within such
speech addressed to YHWH the *second* person form of address is normally used. Apart from Hebrew poetry,[108] the only instance (i.e. within
the Deuteronomistic History) of YHWH's apparently being addressed in
the third person is 2 Sam. 15:8b (cf. v. 7). However, use of the third person here may well derive from the fact that Absalom is not at this moment addressing YHWH, but is *reporting to the king* the substance of a
vow made on a previous occasion.[109] In the case of Deut. 26:5-10a the
narrator's introduction ("and you shall answer and say *before* the
LORD") is ambiguous, and contains no clear indication that the Deity is
being addressed. There is no earlier speech to which vv. 5-10a could be
the reply, and it is not until v. 10a that YHWH is addressed in the vocative ("And behold, now I bring the first of the fruit of the ground, which
thou, *O LORD*, hast given me").[110] In addition, it is only in the latter
verse that the second person form of address is introduced, vv. 5-9 referring to YHWH solely in the *third* person.[111] It would appear that whereas
v. 10a is clearly addressed to the Deity, there is no firm evidence on
which to base a similar affirmation *vis-à-vis* vv. 5-9.

---

[104] E.g. "Then Gideon said *to God*, 'If thou wilt deliver Israel by my hand...'" (Judg. 6:36).
[105] E.g. "Then the LORD called Samuel, *and he said, 'Here I am!'*" (1 Sam. 3:4).
[106] E.g. "And Joshua said, 'Alas, *O Lord GOD*, why hast thou brought this people over the Jordan at all?'" (Josh. 7:7).
[107] Cf. the position of the vocative references to YHWH in Josh. 7:7-9; Judg. 6:22b; 21:3; 1 Sam. 23:10-11a; 2 Sam. 7:18b-29; 23:17aα; 1 Kings 8:23-53; 18:36aβ-37; 19:4bβ; 2 Kings 6:20aβ; 19:15aβ-19. See, however, Deut. 21:7-8; 2 Sam. 15:31b.
[108] Judg. 5:2-31; 1 Sam. 2:1-10; 2 Sam. 22:2-51.
[109] It also helps to avoid the impression, possibly given by the "you" form, that David himself is being addressed.
[110] Cf. Carmichael (1969) 285-286.
[111] Mentioned only by Lohfink (1971): "Daß in den Sätzen 8-13 von dem in Satz 14 angeredeten Gott Jahwe in dritter Person gesprochen wird, fällt zwar auf..." (p. 23), and von Rad (1964): "[E]s fehlt die Anrede, und es wird in [der Erklärung] von Gott in der dritten Person gesprochen" (p. 113).

The identity of the addressee. Within the OT the combination of verbs
(ענה ואמר) which immediately precedes the declaration commanded in
Deut. 26:5-10a is most commonly used to introduce a reply to speech addressed to (or occasionally overheard by) the subject of these verbs. In
this case, however, and regardless of whether v. 5 originally followed on
from v. 4 or from v. 2,[112] nothing is reported as having been said earlier.
It is possible, however, on two grounds, to see the major part of the section as being addressed to the priest referred to in vv. 3-4. First, within
the OT there are eleven instances of the verbal pair ענה ואמר being used to
introduce direct speech in response to an *action*,[113] and in the majority of
cases such speech is addressed to the one(s) carrying out that action. If,
therefore, vv. 3-4 are regarded as an integral part of the text it becomes
possible to see vv. 5-9 as being spoken by the individual Israelite to the
priest, in response to the latter's setting down of the basket before the altar.[114] Secondly, support for the addressee being a priest, or other human
being, i.e. rather than YHWH, comes from the observation that of those
other OT passages with which Deut. 26:5-9 has been compared (and re-

---

[112] Many scholars view vv. 3-4 as a possible post-deuteronom(ist)ic insertion: Cairns
222, Mayes (1979) 332, 334, Hölscher (1922) 188, 215, Smith (1918) 292, 293,
Puukko 231, 247-248, Steuernagel (1900) 94, Bertholet (1899) 80; cf. von Rad
(1964) 113.
[113] Gen. 31:36 (Jacob to Laban in response to Laban's ransacking his tents); 1 Sam.
14:12 (the Philistines to Jonathan and his armour-bearer in response to the two Israelites showing themselves to them); 1 Sam. 14:28 (one of the people to Jonathan in
response to Jonathan's eating some honeycomb); 1 Sam. 30:22 (the "wicked and base
fellows" to David in response to David's approaching the people); 2 Sam. 13:32
(Jonadab to David in response to David's grieving); 1 Kings 13:6 (Jeroboam to the
man of God in response to the shrivelling of the king's hand); Is. 14:10 (dead leaders
and kings to the king of Babylon in response to his arrival in Sheol); Zech. 6:4
(Zechariah to the angel in response to the emergence of four chariots from the mountains); Ezra 10:2 (Shecaniah to Ezra in response to the repentance exhibited by Ezra
and the people); 1 Chron. 12:18 (EVV 17) (David to the men of Benjamin and Judah
in response to their coming to his stronghold); 2 Chron. 29:31 (Hezekiah to the Levites in response to their sanctifying themselves).
[114] If, on the other hand, they are regarded as a late interpolation, then vv. 5-9 originally followed on from v. 2, and can be seen as the worshipper's response to his arrival at the "chosen place", though in this case the identity of the addressee(s) would
be unknown (fellow Israelites/cultic functionaries?). Cf. the identical narrative use of
"answered and said" which occurs in Judg. 18:13-14: "And they…came to the house
of Micah. Then the five men…answered and said to their brethren, 'Do you know
that…'".

gardless of whether they are classified as creeds,[115] free adaptations of such in cult-lyrics[116] or historical summaries[117]), and which refer to YHWH/God in the third person,[118] all are addressed to specific *human* individuals. Num. 20:14b-16[119] is addressed to the king of Edom (v. 14a), Deut. 6:21aβ-24 to "your son" (v. 21aα), 1 Sam. 12:8 to the people (v. 6), and Pss. 78, 105, 135:8-12, 136[120] to other Israelites. Such passages provide ample support for Deut. 26:5-9 being viewed as addressed to a priest[121] (or other human being) rather than to YHWH.[122]

The significance of ועתה *(v. 10a).* A number of scholars have suggested, on the basis of the expression ועתה ("And now") at the beginning of v. 10, that the latter cannot be separated from vv. 5-9.[123] However, while we would not wish to deny that the so-called Credo provides the explanation and motivation for bringing "the first of the fruit of the ground" to YHWH, the two sections are *distinct* in so far as they are addressed to different persons. Moreover, such a conclusion is not inconsistent with the use of ועתה, since there are instances of it introducing a change of ad-

---

[115] Von Rad (1938) 3-7.
[116] Von Rad (1938) 8-11.
[117] Hyatt (1970) 164.
[118] Excluding those passages, which, while *occasionally* referring to YHWH in the third person, primarily do so in the first (Josh. 24:2aβ-13 [cited by von Rad (1938) 6]; Amos 2:9ff.; Mic. 6:4-6 [cited by Anderson 56]) or second (Exod. 15:4, 5, 8-10a, 12-16 [cited by von Rad (1938) 9-10]; Jer. 32:17-25 [cited by Hyatt (1970) 164]). Note that the passages from Exod. 15 and Jer. 32 are addressed to YHWH himself (cf. Exod. 15:1; Jer. 32:16).
[119] Carmichael (1969) 278-287.
[120] For comparisons of Deut.26:5-9 with Deut. 6:21aβ-24; 1 Sam. 12:8 and Pss. 78, 105, 135:8-12, 136 see von Rad (1938) 3-11.
[121] In addition, Carmichael (1969) has argued that the law of the first fruits in Deut. 26 entails a conscious recollection of the narrative of the spies' incursion into Canaan and their return with some of the fruit of the land (Num. 13). He notes, in partial support of his case, that in both accounts the fruit is taken to *priests*, whether to Moses and Aaron (Num. 13:26) or to the priest "who is in office at that time" (Deut. 26:3) (pp. 277-278). His observation thus provides some basis for retaining vv. 3-4 as original to the text; cf. Zimmerli (1982) 110.
[122] Merendino claims that the formula ענה ואמר is never used to introduce a prayer: "Die Formel 'erklären und sagen'...wird an sich nie auf ein Gebet bezogen" (p. 351).
[123] Nicholson (1973) 21-22, Hyatt (1970) 164, Rost (1965) 14-15, Brekelmans 8, Vriezen (1963) 14.

dressee,[124] and these would appear to provide sufficient precedent for the proposed interpretation of vv. 5-10a.

Thus, on the basis of the two different ways of referring to YHWH in Deut. 26:5-10a (i.e. indirectly and directly),[125] and of the introductions to the direct speech in vv. 5 (וענית ואמרת)[126] and 10 (ועתה), a case has been made out for viewing vv. 5-9 as spoken לפני יהוה but addressed either to the priest (vv. 3-4) or to other (unspecified) Israelites, while v. 10 is directed to YHWH himself.

Deut. 26:13

Deut. 26:13a ("then you shall say before the LORD") introduces the direct speech of vv. 13-15, in which it is clear from both content and the second person form of address that YHWH himself is being spoken to:

> "I have given it...according to all *thy* commandment which *thou* hast commanded me; I have not transgressed any of *thy* commandments...I have done according to all that *thou* hast commanded me. *Look down* [imperative] from *thy* holy habitation...and *bless* [imperative] *thy* people Israel and the ground which *thou* hast given us, as *thou* didst swear..."

The significance of saying before the LORD

On two grounds it would appear that, at least in Deut. 26:5, the words to be spoken לפני יהוה are to be delivered in his Presence. First, it has been argued above that both uses of saying לפני the Deity are present in Deut. 26. The direct speech לפני יהוה in vv. 13-15 is addressed *to* him,

---

124 1 Sam. 23:20 (the Ziphites address Saul [...רד...המלך...ועתה] after discussing David's whereabouts *among themselves*. Note that their question [...הלוא] in v. 19 cannot be directed to Saul himself since he could hardly be expected to know that David was hiding on the hill of Hachilah); Jer. 18:11 (YHWH addresses Jeremiah [...אל־איש־יהודה...ועתה אמר] after warning *Israel* using the figure of the potter and the clay [vv. 6-10]); Mal. 2:1 (YHWH addresses the priests [ועתה אליכם המצוה הזאת ...הכהנים] after criticizing *Israel* at the end of ch. 1); Prov. 5:7; 7:24 (the writer addresses his[?] sons [...ועתה בנים שמעו־לי] after advising only *one* of them [בני] in 5:1; 7:1); Neh. 6:9 (Nehemiah prays to God [ועתה חזק את־ידי] after informing his *readers*[?] of Sanballat's plot); cf. Ps. 2:10.

125 Lohfink (1971) suggests that the change in reference to YHWH, i.e. from the third to the second person, could be explained stylistically as a shift from confession in vv. 5-9 to prayer in v. 10 (p. 23).

126 The only instance of this construction being used where there is neither preceding speech nor action occurs in Zech. 4:12, where the prophet repeats in slightly modified form the question (v. 11) to which he has obtained no response of *any* kind.

whereas the speech in vv. 5-9 is intended for a human audience (conceivably the priest in vv. 3-4). It is clear that the two uses established for saying/speaking לפני humans[127] also occur in connection with the Deity. Exod. 6:12, 30 and Deut. 26:13 represent the first category, while Deut. 26:5 and Judg. 11:11 represent the second. It has also been noted that to say/speak לפני one human being, but in fact to address another, involves the *local* use of the preposition and so necessitates the proximity of speaker and human לפני whom he says/speaks.[128] Since, therefore, the individual Israelite is invited to recite the words of Deut. 26:5-9 לפני יהוה but *to* someone else, it is strongly implied that the speaker is in proximity to the Deity.[129] If this is so, then Deut. 26:5 contains a further reference to divine Presence. Secondly, and as in the case of rejoicing "before" God, a non-spatial understanding of the saying לפני יהוה in these verses would appear to be unlikely in view of the preposition chosen. Had the author of Deut. 26:5, 13 wished such saying in relation to YHWH to be understood non-spatially, the more usual אל[130] would have been the obvious choice,[131] particularly since, unlike לפני, it would appear merely to designate the identity of the addressee and would imply nothing about his spatial relationship to the Deity. Alternatively, the phrase לפני יהוה אלהיך could have been omitted altogether without loss of sense, and a vocative reference to YHWH (already employed in v. 10 ["which thou, *O LORD*, hast given me"]) could have been included at the beginning of v. 13 to indicate who was being addressed.

The choice of the preposition לפני in Deut. 26:5, 13 to express the Israelite worshipper's saying in relation to YHWH, i.e. in preference to

---

[127] See above, pp. 179-180.

[128] See above, p. 180.

[129] In his comments on Solomon's prayer of dedication of the temple (1 Kings 8:22-53 // 2 Chron. 6:12-42) Corvin usefully distinguishes two different audiences of the prayer: "In this prayer reference is made, not only to the primary audience, God, but to the secondary audience as well, namely, a circle of hearers [i.e. "all the assembly of Israel" (1 Kings 8:22 // 2 Chron. 6:12)]" (p. 207). Our deliberations imply that a similar distinction can be drawn in respect of the recital of Deut. 26:5-9, though in this case the primary audience is the priest or other (unspecified) Israelites, while the secondary one is YHWH.

[130] Within the OT there are twenty-six occurrences of saying "to" (אמר אל) the Deity: Gen. 4:13; 17:18; Exod. 3:11, 13; 4:10; 19:23; 33:12, 15; Num. 11:11; 14:13; 16:15; 22:10; 23:4; Judg. 6:15, 17, 36, 39; 10:15; 1 Sam. 14:41; 2 Sam. 24:10, 17; Job 9:12; 10:2; 34:31; 1 Chron. 21:8, 17.

[131] אמר ל occurs in 2 Chron. 1:8, but elsewhere only in Hebrew poetry.

using the more common and non-locative אל or omitting any such relational statement altogether, would therefore appear to point to a *literal* rather than to a non-spatial understanding of that saying "before". The correctness of this conclusion, at least as regards Deut. 26:5, can be seen from the particular usage of saying לפני יהוה employed by it. That the direct speech of vv. 5-9 is uttered לפני יהוה but addressed to someone else, *requires* a literal interpretation of the phrase, and so confirms the proximity of speaker and the one "before" whom he speaks.

SETTING DOWN BEFORE

EARLIER VIEWS

Neither Westphal, Nötscher nor Reindl refer to Deut. 26:10, though all three comment on at least one of the other OT instances of setting something down (נוח [Hiph.]) לפני יהוה.

USAGE ELSEWHERE

While there are no OT examples of items being set down לפני human beings, there are two in which they are set down לפני an artefact[132] and four in which they are set down לפני יהוה. In Exod. 16:33-34 the jar of manna which Aaron is told to place לפני יהוה (Exod. 16:33) is left "before *the testimony*" (v. 34), and largely on this basis the pericope is generally considered to presuppose the construction of the ark and the tabernacle/ tent of meeting.[133] In Num. 17:16-28 (EVV 1-13), however, the latter is referred to explicitly (vv. 19, 28 [EVV 4, 13]), and Moses deposits the rods לפני יהוה in the *tent of the testimony* (v. 22 [EVV 7]).[134] Thus, depending on the view taken of the Israelites' portable sanctuary and the reference to the place "where I meet with you" (Num. 17:19 [EVV 4]),[135] both instances of setting down לפני יהוה could be understood in the local sense of proximity to YHWH. In Judg. 6 Gideon, in response to

---

[132] In both cases the "testimony" (Exod.16:34; Num. 17:19 [EVV 4]). Note that in Num. 17:16-28 (EVV 1-13) it is clear from the fact that Moses deposits the rods in the tent of meeting (v. 19 [EVV 4]) which houses the testimony (vv. 22, 23 [EVV 7, 8]) that the rods are in close proximity to that "before" which they are placed.

[133] Burns 127, Gispen 163-164, Knight 119, Clements (1972) 100, Hyatt (1971) 174, Cassuto 199-200, Davies (1967) 141, Noth (1959) 109, Beer 90, Heinisch (1934) 129, Driver (1911) 152.

[134] Note the further reference to the tent in v. 23 (EVV 8).

[135] For the two views of the tabernacle see above, p. 135 n. 22.

YHWH's promise that he would be with him (v. 16), offers to bring out a present and set it לפני him (v. 18). His accompanying entreaty to YHWH, whose identity he appears not to realize, "Do not depart *from here* (מזה)[136]...until I come to thee (עד־באי אליך)", together with the narrator's reference to Gideon's bringing the meat and broth *to him* (אליו) under the oak (v. 19), indicates that his setting "before" is conceived in terms of proximity to the one for whom he is providing the food.[137] Finally, in 1 Sam. 10:25 Samuel lays up לפני יהוה the book containing the rights and duties of kingship. However, despite the surmise that the book was kept in the temple, next to the ark[138] or in closest proximity to God,[139] there is no obvious intimation of divine Presence in the immediate context.

SIGNIFICANCE IN DEUT. 26:10

Outside Deut. 12-26 no clear picture has emerged concerning the use of setting down לפני יהוה.[140] Nevertheless, with reference to Deut. 26:10 it must again be asked why, if the author wished the Israelite's placing of the basket in relation to YHWH to be understood non-spatially, he did not use a less ambiguous expression, such as ליהוה, in order to specify the recipient without implying his spatial proximity to the giver. Or alternatively, we might ask why he did not omit such reference to the Deity altogether by exhorting the worshipper to place the basket before the altar (as in v. 4) or even "there" (using the adverb שם),[141] either of which would have conveyed the idea of the offering being left at the "chosen place". Either way he would have avoided the possibility of misunderstanding raised by the preposition לפני. An interpretation of the setting down לפני יהוה in terms other than literal would thus seem to be unlikely.

---

[136] See above, pp. 107-109.

[137] Regardless of whether his guest is YHWH or the angel of YHWH.

[138] Nötscher 104 n. 1: "Das Buch, das Samuel vor Jahwe niederlegt (1. Sa. 10,25), wird er wohl im Tempel, vielleicht wie die Leviten Dt. 31,9.26 das Gesetzbuch, neben der Lade aufbewahrt haben". Note that despite the book's possible proximity to the ark, Nötscher appears to categorize this particular example as "causal".

[139] Westphal 125-126: "Sonst wurden nur noch die Opfer- und sonstigen kultischen Geräte des Tempels im Hekal aufbewahrt 1 Kö 7,40, vermutlich in den Zellen des Anbaues; ebenso wohl auch alte Urkunden, wie das 'Königsgesetz', das Samuel 'vor Jahwe' niederlegte...alle Gegenstände, die sich im Hauptraume des Tempels befinden...im Hekal 'vor Jahwe' Platz gefunden haben. Sie werden in nächster Nähe Gottes aufgestellt".

[140] Unless the tabernacle is viewed primarily as a dwelling-place.

[141] Cf. Lev. 16:23; Josh. 4:8; 1 Kings 8:9; Ezek. 42:13, 14.

As in the case of rejoicing "before" YHWH, the use of the preposition לפני would appear to militate against a figurative understanding of the injunction to set the basket down לפני יהוה.

WORSHIPPING BEFORE

EARLIER VIEWS

As indicated at the beginning of the previous section, none of the three scholars under consideration deals with Deut. 26:10.

USAGE ELSEWHERE

Prostration before humans

Within the OT there are two examples of prostration (שחה [Hithp.]) לפני human beings. Abraham bows down לפני the Hittites (Gen. 23:12) and Absalom bows לפני David (2 Sam. 14:33). Both instances clearly involve the mutual proximity of the parties concerned.

Worshipping before a Deity

Outside Deut. 12-26 there are five instances of worshipping לפני יהוה and one of worshipping לפני foreign gods. In 1 Sam. 1:19 Elkanah and Hannah worship לפני יהוה. That they do so prior to returning home to Ramah implies that such worship takes place *in Shiloh*.[142] Most scholars, in their comments on chs. 1:1-4:1a, refer to the Shiloh temple as housing the ark,[143] and to the ark as in some way connected with the Presence of YHWH.[144] It would thus appear reasonable to presume that Elkanah's and Hannah's worship לפני יהוה takes place in the vicinity of that sacred object, and thus of the divine Presence. In Is. 66:23 YHWH refers to a time when "all flesh shall come to worship before me", and since the context refers to his *coming* (בא[ה]) to gather all nations and tongues

---

[142] Cf. the chapter's only other references to their worship (שחה [Hithp.]); both indicate that Shiloh is the place where it occurred: "at Shiloh" (v. 3), "there" (v. 28; cf. v. 24).

[143] Baldwin 65-66, Gordon (1986) 73, Klein (1983) 7, McCarter (1980) 59, Ackroyd (1971) 20, 23-24, Mauchline 45, 49-50, Hertzberg (1965) 15, McKane 35, Brockington (1962) 319, Kraus 207, Dhorme (1910) 17, 20, Smith (1899) 3.

[144] Klein (1983) 32, McCarter (1980) 59, Ackroyd (1971) 43, Kraus 207-208, Caird 893; Phythian-Adams (1934) 117, cf. Smith (1899) 26. Dhorme (1910) regards the expression "house/temple of the LORD" (1:7, 9, 24) as indicating that YHWH resided in the temple (p. 42).

(v. 18),[145] it would appear that the predicted worship is envisaged as taking place in his Presence.[146] In Ezek. 46:3 the people are permitted to worship לפני יהוה at the east-facing gate of the inner court of the new temple. YHWH himself is represented as having previously entered the building (44:2), and so the Israelites can be seen as worshipping in proximity to him. In Ps. 22:28 (EVV 27) the psalmist refers to "all the families of the nations worshipping לפני [the LORD]", but since there is no mention of their coming to a particular location to do so, the qualification could well have a more figurative sense or even allude to the divine omnipresence. In Ps. 86:9 the psalmist anticipates a time when all the nations will come and bow down לפני יהוה. There are no clear indications of divine Presence in the psalm, though its reference to all the nations *coming* (יבואו; cf. the same idea in Is. 66:23) is consistent with a local understanding of their bowing לפני him. Finally, in 2 Chron. 25:14 Amaziah worships לפני the gods of the men of Seir. These appear to be idols or images of some kind, since he *brings* and *sets them up*. The most natural understanding of his action would thus be in terms of worshipping in front of them.

SIGNIFICANCE IN DEUT. 26:10

On two grounds it would appear that the injunction to worship לפני יהוה in Deut. 26:10 is intended to be understood in terms of proximity to the Deity. First, and as in the case of rejoicing and saying לפני יהוה, the author has used לפני in preference to the preposition most commonly associated with the verb in question, i.e. ל, which elsewhere is used twenty-three times in connection with YHWH and forty-one times in connection with other gods/non-human objects of worship. This non-use of ל is even more striking when it is considered that, while it is sometimes used in contexts in which both worshipper and worshipped are presumed to be

---

[145] Some commentators retain the *feminine* participle of the MT, understanding its subject to be עת, "the *time* is coming": Pieper 697, Young 531, Slotki (1957) 324, Kissane 319-320, 326. The majority, however, follow the LXX, Syr., Vulg. and Targum, reading the participle as masculine (בא) in agreement with ואכי: Watts (1987) 361, 364, Willis 478, Whybray (1975) 289, Bonnard 482, Westermann (1966) 336, McKenzie 206, Fohrer (1964) 282, Skinner (1929) 252, Lowth 403.

[146] This is implied by the juxtaposition of the two verses regardless of whether v. 23 is considered to come from the same (Bonnard 490-491, Kissane 314-317) or a later (Whybray [1975] 292, Westermann [1966] 336, Skinner [1929] 243) hand.

proximate,[147] it also occurs where such is clearly *not* the case, for example in the eight OT instances of worshipping the sun, moon and stars,
etc.[148] The latter usage would seem to indicate that the principal thought
expressed by the preposition ל in these contexts concerns the direction or
object of the worship rather than the spatial relationship of the parties
concerned. Its use would thus appear to provide an ideal way of avoiding
any suggestion of divine Presence. The author of Deut. 26:10, however,
has chosen to use לפני, with its additional connotations of "in the presence of" or "in front of". Thus, as in the case of rejoicing, it is difficult to
avoid the conclusion that it was precisely because of such additional
connotations that he did so, i.e. in order to specify YHWH as being both
the object of worship *and* in close proximity to the worshipper. Secondly, as the worship לפני יהוה is conceived as occurring at the "chosen
place", it would seem unlikely that the author was referring either to a
figurative meaning or to the divine omnipresence. The proposed interpretation is therefore in line with the only other understanding of the activity
for which a clear OT precedent exists,[149] i.e. that of divine Presence.

The obvious means of avoiding giving the impression that the Israelite's worship takes place in proximity to the Deity has not been utilized.
לפני has been chosen rather than ל, and its strong locative associations
imply that in Deut. 26:10 the worship in relation to YHWH is intended to
occur (as in a number of other places) in the divine Presence.

SUMMARY

Deut. 12-26 contains sixteen instances of לפני יהוה of which two (24:4,
13) are clearly metaphorical, being used in the sense of "in YHWH's
opinion" or "as far as YHWH is concerned". It has been argued that the
significance of the remaining fourteen should be determined independ-

---

[147] Most commonly in relation to man-made artefacts such as "graven images"
(Exod. 20:5; Deut. 5:9), the Golden Calf (Exod. 32:8; Ps. 106:19) or "the work of
one's hands" (Is. 2:8; Jer. 1:16; Mic. 5:12 [EVV 13]), but also in relation to YHWH
(1 Sam. 1:28).
[148] Deut. 4:19; 17:3; 2 Kings 17:16; 21:3; Jer. 8:2; Ezek. 8:16; Zeph. 1:5; 2 Chron.
33:3.
[149] I.e. the two instances of prostration לפני humans and possibly five (1 Sam. 1:19;
Is. 66:23; Ezek. 46:3; Ps. 86:9?; 2 Chron. 25:14) of worshipping לפני divine beings.

ently of references to the divine Name at the "chosen place" or to YHWH himself as being in heaven.[150]

EVIDENCE FOR A LITERAL INTERPRETATION OF לפני יהוה

First, ten of the fourteen instances mention a location,[151] i.e. using an adverb or adverbial phrase, and all but one (18:7) envisage particular occasions on which the activity לפני יהוה is to take place. These features point towards a *literal* understanding of the phrase. Secondly, there is only *one* specified location at which such activities are described as occurring לפני יהוה, i.e. the "chosen place".[152] This is stated explicitly in ten of the fourteen instances, implied by the contexts of three (12:12, 18b; 19:17), and exemplified by the regulations distinguishing between items which are allowed to be eaten "within [the] towns" and those which are commanded to be eaten at the "chosen place". Nowhere is any activity לפני יהוה specified as taking place simply "within [the] towns". Thirdly, while the first two observations are also consistent with the expression understood as "at the sanctuary" or "at the 'chosen place'", neither of

---

[150] See above, p. 156.

[151] Among the instances of לפני יהוה parallel to those under consideration (i.e. outside 12-26) but involving the known presence of the Deity, and thus, by implication, the literal use of the expression, over half specify the location, either explicitly with an adverbial phrase: Ezek. 44:3 ("Only the prince may sit *in [the gate]* to eat bread לפני יהוה"); Ezek. 46:3 ("The people...shall worship *at the entrance of that gate* לפני יהוה"), or implicitly, using a verb of motion: Exod. 18:12 ("Aaron *came*...to eat bread with Moses' father-in-law לפני האלהים"); Judg. 6:18 ("Do not depart from here...until I *come* to thee...and set [my present] לפניך"); Is. 66:23 ("all flesh *shall come* to worship לפני"): Job 23:3-4 ("Oh...that I *might come*...to his seat! I would lay my case לפניו"). If the list is extended to include those instances occurring in the context of the tabernacle, then the proportion rises to two-thirds: Exod. 16:33-34 ("Moses said to Aaron, 'Take a jar...and place it לפני יהוה to be kept throughout your generations.' As the LORD commanded...so Aaron placed it *before the testimony*, to be kept"); Num. 17:22 (EVV 7) ["Moses deposited the rods לפני יהוה *in the tent of the testimony*"]; Num. 27:2, 5 ("[T]hey stood before Moses...at the door of the tent of meeting...[and he] *brought* their case לפני יהוה"); cf. van der Woude (1976) 444: "Die Präp. *lifnē*... bei Verben der Bewegung...wird in lokalem Sinne verwendet".

[152] It is generally accepted that only one sanctuary is in view here, regardless of whether the "chosen place" is considered to refer solely to Jerusalem (Clements [1989] 28, Braulik [1986] 94-95, 98, Clifford (1982) 72-79, Mayes [1979] 61-63, 68, Phillips [1973] 84-85, Nicholson [1967] 95, Cazelles [1966] 16, Smith [1918] xxiv-xxv, 163, Driver [1902] 136-138, 140, Bertholet [1899] 39) or to a central sanctuary whose identity can change from time to time (Craigie [1976] 217, Thompson [1974] 166-167, von Rad [1964] 67, Procksch 452-453).

these alternatives is free from objection.[153] The literal interpretation is the most likely.

FURTHER EVIDENCE FOR A LITERAL INTERPRETATION

In the case of standing (18:7; 19:17) or saying (26:5) לפני יהוה, there are additional indications from their use in context that the literal sense is the one intended:

Deut. 18:7

It has been argued that, although the standing of the urban Levites לפני יהוה is part of their service to the Deity, it does not *of itself* express that service,[154] since the latter is usually indicated by the use of the verb שרת. Rather, the concern to ensure that both they and their rural brethren are allowed to exercise the same responsibility ("minister[ing] in the name of the LORD") at the "chosen place" suggests that the standing in v. 7 should be understood in the same (literal) sense as that in v. 5, and thus that the לפני יהוה which qualifies it should be seen in *its* literal sense of proximity to the Deity.

Deut. 19:17

It has been shown that the sequence לפני...לפני (without connective) does not necessarily entail synonymous apposition, and that within each of the other (admittedly few) OT instances of the same construction there is a consistent usage of the preposition. Since, therefore, the standing לפני the priests and judges occurs in proximity to *them*, it becomes possible to see the concomitant standing לפני יהוה as taking place in proximity to *him*.

Deut. 26:5

It has been argued that the direct speech of vv. 5-9 is spoken לפני יהוה, but addressed to *someone else*, possibly the priest of vv. 3-4. Such a situation is characteristic of the literal use of the preposition, since it *necessitates* the proximity of the speaker and the one לפני whom he speaks. Any Israelite repeating the confession of vv. 5-9 is thus conceived of as being in the divine Presence.

---

[153] See above, pp. 154-156.
[154] I.e. in the sense of 1 Kings 17:1; 18:15, etc.

SUPPORT FROM OUTSIDE DEUT. 12-26

Examination of the other OT instances of the activities under consideration lends support to the proposed understanding of לפני יהוה in Deut. 12-26. Where such activities take place לפני another human being the preposition is generally used in its locative sense,[155] since in the majority of cases (at least eighteen out of twenty-two) the parties concerned are most naturally understood as being in close proximity to each other.[156] Where they occur לפי the Deity the situation is similar, though the literal interpretation is demonstrable in only a smaller proportion of texts. Nearly half (eleven out of twenty-four) entail independent evidence that the divine Presence is localized in the vicinity of the one performing the action.[157] Of the other thirteen, three occur in connection with the tabernacle and so could well involve proximity to the Deity,[158] and one *may* imply the divine omnipresence.[159] The remaining nine provide neither indication of YHWH's whereabouts (whether present or absent) nor evidence that some other (non-literal) meaning of the expression is to be understood.[160] In these cases, therefore, the significance of לפני יהוה must remain uncertain. Suffice it to say that, for the activities referred to in Deut. 12-26, the main use of the preposition for which there is clear attestation in the rest of the OT is the *locative* one.

AN EMPHASIS ON DIVINE TRANSCENDENCE?

In view of the strong locative connotations of the preposition לפני,[161] there are two aspects of its use in relation to the Deity which appear to

---

[155] Apart from rejoicing and setting down which are not recorded as occurring לפי human beings in the OT.

[156] Gen. 23:12; Num. 27:2; 35:12; 36:1; Josh. 20:6, 9; 1 Sam. 20:1; 2 Sam. 11:13; 14:33; 1 Kings 1:25; 3:16, 22; Ezek. 28:9; Eccl. 5:5 (EVV 6); Esth. 1:16; 8:3; Neh. 3:34 (EVV 4:2); 6:19. In contrast, the significance of the Levites' standing "before" for the purpose of ministering (Num. 3:6; 16:9; Ezek. 44:11) is not clear, and there is some debate about 2 Kings 25:29 // Jer. 52:33.

[157] Exod. 18:12; Judg. 6:18; 1 Sam. 1:19; Is. 66:23; Ezek. 44:3, 15; 46:3; Ps. 86:9?; Job 23:4; 2 Chron. 25:14; 29:11.

[158] Exod. 16:33; Num. 17:22 (EVV 7); 27:5.

[159] Ps. 22:28 (EVV 27).

[160] Exod. 6:12, 30; Lev. 23:40; Deut. 10:8; 27:7; Judg. 11:11; 1 Sam. 10:25; Is. 9:2 (EVV 3); 1 Chron. 29:22.

[161] Cf. Reindl 19: "לפני ist eine Präposition zur *Ortsangabe*. Sie bezeichnet in erster Linie...einen Ort mit dem Gesicht der betreffenden Person als Beziehungspunkt...ל allein ist zu vieldeutig, um in allen Fällen eine genaue Ortsangabe zu gewährleisten", Nötscher 6-7, BDB 816: "the most general word for *in the presence of, before*".

conflict with the suggested emphasis on divine transcendence proposed
for Deut. 12-26 by advocates of Name Theology. First, there is the fact
that לפני יהוה is used at all.[162] Had the writer(s) wanted to affirm YHWH's
absence from the "chosen place" it seems unlikely that they would have
risked courting misunderstanding by placing such a preposition before
the divine Name, when the resulting expression (לפני יהוה) could clearly
be taken to affirm the exact opposite of what is supposed to be intended.
Secondly, there is the fact that in six of the fourteen occurrences of לפני
יהוה involving an (arguably) locative sense, לפני appears to have been
chosen *in preference to* other (non-locative) prepositions more commonly used in relation to the Deity. This is particularly strange in a context in which divine transcendence is claimed to be of major concern. If
the author(s) of Deut. 12-26 really did wish to avoid misunderstanding,
why did they not, in the case of "rejoice", "say" and "worship", employ
those non-locative prepositions (ל, אל, ב respectively) which normally
accompany such verbs in relation to YHWH, or, why did they not omit
the expression altogether?[163] On the other hand, the retention of, and bias
towards, לפני, with its strong locative associations, is understandable if
the author(s) of these chapters did wish to affirm that YHWH was indeed
present at the "chosen place".

THE NAME FORMULA AS THEOLOGICAL CORRECTIVE?

McConville (1979) has drawn attention to the close association of the
expression לפני יהוה with the "Name formulae" in Deuteronomy.[164] Thus,
granted that thirteen of its sixteen instances in Deut. 12-26 do refer to the
divine Presence, it might be objected that any nearby references to the divine Name have been deliberately placed there as a theological correc-

---

[162] I.e. excluding the two instances in 24:4, 13.

[163] This would be possible in all fourteen cases, though in 14:23 a divine subject
would need to be added after יבחר, and in 18:7 it might be preferable to insert, for example, "to minister" (cf. 17:12) at the end of the verse. Most of the seven activities
are mentioned elsewhere in Deut. 12-26 without the qualification under discussion
(see above, p. 154 n. 97). Note, however, that worship with merely *implied* reference
to YHWH is not attested in these chapters, but *is* evidenced in Gen. 22:5; Exod. 4:31;
12:27; 24:1; 33:10; 34:8, etc.

[164] P. 159 n. 41.

Table 6.1: Source allocations of לפני יהוה and the divine שם in close proximity

Author	Source allocations[a]					
	Deut. 12		Deut. 14		Deut. 16	Deut. 26
לפני יהוה	7a	12aα	23aα	26bα	11aα	5aα 10bα 10bβ
שם	5a	11a	23aα	24aβ	11b	2b
Mettinger	DtrN?	DtrH	post-D, pre-Dtr?		---	DtrH
Preuß	Layer IV	Layer IV	Layer III	Layer V	Layer III	Layer IV[b]
Mayes	Dtr2	Dtr1	D[c]		D	Dtr2
Merendino	---	---	---	---	pre-D[d]	pre-D[e]
De Tillesse	Dtr		D		D	D
Hölscher	f	f	D[c]		D	D
Puukko	g	g	D		D	D
Steuernagel	Dtr	plur.	sing.		sing.	sing.
Bertholet	g	g	D		D	D?

Key

DtrN The nomistic redaction of DtrH, the Deuteronomistic History. Dtr1 and Dtr2 represent the first and second Deuteronomists respectively.

D The "original Deuteronomy" (Mayes [1979] 47), "le noyau primitif Dt (*Tu*)" (De Tillesse 73), "Urdeuteronomium" (Hölscher [1922] 225, Bertholet [1899] XIX), "Das mutmaßliche Urdeuteronomium" (Puukko 289).

--- Either the source allocation is unclear, or the two verses come from different hands.

plur. Author employing the plural form of address.

sing. Author employing the singular form of address.

[a] Mettinger 54-56, 60 n. 82, Preuß (1982) 51-58, Mayes (1979) 41-48, 220-222, 243-246, 254-260, 331-333, Merendino 23-29, 45-46, 57, 97-102, 105, 135, 147, 149, 347-351, 363-364, 367-369, 371, 398-399, 403, 407, de Tillesse 46-47, 64-69, 72-83, Hölscher (1922) 179-181, 183-184, 186-188, 194, 225, Puukko 242-244, 293-295, Steuernagel (1900) 44-46, 54, 61, 93-94, Bertholet (1899) XIX-XX.

[b] 26:5aα is not specified.

[c] Excluding 14:24aβ. Mayes considers that it "may well be an addition taken from 12:21 ([1979] 246), while Hölscher describes it as a "Glosse aus 12:21" ([1922] 183 n. 1).

[d] Stage 5.

[e] Stage 4, excluding 26:10bα, which is Stage 1.

[f] Vv. 2-7 and 8-12 are separate "Ergänzungen" to 12:13-28 (pp. 180, 181).

[g] Vv. 2-7 and 8-12 represent different editions of the law *re* the unity of the cultplace (Puukko 242-244, Bertholet [1899] 38).

tive[165] in order to suggest that it is not YHWH himself who is present at the "chosen place" but his Name. It is found, however, that among those scholars who have attempted a detailed source analysis of these chapters,[166] there is no one who proposes that the Name references have been *systematically* added to the text subsequent to the incorporation of the various occurrences of לפני יהוה.[167] Rather, it is considered that most references to the divine Name come from the same hand as that of the nearby occurrence of לפני יהוה (Table 6.1).[168] Evidence of any correction of the impression of localized Presence given by the latter is thus lacking.

CONCLUSION

An understanding of לפני יהוה in Deut. 12-26 as referring to the Presence of YHWH localized at the sanctuary is consistent with its general characteristics in these chapters, the particular contextual features evident for the occurrences in 18:7; 19:17 and 26:5, and the usage of identical expressions in connection with both humans and the Deity elsewhere in the OT. In marked contrast to other more metaphorical interpretations (frequently related to an emphasis on divine transcendence), it also makes sense of the use of, and bias towards, the preposition לפני, with its strong locative associations.

---

[165] Note the instances of לפני יהוה in 12:7a (cf. the reference to the divine Name in v. 5a), 12:12aα (cf. v. 11a); 14:23aα (cf. v. 23aα), 14:26bα (cf. v. 24aβ); 16:11aα (cf. v. 11b) and 26:5aα, 10bα, 10bβ (cf. v. 2b).

[166] Mettinger, Preuß (1982), Mayes (1979), Merendino, de Tillesse, Hölscher (1922), Puukko, Steuernagel (1900), Bertholet (1899).

[167] Merendino considers that 12:5a and 7a come from the same hand, as do 12:11a and 12aα; 14:23aα, 14:24a and 26b. At the same time he suggests that the references to the Name in these verses may be secondary. It is important to note, however, that in the remaining cases, 16:11a and 26:2 he regards the entire verse (including the reference to the Name) as having come from the same hand as that of 16:11b and 26:5aα, 10bβ respectively.

[168] See above, p. 196.

7

SUMMARY AND CONCLUSIONS

The results obtained will be summarized in three sections. The first will deal with the various indications of divine Presence noted in Deut. 1-3, 4-5 and 9-10, the second with those instances of לפני יהוה found in chapters 12-26, and the third with the terminology employed in the various passages considered.

PRESENTATION OF RESULTS

THE HISTORICAL PASSAGES

The references to divine Presence noted during the comparisons carried out in chs. 2-4 are summarized in Tables 7.1 and 7.2. Table 7.1 classifies them according to whether they occur in both Deuteronomy and Exodus/Numbers, in Deuteronomy alone or in Exodus/Numbers alone,[1] and Table 7.2 largely according to whether they are expressed using a verb with divine subject or a preposition used locatively.[2] Each group will be commented on individually before an assessment is made of the significance of such terminology in Deuteronomy for its ideas of divine Presence in general and for Name Theology in particular.

Divine Presence in Deuteronomy paralleled in the Tetrateuch

Within the historical sections of Deuteronomy there are five deuteronom(ist)ic examples of divine Presence parallel to similar instances in

---

[1] See below, p. 201.
[2] See below, pp. 207-208.

the corresponding accounts in Exodus or Numbers (Table 7.1).[3] In one case (Deut. 1:42 // Num. 14:42) the same construction (בקרב) is used to express that Presence in the two narratives, while in the other four a variety of means is employed. It is important to note, however, that in all five, the expression used in Deuteronomy fulfils the same function within its context as does the corresponding one in Exodus or Numbers.[4] In both Deut. 1:30 and Num. 14:9 the promise that YHWH will "fight for" (Deut.) or "be with" (Num.) the people is part of the leaders' attempt to allay Israelite fears regarding the perceived prowess of the Canaanites. In both Deut. 1:42 and Num. 14:42, 43 the warning that YHWH will not be "in the midst of" (Deut., Num.) or "with" (Num.) Israel is part of Moses' attempt to dissuade the people from going up into the land. And it is to this absence of the Deity that both accounts attribute the subsequent Israelite defeat. In both Deut. 4:10aβ and Exod. 19:17a the assembling of the people "to" (Deut.) or "to meet" (Exod.) the Deity is to take place at the foot of the mountain prior to the proclamation of the Ten Commandments. And in both Deut. 10:1 and Exod. 34:1-2 the instruction to come up "to me" (Deut.) or "[to] present yourself...to me" (Exod.) involves Moses in ascending the mountain with two freshly-hewn tables of stone. In addition, although Deut. 9:18a and Exod. 34:28a stand in different literary contexts,[5] they both represent Moses as "before" (Deut.) or "with" (Exod.) YHWH, fasting for forty days and forty nights.

Divine Presence in Deuteronomy not paralleled in the Tetrateuch

There are ten instances of this, four of which would not be *expected* to occur in Exodus/Numbers. 1:33 (containing the reference to YHWH's "going before [the Israelites]...in fire...and...cloud") and 4:10aα (the people's "standing before" YHWH) are represented as comments made not at the time of the original incidents, but in the *present* (i.e. in Moab, 1:5). The former is Moses' reminder to the people of their past failure to accept the reassurances of vv. 29-31, while the relative clause in the latter enables him to specify more closely the past day on which YHWH

---

[3] See opposite, p. 201.
[4] In addition to the arguments adduced earlier, (pp. 24-28, 32-36, 45-50, 114-115) this observation provides further evidence that the deuteronom(ist)ic expressions also refer to divine Presence.
[5] In the middle (Deut.) and end (Exod.) of the Golden Calf incident respectively.

Table 7.1: Divine Presence in Deuteronomy: Summary of Synoptic Comparison

Divine Presence in Deuteronomy paralleled in the Tetrateuch

Deut. 1:29-30 (2x)	Num. 14:9
Deut. 1:42	Num. 14:42-43 (2x)
Deut. 4:10aβ	Exod. 19:17a
Deut. 9:18a[a]	Exod. 34:28a
Deut. 10:1	Exod. 34:1-2

Divine Presence in Deuteronomy not paralleled in the Tetrateuch

Deut. 1:33	---
Deut. 1:45	---
Deut. 4:10aα	---[b]
Deut. 4:12; 5:4 (2x), 5, 22	[Exod. 20:1]
Deut. 5:23	[Exod. 20:18]
Deut. 5:24, 26	[Exod. 20:19]
Deut. 5:31	---
Deut. 9:10; 10:4	[Exod. 31:18; 34:28b]
Deut. 9:12	[Exod. 32:7]
Deut. 9:25	[Exod. 32:11]

Divine Presence in the Tetrateuch not paralleled in Deuteronomy

---	Exod. 18:19
---	Exod. 19:3, 11, 21, 22, 24
[Deut. 4:10-11]	Exod. 19:9, 18, 20a
---	Exod. 20:20, 21
---	Exod. 20:24
---	Exod. 32:30, 31
---	Exod. 33:3, 5, 14, 15, 16; 34:9
---	Exod. 33:9, 11; 34:34
---	Exod. 33: 20, 21, 22 (2x), 23 (3x); 34:5 (2x), 6
---	Num. 11:17, 25
---	Num. 14:10b
---	Num. 14:14aβb
[Deut. 3:18-20]	Num. 32:20, 21, 22 (2x)

Key

---   No parallel text occurs because of the differing concerns of the deuterono-m(ist)ic and/or tetrateuchal pericopes involved.

[ ]   References enclosed in square brackets are parallel to ones in the same horizontal row, but contain no comparable allusions to divine Presence.

a Deut. 9:18a is found in a different literary context from that of Exod. 34:28a. The strictly parallel verse, Deut. 10:4, makes no mention of divine Presence.
b There is no closely analogous verse in Exodus (see pp. 200 and 202), but note 19:17b.

communicated to him the content of 4:10aβb. It is thus only to be expected that these references to divine Presence are absent from Exodus/ Numbers. In addition, 1:45 (which refers to Israel's "weeping before the LORD") and 5:31 (in which YHWH instructs Moses, "stand here by me") have no real parallels in the Exodus/Numbers accounts. Both Deut. 1 and Num. 14 refer to the Israelites being defeated and pursued as far as Hormah, but only Deuteronomy mentions their return to Kadesh. And although both Deut. 5 and Exod. 20 indicate YHWH's response to the people's request, the content of his remarks in the two accounts differs significantly.

The six remaining instances all occur in contexts which are in some way paralleled in Exodus, though without any reference to the divine Presence. In Deuteronomy YHWH communicates the Decalogue "out of the midst of the fire" (4:12; 5:4, 22), "face to face" with the people (5:4), and with Moses standing "between [him and Israel]" (5:5), while in Exodus he merely "[speaks] all these words" (20:1). In Deuteronomy Moses introduces the people's reaction to the revelation of the Decalogue by referring to their hearing "[YHWH's] voice out of the midst of the darkness" (5:23), whereas in Exodus the narrator mentions only their perception of the "thunderings and...lightnings and...sound of the trumpet" (20:18). In Deuteronomy the people's own reaction to that revelation includes two references to the Deity having spoken "out of the midst of the fire" (5:24, 26), while in Exodus it refers only to his speaking (20:19). In Deuteronomy the two tables of stone are inscribed with all the words "which the LORD had spoken...out of the midst of the fire" (9:10, cf. 10:4), whereas in Exodus the origin of the commandments is not mentioned (31:18, cf. 34:28b). In Deuteronomy, after the making of the Golden Calf, YHWH instructs Moses to "go down...from here" (9:12), but in Exodus he merely tells him to "go down" (32:7). Finally, in Deuteronomy, in an attempt to avert the threatened judgement, Moses "lies prostrate before the LORD...and...prays to the LORD" (9:25-26), whereas in Exodus he merely "beseeches the LORD his God" (32:11). In all six cases it is clear that Deuteronomy exhibits a heightened sense of divine Presence.

Divine Presence in the Tetrateuch not paralleled in Deuteronomy

Within Exodus and Numbers there are twelve instances of divine Presence which are without parallel in Deuteronomy, but which occur in contexts similar to those found in that book. In the majority of cases, however, it is possible to explain the absence of the sections containing them (and thus of the expressions themselves) without having to appeal to a deuteronom(ist)ic emphasis on divine transcendence. They are absent either because Deuteronomy does not share some perceived concern of Exodus or Numbers (six examples), or because of some special emphasis of its own (five examples).

In the first category, the absence from Deut. 1:9-18 of the people's "bringing their cases to God" (Exod. 18:19) is consistent with the section's initial lack of interest in the details of Moses' task. The omission from 3:18-20 of the four instances of "before YHWH" (Num. 32:20-24) is consistent with the section's silence as regards a possible Transjordanian reluctance to participate in the conquest of Cisjordan, as also of any reference to sin or to the land as a gift conditional upon such cooperation. The absence from 9:8-10:11 of the intercession recorded in Exod. 32:30-34 (together with its references to Moses "going up to" and "returning to" YHWH) is understandable in view of the section's indifference to, among other things, the journey to the land. The same indifference also accounts for the exclusion of two further groups of texts (Exod. 33:3, 5, 14, 15, 16; 34:9 and 33:20, 21, 22, 23; 34:5, 6) both of which relate to the question as to how a holy God might accompany a sinful people on their travels. Exod. 20:24, in which YHWH promises to come to the Israelites, has no direct parallel in Deuteronomy.

In the second category, the exclusive preoccupation of Deut. 1:9-18 with the *human* sphere, together with the general dissimilarity of the two narratives, is sufficient to explain the absence of the references to divine descent found in Num. 11:17, 25. The portrayal in Deut. 1-3 of the efficacy of the divine word adequately accounts for the absence from Deut. 1:19-40 of Moses' successful intercession (Num. 14:13-19), with its references to YHWH being in the midst of the people, being seen face to face and going ahead of the Israelites (v. 14aβb). Deut. 4:10-14 and 5 are primarily concerned with the experience of the *people*, and so do not include a number of passages from Exod. 19 (vv. 3-8, 10-15, 20b-25) and 20 (vv. 20-21) in which Moses is the principal actor and which contain several indications of divine Presence (Exod. 19:3, 11, 21, 22, 24; 20:20, 21). Finally, the recounting of the Golden Calf incident in Deut. 9:8-10:11 as a prime example of Israelite rebellion is sufficient to exclude from it both the tent of meeting pericope (Exod. 33:7-11), with its suggestion of divine descent and YHWH speaking face to face with Moses, and the reference to Moses going in before YHWH (Exod. 34:34). This leaves just two groups of divine Presence expressions for whose absence from Deuteronomy no adequate reason can be proffered, i.e. those referring to the coming and the divine descent of YHWH (Exod. 19:9, 18, 20a) and that to the appearing of his glory (Num. 14:10b). In these instances, Exodus and Numbers would appear to manifest a heightened emphasis on divine Presence relative to that in Deuteronomy.

Summary

There are thirteen pairs of passages which can be regarded as in some way comparable (Table 7:3).[6] Five refer to divine Presence in both accounts, six do so only in Deuteronomy and two only in the Tetrateuch. Moreover, there are fifteen instances of divine Presence (four in Deuteronomy and eleven in Exodus/Numbers)[7] whose absence from the other account can generally be explained in terms of differing emphases within the narratives.

לפני יהוה IN DEUT. 12-26

It has been argued that the majority of the sixteen instances of לפני יהוה in Deut. 12-26 should be understood in the literal sense and thus that they point to the localized Presence of the Deity at the "chosen place". Such an interpretation makes best sense of the following observations. First, there is a clear bias in favour of the preposition לפני to qualify the seven activities (eating, rejoicing, etc.) anticipated as being carried out before YHWH. In six out of the fourteen instances of the expression לפני is used instead of the prepositions (אל, ב, ל) more commonly associated with such behaviour. This preference for acting *before* God, and thereby using a preposition whose possible range of meaning undoubtedly includes the literal "in the presence of", is consistent with a belief in the Deity being localized in the immediate vicinity of the worshipper, but is antithetical to a concern to emphasize his *absence* from the earthly sphere. In the latter case, confusion as to the view being presented of the divine whereabouts would certainly result from a literal interpretation of the phrase, but could easily be avoided either by using the aforementioned prepositions or by omitting reference to YHWH altogether.[8] However, the fact

---

[6] See below, pp. 211-212.
[7] Indicated by --- in Table 7:1.
[8] See above, pp. 166-167, 185-187, 190-191, 194-195.

that neither of these precautions has been taken would seem to suggest that within Deut. 12-26 the affirmation of divine transcendence is not of major concern. By contrast, if the writer wished to indicate the Deity's *Presence* rather than his absence, then such a preference for a preposition ideally suited to express the divine proximity would be understandable.

Secondly, apart from the three instances of לפני יהוה in 24:4, 13 (metaphorical) and 26:13 (location unspecified), the expression is used in connection with only one particular locality. Activities carried out לפני יהוה are not permitted to take place anywhere within the land (e.g. "within your towns"), but are confined to "the place which the LORD your God will choose". Such a restriction, however, is not intended to suggest an identification of לפני יהוה with the "chosen place", since the occasional close literary proximity of the two phrases (i.e. in 12:18a; 14:23 and 15:20), would seem to imply a distinction between them. On the other hand, it *is* consistent with the notion that God himself is there and that it is the sole place at which he has condescended to localize himself. Both the preference, where choice is possible, for the preposition לפני and the use of the resulting expression, לפני יהוה, only in connection with the "chosen place" are intelligible if the writer(s) wanted to indicate, not just that the Israelites' eating, rejoicing, etc. were to be in relation to the Deity, but also that there they were to be in his Presence.

Finally, it is important to note that such an interpretation is supported in the case of three of the instances (those in 18:7; 19:17 and 26:5) by more detailed argumentation based on particular contextual considerations, and is, moreover, the main use of לפני יהוה, when qualifying the same seven activities, for which there is clear attestation in the rest of the OT.

Our studies have therefore suggested that God is represented as being present on the earth not only in the context of the Wilderness wanderings and Holy War but also in that of the cult, and at the very place at which the divine Name is known to be present.

THE TERMINOLOGY OF DIVINE PRESENCE

A number of scholars have sought to classify the OT terminology used to express the notion of divine Presence. The terms most frequently identified are verbs (e.g. בוא, ירד, ראה [Niph.]),[9] though Davies has referred to a number of nouns (e.g. face, glory, name, tabernacle)[10] and prepositions (e.g. before, in the midst of, with). It can be seen from Table 7.2 that it is verbs and prepositions which have figured most prominently in our particular analysis.[11] The data tabulated comes primarily from the passages discussed in chapters 2-4, but also includes other deuteronom(ist)ic examples of the same or similar expressions found elsewhere in Deuteronomy.

Several points can be made. First, if we look in Table 7.2 at the Exodus/Numbers passages as a whole, two-thirds of the expressions used occur in identical or similar[12] form in Deuteronomy, in either the synoptic passages studied or other deuteronom(ist)ic sections of the book. Of the remaining one-third, the most significant omissions from Deuteronomy are ירד and the range of anthropomorphic expressions concentrated in Exod. 33 (פנים, כף, אחר), of which only פנים is represented in Deuteronomy (4:37).[13] Secondly, in Deuteronomy as a whole three of YHWH's activities are particularly well attested: his *being* (אין, היה or implied) with/among the people, his *going* (הלך) with/among/before them, and his *speaking* (דבר [Piel]) from an earthly site (in this case the fire), the latter mode of communication having, as has been argued above,[14] the same connotation of divine Presence as does his speaking from the "burning bush" (Exod. 3:4). As far as prepositions are concerned, *"before"* (לפני) is used the most frequently, there being numerous instances of humans carrying out activities "before the LORD" in what, as we have proposed, is predominantly its literal (i.e. spatial) sense. It should also be noted that, as in the Exodus/Numbers passages studied, so also in Deuteronomy, there is some variation in the divine mode of travel, with בוא (4:34) and עבר לפני (9:3; 31:3) being used as well as the more frequent

[9] Mann 252-258, Schnutenhaus 1-21 (*re* the coming and appearing of God), cf. Brueggemann (1976) 680 (*re* the Sinai theophany).
[10] (1962b) 874. See also Mann, pp. 256-258.
[11] See below, pp. 207-208.
[12] Printed in italics in the table.
[13] The finger (אצבע) of God, which is referred to in Exod. 31:18, also occurs in Deut. 9:10, though whether in either case implying the divine proximity is doubtful.
[14] Pp. 60-66.

Table 7.2: The Terminology of Divine Presence

Expression employed		Deuteronomy		Tetrateuch
Hebrew	English	Discussed	Other	Discussed

Verbal (God as subject)

Hebrew	English	Discussed	Other	Discussed
קרא מן	speak from an earthly site	*4:12, 15, 33*[a] *5:4, 22, 26 9:10 10:4*		Exod. 19:3
בוא	come		4:34	Exod. 19:9 Exod. 20:20, 24
ירד	come down/descend			Exod. 19:11, 18, 20 Exod. 33:9[b] Exod. 34:5 Num. 11:17, 25
ערפל	be in thick darkness	*5:22*		Exod. 20:21[c]
עלה בקרב	go up among			Exod. 33:3, 5
הלך עם	go with		20:4 31:6	Exod. 33:16
הלך בקרב	go in the midst of		*23:15*[d]	Exod. 34:9
הלך לפני	go before	1:30, 33	31:8	Num. 14:14
עבר	pass by			Exod. 33:22
עבר על־פני	pass before		*9:3*[e] *31:3*[e]	Exod. 34:6
יצב (Hithp.) עם	stand with			Exod. 34:5
היה [f]את/עם	be with		2:7[c] 20:1[c] 31:8, 23	Num. 14:9[c], 43
אין בקרב	be in the midst of/among	1:42	6:15[c] 7:21[c]	Num. 14:14[c], 42
ראה (Niph.)	appear (God's glory)		*5:24*[g]	Num. 14:10

Key
Italicized references include similar, though not identical, terminology.

[a] No distinction is drawn between YHWH speaking (דבר [Piel]) "out of the midst of (מתוך) the fire" and his voice doing the same.
[b] *Divine* descent is implied by that of the cloud. See above, p. 77 n. 129.
[c] היה (or אין) is understood.
[d] Hithp. (EVV 23:14).
[e] לפני.
[f] There is no significant difference between את and עם according to Preuß (1968) 140, 144, 152; cf. van Unnik 300 n. 36. See, however, BDB 87.
[g] Hiph.

Continued on next page

Table 7.2: *Continued*

Expression employed		Deuteronomy		Tetrateuch
Hebrew	English	Discussed	Other	Discussed

Prepositional

Hebrew	English	Discussed	Other	Discussed
אל	to God	10:1		Exod. 18:19
ל	to God	4:10		Exod. 19:3, 21, 22, 24 Exod. 34:2
לקראת	to meet God			Exod. 19:17
את/עם	by/with God	5:31		Exod. 33:21 Exod. 34:28
לפני[a]	before God	1:45 4:10 9:18, 25 12:7, 12, 18 (2x) 14:23, 26 15:20 16:11 18:7 19:17 26:5, 10 (2x), 13	10:8 27:7 29:9, 14[b]	Exod. 34:34 Num. 32:20, 21, 22 (2x)
...בין...ובין	between God and...	5:5		

Anthropomorphisms

Hebrew	English	Discussed	Other	Discussed
פנים	Presence/face		4:37	Exod. 33:14, 15, 20, 23
כף	hand			Exod. 33:22, 23
אחר	back			Exod. 33:23

Adverbial

Hebrew	English	Discussed	Other	Discussed
מזה	hence	9:12		Exod. 33:1
פנים אל־פנים	face to face	5:4[c]		Exod. 33:11
עין בעין	face to face			Num. 14:14

[a] Excluding metaphorical instances (6:25?; 24:4, 13).

[b] EVV 29:10, 15.

[c] פנים בפנים. See above, p. 77 n. 126.

הלך.[15] Moreover, if attention is directed only to those passages from Exodus/Numbers which are deemed to be "comparable" (Table 7.3),[16] then most of the divine Presence terminology which they employ is represented *somewhere* in Deuteronomy, whether in the synoptic passages or elsewhere, with the notable exception of ירד.[17]

IMPLICATIONS

DIVINE PRESENCE

In trying to assess whether Deuteronomy is playing down YHWH's earthly Presence in the service of a conscious theology of transcendence, the question cannot be whether it has a lesser emphasis on divine Presence than have other OT books, since for some of these latter the subject of divine Presence is a major preoccupation.[18] Rather, the question is whether Deuteronomy refers to divine Presence in contexts where it might reasonably be expected to do so if its author(s) had no particular objection to the notion. If it *does*, then he (they) presumably did not object to it, but if it does *not*, then there may be a case for saying that he (they) had some aversion to the idea. Now, in specifying only those pas-

---

[15] In this connection, it is difficult to see what evidence Clements (1965) could adduce for his view regarding "[t]he older ideas of Yahweh's accompanying presence… found in Deuteronomic material", i.e. that "it is with the doctrine of Yahweh's name set in Israel's sanctuary that the Deuteronomic interpretation of this belief is given" (p. 94 n. 4; see above, p. 10). As he himself hints, the historical sections of Deuteronomy contain no reference either to the divine Name, i.e. as understood by Name Theology, or to YHWH himself being in heaven. The only possible exception is 4:39, but this follows 4:36 which, as we have seen, represents YHWH as being both in heaven *and* on earth, and so could hardly be cited in support.

[16] See below, pp. 211-212.

[17] And also לקראת, except that the passage in which it occurs (Exod. 19:17) is paralleled in Deut. 4:10aβ-11, though a different expression is used there.

[18] Some scholars regard divine Presence as a or even *the* overriding theme of the book of Exodus: Durham: "The centerpiece of [the book's theological] unity is the theology of Yahweh present with and in the midst of his people Israel. Throughout the Book of Exodus…this theme is constantly in evidence, serving as a theological anchor and also as a kind of compass indicating the directions in which the book is to go" (p. xxi), Cole: "[T]he 'theology of the presence'…is a recurrent note throughout the entire book of Exodus" (p. 39), Davies (1962a): "[T]hrough the rich diversity there is one theme which appears persistently throughout the book, the theme of the Presence of Yahweh…this theme confers upon the diversity of the book its fundamental yet manifest unity" (p. 21); cf. Zenger (1978): "Nicht Israel ist das Thema dieser Geschichten, sondern Jahwe, der 'Er ist da bei uns'" (p. 20).

sages where divine Presence might reasonably be expected to occur, we
are restricting ourselves to the kind of synoptic approach employed in
chapters 2-4, in which Deuteronomy's view of divine Presence is determined by comparing passages with parallel accounts (in our case from
Exodus and Numbers) which *themselves* refer to divine Presence. Deu-
teronom(ist)ic passages which do not have such parallel material and
which lack references to divine Presence can contribute little to our investigation, since there is no way of knowing whether they might have
included the subject or not. This means that the data most pertinent to the
question whether YHWH's Presence has been played down (or even
eliminated) in the historical sections of Deuteronomy is that recorded in
Table 7.3. The eleven passages in Exodus/Numbers with no real parallels
in Deuteronomy can be set aside, since there is no way of knowing
whether the latter would have mentioned divine Presence had its concerns been the same as those of the tetrateuchal passages.

In the light of these observations a number of conclusions can be
drawn from the results outlined above. First, inspection of the deuterono-
m(ist)ic "comparable" (Table 7.3) and other (Deut. 1:33, 45, 4:10aα,
5:31) passages shows that the affirmation of divine Presence is a clear
feature of some at least of the historical sections of Deuteronomy. Secondly, Table 7.3 also shows that, where comparison *can* be made, reference to YHWH's earthly Presence has been neither eliminated nor
systematically reduced. In relation to Exodus/Numbers the deuterono-
m(ist)ic allusions to divine Presence are parallel in five instances, heightened in six, and absent in only two. Thirdly, this affirmation of divine
Presence in the historical sections of Deuteronomy finds support in the
legal section of the book. If it be granted that in chs. 12-26 לפני יהוה generally refers to the localized Presence of YHWH, then the majority of
allusions to the divine whereabouts locate him at the "chosen place", i.e.
on earth rather than in heaven. Fourthly, there is no evidence of any
weakening in Deuteronomy of the way in which the divine Presence is
expressed. A variety of terms is employed (Table 7.2). It includes references both to YHWH[19] being (אין, היה) in proximity to people, moving
(עבר, הלך, בוא) about the land, or speaking from (מתוך) an earthly site, and
to human beings acting in relation to (עם, לפני, אל/ל) him. Moreover, the

---

[19] As subject.

Table 7.3: Comparable passages in Deuteronomy and the Tetrateuch

Divine Presence in Deuteronomy paralleled in the Tetrateuch

"Do not be in dread or afraid of them. The LORD your God *who goes before you will himself fight for you...*" (Deut. 1:29-30)	"[D]o not fear the people of the land... the LORD is *with us*; do not fear them." (Num. 14:9)
"[T]he LORD said to me, 'Say to them, Do not go up or fight, for I am not *among you*; lest you be defeated before your enemies.'" (Deut. 1:42)	Moses said, "...Do not go up lest you be struck down before your enemies, for the LORD is not *among you*...you shall fall by the sword...the LORD will not be *with you*." (Num. 14:41-43)
"[T]he LORD said to me, '*Gather the people to me...*' And you came near and stood at the foot of the mountain..." (Deut. 4:10-11)	Moses brought the people out of the camp to *meet God*; and they took their stand at the foot of the mountain. (Exod. 19:17)
"I lay prostrate *before the LORD*...forty days and forty nights; I neither ate bread nor drank water..." (Deut. 9:18)	[Moses] was there *with the LORD* forty days and forty nights; he neither ate bread nor drank water. (Exod. 34:28a)
"[T]he LORD said to me, 'Hew two tables of stone like the first, and *come up to me* on the mountain'..." (Deut. 10:1)	The LORD said to Moses, "Cut two tables of stone like the first...and come up...to Mount Sinai, and *present yourself there to me* on the top of the mountain." (Exod. 34:1-2)

Divine Presence in Deuteronomy not paralleled in the Tetrateuch

"The LORD spoke with you *face to face...out of the midst of the fire*, while I stood *between the LORD and you* at that time...He said..." (Deut. 5:4-5; cf. 4:12; 5:22)	God spoke all these words, saying... (Exod. 20:1)
"[W]hen you heard the voice *out of the midst of the darkness*, while the mountain was burning with fire, you came near to me...and you said..." (Deut. 5:23-24)	[W]hen all the people perceived the thunderings and the lightnings and the sound of the trumpet and the mountain smoking, the people were afraid and trembled; and they stood afar off, and said to Moses... (Exod. 20:18-19)

Continued on next page

Table 7.3: *Continued*

"[Y]ou said, '...we have heard [the LORD's] voice *out of the midst of the fire*...if we hear the voice of the LORD...any more, we shall die. For who is there...that has heard the voice of the living God speaking *out of the midst of fire,* as we have, and has still lived? Go near, and hear all that the LORD...will say; and speak to us all that the LORD...will speak to you; and we will hear...'" (Deut. 5:24-27)

[The people] said to Moses, "You speak to us, and we will hear; but let not God speak to us, lest we die." (Exod. 20:19)

"[T]he LORD gave me the two tables of stone written with the finger of God; and on them were all the words which the LORD had spoken with you...*out of the midst of the fire...*" (Deut. 9:10, cf. 10:4)

[The LORD] gave to Moses...the two tables of the testimony, tables of stone, written with the finger of God. (Exod. 31:18, cf. 34:28b)

"[T]he LORD said to me, 'Arise, go down quickly *from here*; for your people whom you have brought from Egypt have acted corruptly...'" (Deut. 9:12)

[T]he LORD said to Moses, "Go down; for your people, whom you brought up out of...Egypt, have corrupted themselves..." (Exod. 32:7)

"I lay prostrate *before the LORD*...And I prayed to the LORD..." (Deut. 9:25-26)

Moses besought the LORD his God, and said... (Exod. 32:11)

Divine Presence in the Tetrateuch not paralleled in Deuteronomy

"I commanded you at that time, saying, 'The LORD your God has given you this land to possess; all your men of valour shall pass over armed before your brethren the people of Israel.'" (Deut. 3:18)

Moses said to them, "If...every armed man of you will pass over the Jordan *before the LORD*, until he has driven out his enemies from before him" (Num. 32:20-21)

"[T]he LORD said to me, 'Gather the people to me, that I may let them hear my words...' And you came near and stood at the foot of the mountain, while the mountain burned with fire to the heart of heaven, wrapped in darkness, cloud, and gloom." (Deut. 4:10-11)

[T]he LORD said to Moses, "Lo, I am *coming* to you *in a thick cloud,* that the people may hear when I speak with you..."
Mount Sinai was wrapped in smoke, because the LORD *descended upon it in fire*; and the smoke of it went up like the smoke of a kiln...And the LORD *came down upon Mount Sinai...* (Exod. 19:9, 18-20a)

varying degrees of directness by which that Presence is expressed (from the mere hint in the use of מזה to the intimacy suggested by both God's speaking פנים בפנים and the instruction "stand here by me") do not seem particularly different from those employed in the comparable passages from Exodus/Numbers. As already observed, the one significant omission is ירד, and this is especially conspicuous as regards Deut. 4:10-11 in which a reference to divine descent could well have provided an additional and striking example of something "which your eyes have seen" (v. 9).[20] However, in view of the other indications of divine Presence scattered throughout Deuteronomy in general and 4:9-14 in particular, the most that could be said is that, like E,[21] the deuteronom(ist)ic author(s) wished to eliminate *that particular type* of expression, in line with its omission from the Deuteronomistic History as a whole.[22] Finally, it should be remembered that in the majority of cases where mention of divine Presence is absent from Deuteronomy (cf. Exod. 18:19, 19:3, 11, etc.) there is no need to posit that the relevant sections were omitted in order to avoid reference to it. Rather, their omission can be explained in terms of the differing interests, unrelated to the question of the divine whereabouts, displayed by the respective accounts. No appeal to a supposed deuteronom(ist)ic emphasis on YHWH's transcendence is necessary.

Our deliberations thus provide no support for the view that Deuteronomy, whether in its historical sections, especially those dealing with the Wilderness wanderings, Holy War or events at Horeb) or in its legal section (particularly where it has to do with the cult), has eliminated the Deity from the earthly sphere.

NAME THEOLOGY

Broadly speaking, most of the deuteronom(ist)ic instances of divine Presence fall into one of two main categories: those which occur in material dealing with events at Horeb/Sinai, whether it be the first giving of the Law (4:10, 12, 15, 33, 36, 5:4, 5, 22, 23, 24, 26, 31) or the incident of the Golden Calf (9:10, 12, 18, 25, 10:1, 4), and those which are found in the context of the Wilderness wanderings or Holy War (1:30, 33, 42, 45,

---

[20] See above, pp. 52-53.
[21] E generally represents God as dwelling on the mountain (see above, p. 3) and so clearly has no aversion to divine Presence as such.
[22] See above, p. 53.

as well as a number of other references cited in Table 7.2 but not discussed in detail).[23] With respect to the first group, it has already been mentioned that, in support of the view that Deuteronomy espouses Name Theology, a number of scholars appeal not only to 26:15,[24] which occurs in the legal section of the book and designates heaven as YHWH's dwelling-place, but also to aspects of the deuteronom(ist)ic version of the first giving of the Law.[25] Some point to certain features of the account,[26] particularly the absence of divine descent, while others refer only to 4:36,[27] to show that, consistent with what is being proposed, YHWH is represented as dwelling in heaven rather than on earth. Such an appeal to the portrayal of the Deity in an *historical* section, in support of a particular view of his relation to the *sanctuary*, clearly presupposes a universally consistent presentation of YHWH and his relationship to the world in Deuteronomy.[28] Indeed, as has already been pointed out, some scholars have referred to a general deuteronom(ist)ic emphasis on divine transcendence in their discussions of Name Theology.[29]

Our analysis, however, has shown that Deuteronomy's presentation of the Horeb material reveals no such emphasis on divine transcendence. On the contrary, its allusions to the divine Presence on the earth are as numerous as those in the Exodus account (i.e. in comparable material). In addition, the appeal to 4:36 as confirming a "relocation"[30] of YHWH in heaven has been shown to be unwarranted.[31] Rather than portraying YHWH as being in heaven and therefore not on the mountain, the verse represents him as being both in heaven *and* on the earth,[32] in accordance

---

[23] 2:7; 4:37; 6:15; 7:21; 9:3; 20:1, 4; 23:15 (EVV 14); 31:3, 6, 8, 23.

[24] Braulik (1986) 98-99, Preuß (1982) 16-17, Weinfeld (1972a) 197-198, Clements (1965) 90 n. 1, Dumermuth 69, 70 n. 60, Bietenhard 255, Schmidt 93, von Rad (1929) 35 n. 1, Westphal 266, Steuernagel (1900) 44, Smend (1893) 281 n. 1.

[25] See above, pp. 14, 89-90.

[26] Mettinger 46, 48, 124-125, Terrien (1978) 201-202, Weinfeld (1972a) 198, 206-208, McBride 2, Clements (1965) 90, Westphal 266 (cf. 65-66); cf. Dus 200.

[27] Preuß (1982) 16-17, Bietenhard 255, Procksch 452, Schmidt 93 (cf. 95), von Rad (1929) 35 n. 1.

[28] See above, p. 11 n. 48.

[29] See above, p. 7 n. 29.

[30] Mettinger 47.

[31] See above, pp. 68-73.

[32] By the same token, the evidence of 26:15 for a completely transcendent Deity would be weakened if it could be shown that יהוה לפני in v. 13 referred to the localized Presence of YHWH at the sanctuary.

with what has been observed elsewhere in the OT. Moreover, the supposed deuteronom(ist)ic emphasis on the auditory (i.e. as opposed to visual) aspects of the event, sometimes cited in support of the idea of relocation, has been shown to be unfounded and therefore insignificant as regards the point at issue.[33]

Other scholars who espouse Name Theology accept that there *is* evidence for divine Presence in Deuteronomy (usually in the context of Holy War).[34] However, while some of these do not relate it to their understanding of the Name in chs. 12-26, there are those who realize that the two themes represent conflicting views of God's relationship to the earthly sphere, and so comment on their inclusion together within the book.[35] Nicholson, for example, remarks:

> Deuteronomy's strong attachment to the ideology of the Holy War would seem to imply that the Ark, so central in this ideology, must have retained some of its older mystique for the Deuteronomic circle. This seems clear from such passages as Deut. vii. 12 [sic] where Yahweh is conceived of as being in the 'midst' of Israel in battle. Nevertheless, it is evident that in actual cultic practice the authors of Deuteronomy have dispensed with the older notion.[36]

Here he distinguishes, in contrast to Mettinger and others,[37] between the portrayal of YHWH in relation to war and in relation to the cult. Our studies have shown, however, that such a distinction cannot be drawn. The use of לפני יהוה in Deut. 12-26 implies that the Deity is present at the "chosen place"[38] as well as on the battlefield. Moreover, the fact that many of the activities carried out there are not seasonal, but occur לפני

---

[33] See above, pp. 89-97.
[34] Particularly von Rad, whose *Deuteronomium-Studien* contains unrelated chapters on both Name Theology and Holy War.
[35] See above, pp. 10-11.
[36] (1967) 73 n. 1. Presumably v. 21 is intended.
[37] See above, p. 214 nn. 26, 27.
[38] The same point has been made by others, though not in any detail. See above, p. 10 n. 43. In this connection, it is curious that several scholars who espouse Name Theology specifically refer to לפני יהוה in other (usually Priestly) contexts as evidence for the divine Presence at the cult, but make no comment on its several occurrences in Deut. 12-26: Weinfeld (1972a), referring to the ministrations of the high priest as prescribed in P: "All these acts are performed 'before the Lord (לפני יהוה)', that is, in his presence" (p. 192), von Rad, quoted above on p. 136 n. 22, and cited by Clements (1965) 118 n. 2; cf. Metzger's comment on 2 Kings 19:15 (p. 139).

יהוה at any time of the year, would appear to imply a more or less continuous Presence at the cult place. Such an understanding is consistent with 23:15 (EVV 14),[39] which, while not specifically referring to the "chosen place", does imply YHWH's continual Presence within the Israelite camp *after* the settlement, i.e. rather than in the more distant past.[40]

It would therefore appear, given that 26:15 also locates God in heaven, and despite affirmations to the contrary,[41] that there is some evidence for saying that in Deuteronomy he is represented, in relation to both Horeb (4:36) and the cult (ch. 26), as being both in heaven *and* on the earth.[42,43]

Thus, the biblical foundation on which discussions of the significance of the divine Name at the "chosen place" have so far been based is shown to be inadequate. Not only do both the historical and the cultic material in Deuteronomy portray YHWH as being present on the earth, but seri-

---

[39] Referred to by Rofé 25, 27, Mayes (1979) 59, Gordon (1974) 118, Wenham (1971) 112, Fretheim (1968a) 7 n. 41, Myers (1961) 26, 28; cf. von Rad (1952) 69-70.

[40] Outside Deut. 12-26 the following deuteronom(ist)ic texts also promise the divine Presence in the land: 6:15; 7:21; 9:3; 31:3, 6, 8 (cf. v. 17).

[41] Mettinger: "[T]he ideas of the Sabaoth theology concerning the presence of God were primarily unitary: heaven and earth were conjoined in the Temple, where God ruled from his throne. Again, the Deuteronomistic theology shattered this unitary conception by emphasizing the transcendence of God...[who] became 'relocated' to the heavens above" (pp. 46-47), Weinfeld (1972a): "The belief of the divine presence in the sanctuary did not...preclude the belief in the Deity's heavenly abode. Israel appears to have shared this dialectical conception of the divine abode...with other peoples of the Ancient East...This dialectical belief, however, is a non-deuteronomic conception and is completely rejected by the deuteronomic school...which regarded heaven as the exclusive place of God's abode" (p. 197 n. 3), Metzger: "Im Unterschied zur Gottesbergvorstellung, derzufolge der Jahwethron vom Zion bis in den Himmel hineinragt und derzufolge im Heiligtum die Grenze zwischen Himmlisch und Irdisch aufgehoben ist, zieht der Deuteronomist eine Grenze zwischen dem von Menschenhand erbauten Tempelgebäude und dem Himmel als Wohnstatt und Thronsitz Jahwes" (p. 150); cf. Clements, quoted above, p. 6 n. 23.

[42] See above, pp. 68-73.

[43] Mayes (1979): "[T]he basic idea [expressed by the Name formulae] is an affirmation of the real and actual presence of Yahweh at the sanctuary; the primary concern is not with the problem of how God can dwell in heaven and at the same time be present with his people" (p. 225); Wenham (1971): "In Deuteronomy 26 the sanctuary is described as the place where Yahweh's name dwells, yet the Israelite worships and speaks 'before the LORD', concluding his worship with a prayer asking God to look down 'from heaven his holy habitation'. It seems that Deuteronomy regards God as present in heaven and in His sanctuary" (p. 113).

ous doubt has also been cast on the two lines of approach (i.e. the appeal to 4:36/26:15 and the presumed deuteronom[ist]ic emphasis on the auditory aspect of the first giving of the law) that argue for his sole localization in heaven.

CONCLUSIONS

Divine Presence is clearly referred to in Deuteronomy. In the historical sections it is expressed in a variety of ways, similar to those found in the comparable sections of Exodus/Numbers, and in some cases without parallel in the tetrateuchal accounts. Many of its occurrences are embedded in material generally regarded as deuteronomistic and so represent the Deuteronomists' own version of Israel's past. Such usage indicates that the Deuteronomists cannot have been committed to the idea of a solely transcendent Deity.[44]

Moreover, although it is difficult to prove conclusively that לפני יהוה in the legal section (chs. 12-26) refers to the proximate Presence of the Deity at the "chosen place", no convincing arguments have been put forward against such an interpretation, while the available evidence tends to support it. The claim that the deuteronomic cult envisages YHWH as being *only* in heaven thus requires modification.

In view of these observations, therefore, the existence in Deuteronomy of a thoroughgoing Name Theology as traditionally defined begins to look unlikely, and the significance of the divine Name in relation to the "chosen place" calls for further investigation.

---

[44] Cf. Fretheim (1968a): "It is clear that the Deuteronomists did not think that the only way that God could be present among his people was by means of his name. Such references to God's presence are found not only in Deuteronomy, but also in the introduction to the Deuteronomistic historical work" (p. 7).

BIBLIOGRAPHY

Ackroyd, P.R.
1971   *The First Book of Samuel*, CBC. Cambridge: Cambridge University Press.
1973   *I and II Chronicles, Ezra, Nehemiah*, TBC. London: SCM.
Albright, W.F.
1950   "The Judicial Reform of Jehoshaphat", *Alexander Marx Jubilee Volume*, ed.
       S. Lieberman. New York: The Jewish Theological Seminary of America,
       61-82.
Allen, L.C.
1990   *Ezekiel 20-48*, WBC 29. Dallas: Word.
Alt, A.
1953   "Die Ursprünge des israelitischen Rechts", Kleine Schriften zur Geschichte
       des Volkes Israel, 1. München: Beck, 278-332.
Amsler, S.
1976   "עמד *ʿmd* stehen", *THAT* 2, 328-332.
Anderson, G.W.
1959   *A Critical Introduction to the Old Testament*. London: Duckworth.
Baldwin, J.G.
1988   *1 and 2 Samuel*, TOTC. Leicester: Inter-Varsity.
Balentine, S.E.
1985   "Prayer in the Wilderness Traditions: In Pursuit of Divine Justice", HAR 9
       (Fs S.D. Goitein), ed. R. Ahroni, 53-74.
1989   "Prayers for Justice in the Old Testament: Theodicy and Theology", *CBQ*
       51, 597-616.
Barr, J.
1959   "Theophany and Anthropomorphism in the Old Testament", VTSup 7.
       Leiden: Brill, 31-38.
Barucq, A.
1968   *Ecclésiaste*, VS. Paris: Beauchesne.
Baudissin, W.W. Graf
1915   "'Gott schauen' in der alttestamentlichen Religion", *ARW* 18, 173-239.

220   *Out of the Midst of the Fire*

Beer, G.
1939   *Exodus*, HAT 3. Tübingen: Mohr-Siebeck.
Benzinger, I.
1901   *Die Bücher der Chronik*, KHC 20. Tübingen: Mohr-Siebeck.
Bertholet, A.
1899   *Deuteronomium*, KHC 5. Freiburg: Mohr-Siebeck.
1901   *Leviticus*, KHC 3. Tübingen: Mohr-Siebeck.
Beyerlin, W.
1961   *Herkunft und Geschichte der ältesten Sinaitraditionen*. Tübingen: Mohr-Siebeck.
Bietenhard, H.
1954   "ὄνομα, ὀνομάζω, ἐπονομάζω, ψευδώνυμος, *TWNT* 5, 242-283.
Binns, L.E.
1927   *The Book of Numbers*, WC. London: Methuen.
Blenkinsopp, J.
1989   *Ezra-Nehemiah*, OTL. London: SCM.
Boling, R.G. and Wright, G.E.
1982   *Joshua*, AB 6. Garden City: Doubleday.
Bonnard, P.-E.
1972   *Le Second Isaïe*, Ebib. Paris: Gabalda.
Braulik, G.
1971   "Spuren einer Neubearbeitung des deuteronomistischen Geschichtswerkes in 1 Kön 8,52-53. 59-60", *Bib* 52, 20-33.
1977   "Weisheit, Gottesnähe und Gesetz - Zum Kerygma von Deuteronomium 4,5-8", *Studien zum Pentateuch* (Fs W. Kornfeld), ed. G. Braulik. Wien: Herder, 165-195.
1981   "Leidensgedächtnisfeier und Freudenfest. 'Volksliturgie' nach dem deuteronomischen Festkalender (Dtn 16,1-17)", *ThPh* 56, 335-357.
1983   "Die Freude des Festes. Das Kultverständnis des Deuteronomium - die älteste biblische Festtheorie", *ThJb*. Leipzig: St. Benno-Verlag, 13-54.
1986   *Deuteronomium 1-16,17*, Die Neue Echter Bibel. Würzburg: Echter Verlag.
Brekelmans, C.H.W.
1963   "Het 'historische Credo' van Israël", *TTh* 3, 1-11.
Bright, J.
1953   The Book of Joshua, *IB* 2, 539-673.
Brockington, L.H.
1962   I and II Samuel, *PCB*, 318-337.
1969   *Ezra, Nehemiah and Esther*, CeB (New Series). London: Nelson.
Brueggemann, W.
1968   "The Kerygma of the Deuteronomistic Historian", *Int* 22, 387-402.
1976   "Presence of God, Cultic", *IDBSup*, 680-683.
1982   *Genesis*, Interpretation. Atlanta: Knox.
Budd, P.J.
1984   *Numbers*, WBC 5. Waco: Word.
Buis, P. and Leclercq, J.
1963   *Le Deutéronome*, SB. Paris: Gabalda.
Burns, R.J.
1983   *Exodus, Leviticus, Numbers, with Excursuses on Feasts/Ritual and Typology*, OTM 3. Wilmington: Glazier.

Butler, T.C.
1983   *Joshua*, WBC 7. Waco: Word.
Caird, G.B.
1953   The First and Second Books of Samuel, *IB* 2, 853-1176.
Cairns, I.
1992   *Word and Presence: A Commentary on the Book of Deuteronomy*, ITC. Grand Rapids: Eerdmans.
Carley, K.W.
1974   *The Book of the Prophet Ezekiel*, CBC. Cambridge: Cambridge University Press.
Carmichael, C.M.
1969   "A New View of the Origin of the Deuteronomic Credo", *VT* 19, 273-289.
1974   *The Laws of Deuteronomy*. Ithaca: Cornell University Press.
Carroll, R.P.
1977   "The Aniconic God and the Cult of Images", *ST* 31, 51-64.
Cassuto, U.
1967   *A Commentary on the Book of Exodus*. Jerusalem: Magnes.
Cazelles, H.
1948   "Sur un Rituel du Deutéronome (*Deut.* XXVI, 14)", *RB* 55, 54-71.
1966   *Le Deutéronome*, SB(J). Paris: Cerf.
1967   "Passages in the Singular within Discourse in the Plural of Dt 1-4", *CBQ* 29, 207-219.
Childs, B.S.
1960   *Myth and Reality in the Old Testament*, SBT 27. London: SCM.
1974   *Exodus*, OTL. London: SCM.
Christensen, D.L.
1991   *Deuteronomy 1-11*, WBC 6A. Dallas: Word.
Clamer, A.
1940   Le Deutéronome, *SB(PC)* 2. Paris: Letouzey et Ané.
Clements, R.E.
1965   *God and Temple*. Oxford: Blackwell.
1968   *God's Chosen People*. London: SCM.
1972   *Exodus*, CBC. Cambridge: Cambridge University Press.
1978   *Old Testament Theology: A Fresh Approach*. London: Marshall, Morgan & Scott.
1989   *Deuteronomy*, Old Testament Guides. Sheffield: JSOT.
Clifford, R.J.
1972   *The Cosmic Mountain in Canaan and the Old Testament*, HSM 4. Cambridge (Mass.): Harvard University Press.
1982   *Deuteronomy, with an Excursus on Covenant and Law*, OTM 4. Wilmington: Glazier.
Coats, G.W.
1968   *Rebellion in the Wilderness*. Nashville: Abingdon.
Cody, A.
1984   *Ezekiel, with an Excursus on Old Testament Priesthood*, OTM 11. Wilmington: Glazier.
Cogan, M. and Tadmor, H.
1988   *II Kings*, AB 11. Garden City: Doubleday.

Coggins, R.J.
1976   *The First and Second Books of the Chronicles*, CBC. Cambridge: Cambridge University Press.
Cohn, R.L.
1981   *The Shape of Sacred Space: Four Biblical Studies*, AARSR 23. Chico: Scholars Press.
Cole, R.A.
1973   *Exodus*, TOTC. London: Tyndale.
Cooke, G.A.
1936   *A Critical and Exegetical Commentary on the Book of Ezekiel*, ICC. Edinburgh: T. & T. Clark.
Cornill, C.H.
²1892   *Einleitung in das Alte Testament*, GThW 2.1. Freiburg: Mohr-Siebeck.
Corvin, J.W.
1972   "A Stylistic and Functional Study of the Prose Prayers in the Historical Narratives of the Old Testament" (PhD. Diss.). Emory.
Craigie, P.C.
1969   "'Yahweh is a Man of Wars'", *SJT* 22, 183-188.
1976   *The Book of Deuteronomy*, NICOT. Grand Rapids: Eerdmans.
Crenshaw, J.L.
1988   *Ecclesiastes*, OTL. London: SCM.
Cross, F.M.
1973   *Canaanite Myth and Hebrew Epic: Essays in the History of the Religion of Israel*. Cambridge (Mass.): Harvard University Press.
Cundall, A.E.
1968   *Judges*, TOTC. London: Tyndale.
Cunliffe-Jones, H.
1951   *Deuteronomy*, TBC. London: SCM.
Curtis, E.L. and Madsen, A.A.
1910   *A Critical and Exegetical Commentary on the Books of Chronicles*, ICC. Edinburgh: T. & T. Clark.
Curtis, E.M.
1985   "The Theological Basis for the Prohibition of Images in the Old Testament", *JETS* 28, 277-287.
Davies, G.H.
1942   "The Presence of God in Israel", *Studies in History and Religion* (Fs H.W. Robinson), ed. E.A. Payne. London: Lutterworth, 11-29.
1962a Deuteronomy, *PCB*, 269-284.
1962b "Presence of God", *IDB* 3, 874-875.
1962c "Tabernacle", *IDB* 4, 498-506.
1967   *Exodus*, TBC. London: SCM.
Dhorme, P.
1910   *Les Livres de Samuel*, Ebib. Paris: Gabalda.
1921   "L'emploi métaphorique des noms de parties du corps en hébreu et en akkadien. III. Le visage", *RB* 30, 374-399.
Dietrich, W.
1972   *Prophetie und Geschichte: Eine redaktionsgeschichtliche Untersuchung zum deuteronomistischen Geschichtswerk*, FRLANT 108. Göttingen: Vandenhoeck & Ruprecht.

Dillard, R.B.
1987   *2 Chronicles*, WBC 15. Waco: Word.
Dillmann, A.
1886   *Die Bücher Numeri, Deuteronomium und Josua*, KEH. Leipzig: Hirzel.
Driver, S.R.
[3]1902 *A Critical and Exegetical Commentary on Deuteronomy*, ICC. Edinburgh: T. & T. Clark.
1911   *The Book of Exodus*, CBSC. Cambridge: Cambridge University Press.
[9]1913 *An Introduction to the Literature of the Old Testament*, ITL. Edinburgh: T. & T. Clark.
Dumermuth, F.
1958   "Zur deuteronomischen Kulttheologie und ihren Voraussetzungen," *ZAW* 70, 59-98.
Durham, J.I.
1987   *Exodus*, WBC 3. Waco: Word.
Dus, J.
1964   "Der ferne Gott und das nahe Gebot (Eine Studie zum Deuteronomium)", *CV* 7, 193-200.
Eaton, M.A.
1983   *Ecclesiastes*, TOTC. Leicester: Inter-Varsity.
Eichrodt, W.
1933   *Theologie des Alten Testaments*, 1: *Gott und Volk*. Leipzig: Hinrichs.
1935   *Theologie des Alten Testaments, 2: Gott und Welt*. Leipzig: Hinrichs.
1939   *Theologie des Alten Testaments*, 3: *Gott und Mensch*. Leipzig: Hinrichs.
1966   *Der Prophet Hesekiel*, ATD 22. Göttingen: Vandenhoeck & Ruprecht.
Eißfeldt, O.
1922   *Hexateuch-Synopse: Die Erzählung der fünf Bücher Mose und des Buches Josua mit dem Anfange des Richterbuches*. Leipzig: Hinrichs.
1934   *Einleitung in das Alte Testament*, NTG. Tübingen: Mohr-Siebeck.
Eliade, M.
[2]1949 *Le Mythe de l'éternel retour: archétypes et répétition*. Paris: Gallimard.
Fensham, F.C.
1959   "New Light on Exodus 21 6 and 22 7 from the Laws of Eshnunna", *JBL* 78, 160-161.
1982   *The Books of Ezra and Nehemiah*, NICOT. Grand Rapids: Eerdmans.
Fisch, S.
1950   *Ezekiel*, SBBS. London: Soncino.
Fohrer, G.
1964   *Das Buch Jesaja*, 3: *Kapitel 40-66*, ZBK. Stuttgart: Zwingli.
[10]1965 *Einleitung in das Alte Testament*. Heidelberg: Quelle & Meyer.
Fowler, M.D.
1987   "The Meaning of *lipnê* YHWH in the Old Testament", *ZAW* 99, 384-390.
Fredriksson, H.
1945   *Jahwe als Krieger*. Lund: Gleerup.
Fretheim, T.E.
1968a   "The Ark in Deuteronomy", *CBQ* 30, 1-14.
1968b   "The Priestly Document: anti-temple?", *VT* 18, 313-329.
1983   *Deuteronomic History*, Interpreting Biblical Texts. Nashville: Abingdon.
1984   *The Suffering of God*, OBT 14. Philadelphia: Fortress.

Friedman, R.E.
1981 "From Egypt to Egypt: Dtr[1] and Dtr[2]", *Traditions in Transformation* (Fs F.M. Cross), eds. B. Halpern and J.D. Levenson. Winona Lake: Eisenbrauns, 167-192.

Fritz, V.
1970 *Israel in der Wüste: Traditionsgeschichtliche Untersuchung der Wüstenüberlieferung des Jahwisten*, MThSt 7. Marburg: Elwert.

Fuhs, H.F.
1988 *Ezechiel II: 25-48*, Die Neue Echter Bibel. Würzburg: Echter Verlag.

Gese, H.
1975 "Der Name Gottes im Alten Testament", *Der Name Gottes*, ed. H. von Stietencron. Düsseldorf: Patmos-Verlag, 75-89.

Giesebrecht, F.
1901 *Die alttestamentliche Schätzung des Gottesnamens und ihre religionsgeschichtliche Grundlage*. Königsberg: Thomas & Oppermann.

Gispen, W.H.
1982 *Exodus*, Bible Student's Commentary. Grand Rapids: Zondervan.

Goettsberger, J.
1939 *Die Bücher der Chronik oder Paralipomenon*, HSAT 4.1. Bonn: Hanstein.

Gordon, R.P.
1974 "Deuteronomy and the Deuteronomic School", *TynBul* 25, 113-120.
1986 *1 & 2 Samuel*. Exeter: Paternoster.

Görg, M.
1967 *Das Zelt der Begegnung*, BBB 27. Bonn: Hanstein.
1980 "'Ich bin mit Dir'. Gewicht und Anspruch einer Redeform im Alten Testament", *TGl* 70, 214-240.

Gray, G.B.
1903 *A Critical and Exegetical Commentary on Numbers*, ICC. Edinburgh: T. & T. Clark.
1913 *A Critical Introduction to the Old Testament*. London: Duckworth.

Gray, J.
[2]1970 *I and II Kings*, OTL. London: SCM.
[2]1986 *Joshua, Judges, Ruth*, NCB. Basingstoke: Marshall, Morgan & Scott.

Greenstone, J.H.
1948 *Numbers*. Philadelphia: The Jewish Publication Society of America.

Grether, O.
1934 *Name und Wort Gottes im Alten Testament*, BZAW 64. Gießen: Töpelmann.

Gulin, E.G.
1923 *Das Antlitz Jahwes im Alten Testament*, STAT Ser. B 17.3. Helsinki: Suomalainen Tiedeakatemia.

Habel, N.C.
1985 *The Book of Job*, OTL. London: SCM.

Hahn, J.
1981 *Das "Goldene Kalb"*, EHS.T 154. Frankfurt am Main: Peter Lang.

Haran, M.
1978 *Temples and Temple-Service in Ancient Israel*. Oxford: Oxford University Press.

Hartley, J.E.
1988 *The Book of Job*, NICOT. Grand Rapids: Eerdmans.

Heinisch, P.
1923 *Das Buch Ezechiel*, HSAT 8.1. Bonn: Hanstein.
1934 *Das Buch Exodus*, HSAT 1.2. Bonn: Hanstein.
1935 *Das Buch Leviticus*, HSAT 1.3. Bonn: Hanstein.
1936 *Das Buch Numeri*, HSAT 2.1. Bonn: Hanstein.
Hempel, J.
1926 *Gott und Mensch im Alten Testament*, BWANT 38. Stuttgart: Kohlhammer.
Hendel, R.S.
1988 "The Social Origins of the Aniconic Tradition in Early Israel", *CBQ* 50, 365-382.
Hertzberg, H.W.
[2]1959 *Die Bücher Josua, Richter, Ruth*, ATD 9. Göttingen: Vandenhoeck & Ruprecht.
[3]1965 *Die Samuelbücher*, ATD 10. Göttingen: Vandenhoeck & Ruprecht.
Hoffmann, D.
1913 *Das Buch Deuteronomium*, 1: *Deut. I-XXI,9*. Berlin: Poppelauer.
Holmgren, F.C.
1987 *Israel Alive Again: A Commentary on the Books of Ezra and Nehemiah*, ITC. Grand Rapids: Eerdmans.
Hölscher, G.
1922 "Komposition und Ursprung des Deuteronomiums", *ZAW* 40, 161-255.
1952 *Das Buch Hiob*, HAT 1.17. Tübingen: Mohr-Siebeck.
Holzinger, H.
1893 *Einleitung in den Hexateuch*. Freiburg: Mohr-Siebeck.
1900 *Exodus*, KHC 2. Tübingen: Mohr-Siebeck.
1903 *Numeri*, KHC 4. Tübingen: Mohr-Siebeck.
Horst, F.
1968 *Hiob*, BKAT 16.1. Neukirchen-Vluyn: Neukirchener Verlag.
Hossfeld, F.-L.
1982 *Der Dekalog*, OBO 45. Freiburg: Universitätsverlag.
Hyatt, J.P.
1970 "Were There an Ancient Historical Credo in Israel and an Independent Sinai Tradition?", *Translating and Understanding the Old Testament* (Fs H.G. May), eds. H.T. Frank and W.L. Reed. Nashville: Abingdon, 152-170.
1971 *Exodus*, NCB. London: Oliphants.
Jacob, B.
1903 *Im Namen Gottes: Eine sprachliche und religionsgeschichtliche Untersuchung zum Alten und Neuen Testament*. Berlin: Calvary.
Jacob, E.
[2]1968 *Théologie de l'Ancien Testament*. Neuchâtel: Delachaux et Niestlé.
Janowski, B.
1982 *Sühne als Heilsgeschehen*, WMANT 55. Neukirchen-Vluyn: Neukirchener Verlag.
1987 "Ich will in eurer Mitte wohnen", *JBTh* 2, 165-193.
Jenni, E.
1970 "'Kommen' im theologischen Sprachgebrauch des Alten Testaments", *Wort-Gebot-Glaube* (Fs W. Eichrodt), eds. H.-J. Stoebe, J.J. Stamm und E. Jenni. Zürich: Zwingli, 251-261.
1971 "בוא *bōʾ* kommen", *THAT* 1, 264-269.

Jepsen, A.
1927   *Untersuchungen zum Bundesbuch*, BWANT 41. Stuttgart: Kohlhammer.
Jeremias, J.
1965   *Theophanie: Die Geschichte einer alttestamentlichen Gattung*, WMANT 10. Neukirchen-Vluyn: Neukirchener Verlag.
1976   "Theophany in the OT", IDBSup, 896-898.
Johnson, A.R.
1947   "Aspects of the use of the term פָּנִים in the Old Testament" (Fs O. Eißfeldt), ed. J. Fück. Halle an der Saale: Niemeyer, 155-159.
²1961   *The One and the Many in the Israelite Conception of God*. Cardiff: University of Wales Press.
Jones, G.H.
1975   "'Holy War' or 'Yahweh War'?", *VT* 25, 642-658.
1984   *1 and 2 Kings*, 1, NCB. London: Marshall, Morgan & Scott.
Junker, H.
1933   *Das Buch Deuteronomium*, HSAT 2.2. Bonn: Hanstein.
Kaiser, O.
⁵1984   *Einleitung in das Alte Testament*. Gütersloh: Mohn.
Keil, C.F.
1862   *Biblischer Commentar über die Bücher Mose's*, 2: *Leviticus, Numeri und Deuteronomium*. Leipzig: Dörffling und Franke.
Kennedy, A.R.S.
n.d.   *Leviticus and Numbers*. CeB. Edinburgh: T.C. & E.C. Jack.
Ketter, P.
1953   *Die Königsbücher*, HBK 3.2. Freiburg: Herder.
Kidner, D.
1967   *Genesis*, TOTC. London: Tyndale.
Kissane, E.J.
1943   *The Book of Isaiah*, 2: *XL-LXVI*. Dublin: Browne and Nolan.
Klein, M.L.
1979   "The Preposition קְדָם ('before'). A Pseudo-Anti-Anthropomorphism in the Targums", *JTS* (New Series) 30, 502-507.
Klein, R.W.
1983   *1 Samuel*, WBC 10. Waco: Word.
Knapp, D.
1987   *Deuteronomium 4: Literarische Analyse und theologische Interpretation*, GTA 35. Göttingen: Vandenhoeck & Ruprecht.
Knierim, R.
1961   "Exodus 18 und die Neuordnung der mosaischen Gerichtsbarkeit", *ZAW* 73, 146-171.
Knight, G.A.F.
1976   *Theology as Narration: A Commentary on the Book of Exodus*. Edinburgh: Handsel .
Knudtzon, J.A.
1915   *Die El-Amarna-Tafeln*, 1: *Die Texte*. Leipzig: Hinrichs.
Koch, K.
1959   *Die Priesterschrift von Exodus 25 bis Leviticus 16*, FRLANT 71. Göttingen: Vandenhoeck & Ruprecht.

Kornfeld, W.
1983   *Levitikus*, Die Neue Echter Bibel. Würzburg: Echter Verlag.

Kraus, H.-J.
²1962   *Gottesdienst in Israel. Grundriß einer Geschichte des alttestamentlichen Gottesdienstes*. München: Kaiser.

Kuhn, T.S.
²1970   *The Structure of Scientific Revolutions*, IEUS 2.2. Chicago: University of Chicago Press.

Kuntz, J.K.
1967   *The Self-revelation of God*. Philadelphia: Westminster.

Kuschke, A.
1952   "Die Lagervorstellung der priesterschriftlichen Erzählung", *ZAW* 63, 74-105.

Leupold, H.C.
1952   *Exposition of Ecclesiastes*. Welwyn: Evangelical Press.
1953   *Exposition of Genesis*, 2: *Chapters 20-50*. Grand Rapids: Baker.

Levenson, J.D.
1975   "Who inserted the Book of the Torah?", *HTR* 68, 203-233.
1985   *Sinai and Zion: An Entry into the Jewish Bible*. Minneapolis: Winston.

Levine, B.A.
1968   "On the Presence of God in Biblical Religion", *Religions in Antiquity* (Fs E.R. Goodenough), ed. J. Neusner, SHR 14. Leiden: Brill, 71-87.

L'Hour, J.
1963   "Une législation criminelle dans le Deutéronome", *Bib* 44, 1-28.

Lind, M.C.
1980   *Yahweh is a Warrior*. Scottdale: Herald.

Lindblom, J.
1961   "Theophanies in Holy Places in Hebrew Religion", *HUCA* 32, 91-106.

Loader, J.A.
1986   *Ecclesiastes: A Practical Commentary*, Text and Interpretation. Grand Rapids: Eerdmans.

Lohfink, N.
1960a   "Darstellungskunst und Theologie in Dtn 1,6-3,29", *Bib* 41, 105-134.
1960b   "Wie stellt sich das Problem Individuum - Gemeinschaft in Deuteronomium 1,6-3,29?" *Schol* 35, 403-407.
1963   *Das Hauptgebot: Eine Untersuchung literarischer Einleitungsfragen zu Dtn 5-11*, AnBib 20. Roma: Pontificio Instituto Biblico.
1965   *Höre, Israel! Auslegung von Texten aus dem Buch Deuteronomium*, WB 18. Düsseldorf: Patmos-Verlag.
1971   "Zum 'kleinen geschichtlichen Credo' Dtn 26, 5-9", *ThPh* 46, 19-39.
1980   *Kohelet*, Die Neue Echter Bibel. Stuttgart: Echter Verlag.
1984   "Zur deuteronomischen Zentralisationsformel", *Bib* 65, 297-329.

Lowth, R.
¹⁷1868   *Isaiah: A New Translation*. London: Tegg.

Macholz, G.C.
1972   "Zur Geschichte der Justizorganisation in Juda", *ZAW* 84, 314-340.

Maclear, G.F.
1878   *The Book of Joshua*, CBSC. Cambridge: Cambridge University Press.

Maher, M.
1982   *Genesis*, OTM 2. Wilmington: Glazier.
Maier, J.
1965   *Das Altisraelitische Ladeheiligtum*, BZAW 93. Berlin: Töpelmann.
Maly, E.H.
1981   "'...The Highest Heavens Cannot Contain You...' (2 [sic] Kgs 8,27):
        Immanence and Transcendence in the Deuteronomist", *Standing before God*
        (Fs J.M. Oesterreicher), eds. A. Finkel and L. Frizzel. New York: Ktav, 23-
        30.
Mann, T.W.
1977   *Divine Presence and Guidance in Israelite Traditions: The Typology of
        Exaltation*, JHNES. Baltimore: Johns Hopkins University Press.
Martin, J.D.
1975   *The Book of Judges*, CBC. Cambridge: Cambridge University Press.
Martin, W.J.
1969   "'Dischronologized' Narrative in the Old Testament", VTSup 17. Leiden:
        Brill, 179-186.
Mauchline, J.
1971   *1 and 2 Samuel*, NCB. London: Oliphants.
Mayes, A.D.H.
1979   *Deuteronomy*, NCB. London: Oliphants.
1980   "Deuteronomy 5 and the Decalogue", *PIBA* 4, 68-83.
1983   *The Story of Israel between Settlement and Exile*. London: SCM.
McBride, S.D.
1969   "The Deuteronomic Name Theology" (PhD. Diss.). Harvard.
McCarter, P.K., Jr.
1980   *I Samuel*, AB 8. Garden City: Doubleday.
1984   *II Samuel*, AB 9. Garden City: Doubleday.
McConville, J.G.
1979   "God's 'Name' and God's 'Glory'", *TynBul* 30, 149-163.
1984   *Law and Theology in Deuteronomy*, JSOTSup 33. Sheffield: JSOT.
McCurley, F.R., Jr.
1974   "The Home of Deuteronomy Revisited: A Methodological Analysis of the
        Northern Theory", *A Light unto My Path* (Fs J.M. Myers), eds. H.N. Bream,
        R.D. Heim and C.A. Moore. Philadelphia: Temple University Press, 295-
        317.
McKane, W.
1963   *I and II Samuel*, TBC. London: SCM.
McKenzie, J.L.
1968   *Second Isaiah*, AB 20. Garden City: Doubleday.
McNeile, A.H.
1908   *The Book of Exodus*, WC. London: Methuen.
1911   *The Book of Numbers*, CBSC. Cambridge: Cambridge University Press.
Mendenhall, G.E.
1973a   "The Mask of Yahweh", *The Tenth Generation*. Baltimore: Johns Hopkins
        University Press, 32-66.
1973b   "Toward a Biography of God: Religion and Politics as Reciprocals", *The
        Tenth Generation*. Baltimore: Johns Hopkins University Press, 198-214.

Merendino, R.P.
1969   *Das deuteronomische Gesetz. Ein literarkritische gattungs- und überliefe-rungsgeschichtliche Untersuchung zu Dt 12-26*, BBB 31. Bonn: Hanstein.
Mettinger, T.N.D.
1982   *The Dethronement of Sabaoth: Studies in the Shem and Kabod Theologies*, ConBOT 18. Lund: Gleerup.
Metzger, M.
1970   "Himmlische und irdische Wohnstatt Jahwes", *UF* 2, 139-158.
Michaeli, F.
1967   *Les Livres des Chroniques, d'Esdras et de Néhémie*, CAT 16. Neuchâtel: Delachaux et Niestlé.
1974   *Le Livre de L'Exode*, CAT 2. Neuchâtel: Delachaux et Niestlé.
Milgrom, J.
1976   *Cult and Conscience: The Asham and the Priestly Doctrine of Repentance*, SJLA 18. Leiden: Brill.
Miller, J.M. and Tucker, G.M.
1974   *The Book of Joshua*, CBC. Cambridge: Cambridge University Press.
Miller, P.D.
1969   "The Gift of God: The Deuteronomic Theology of the Land", *Int* 23, 451-465.
1973   *The Divine Warrior in Early Israel*, HSM 5. Cambridge (Mass.): Harvard University Press.
Mittmann, S.
1975   *Deuteronomium 1₁-6₃ literarkritisch und traditionsgeschichtlich unter-sucht*, BZAW 139. Berlin: de Gruyter.
Moberly, R.W.L.
1983   *At the Mountain of God: Story and Theology in Exodus 32-34*, JSOTSup 22. Sheffield: JSOT.
Morgenstern, J.
1911   "Biblical Theophanies", *ZA* 25, 139-193.
1918   "The Tent of Meeting", *JAOS* 38, 125-139.
Myers, J.M.
1961   "The Requisites for Response: On the Theology of Deuteronomy", *Int* 15, 14-31.
1965a *I Chronicles*, AB 12. Garden City: Doubleday.
1965b *II Chronicles*, AB 13. Garden City: Doubleday.
Nelson, R.D.
1981   *The Double Redaction of the Deuteronomistic History*, JSOTSup 18. Shef-field: JSOT.
Newman, M.L., Jr.
1962   *The People of the Covenant: A Study of Israel from Moses to the Monarchy*. New York: Abingdon.
Nicholson, E.W.
1967   *Deuteronomy and Tradition*. Oxford: Blackwell.
1973   *Exodus and Sinai in History and Tradition*. Oxford: Blackwell.
1974   "The interpretation of Exodus xxiv 9-11", *VT* 24, 77-97.
1977   "The Decalogue as the direct address of God", *VT* 27, 422-433.
Noth, M.
³1948   *Überlieferungsgeschichte des Pentateuch*. Stuttgart: Kohlhammer.

1959 *Das zweite Buch Mose: Exodus*, ATD 5. Göttingen: Vandenhoeck & Ruprecht.
1962 *Das dritte Buch Mose: Leviticus*, ATD 6. Göttingen: Vandenhoeck & Ruprecht.
1966 *Das vierte Buch Mose: Numeri*, ATD 7. Göttingen: Vandenhoeck & Ruprecht.
³1967 *Überlieferungsgeschichtliche Studien.* Tübingen: Niemeyer.
³1971 *Das Buch Josua*, HAT 7. Tübingen: Mohr-Siebeck.
Nötscher, F.
1924 *"Das Angesicht Gottes schauen" nach biblischer und babylonischer Auffassung.* Würzburg: Wissenschaftliche Buchgesellschaft.
O'Brien, M.A.
1989 *The Deuteronomistic History Hypothesis: A Reassessment*, OBO 92. Freiburg: Universitätsverlag.
Oesterley, W.O.E. and Robinson, T.H.
1934 *An Introduction to the Books of the Old Testament.* London: SPCK.
Ogden, G.
1987 *Qoheleth,* Readings - A New Biblical Commentary. Sheffield: JSOT.
1992 "Idem per Idem: Its Use and Meaning", *JSOT* 53, 107-120.
Patrick, D.
1986 *Old Testament Law.* London: SCM.
Paul, S.M.
1970 *Studies in the Book of the Covenant in the Light of Cuneiform and Biblical Law*, VTSup 18. Leiden: Brill.
Peckham, B.
1975 "The Composition of Deuteronomy 9:1-10:11", *Word and Spirit* (Fs D.M. Stanley), ed. J. Plevnik. Willowdale: Regis College Press, 3-59.
Perlitt, L.
1969 *Bundestheologie im Alten Testament*, WMANT 36. Neukirchen-Vluyn: Neukirchener Verlag.
Phillips, A.
1970 *Ancient Israel's Criminal Law: A New Approach to The Decalogue.* Oxford: Blackwell.
1973 *Deuteronomy*, CBC. Cambridge: Cambridge University Press.
Phythian-Adams, W.J.
1934 *The Call of Israel: An Introduction to the Study of Divine Election.* London: Oxford University Press.
1942 *The People and the Presence: A Study of the At-one-ment.* London: Oxford University Press.
Pieper, A.
1979 *Isaiah II: An Exposition of Isaiah 40-66.* Milwaukee: Northwestern.
Polzin, R.
1980 *Moses and the Deuteronomist: A Literary Study of the Deuteronomic History*, 1: *Deuteronomy, Joshua, Judges.* New York: Seabury.
Porter, J.R.
1976 *Leviticus*, CBC. Cambridge: Cambridge University Press.
Preuß, H.D.
1968 "'...ich will mit dir sein!'", *ZAW* 80, 139-173.
1973 "בוֹא", *TWAT* 1, 536-568.

1982   *Deuteronomium*, ErFor 164. Darmstadt: Wissenschaftliche Buchgesell-
        schaft.
Procksch, O.
1950   *Theologie des Alten Testaments*. Gütersloh: Bertelsmann.
Provan, I.W.
1988   *Hezekiah and the Books of Kings*, BZAW 172. Berlin: de Gruyter.
Puukko, A.F.
1910   *Das Deuteronomium: Eine literarkritische Untersuchung*, BWAT 5.
        Leipzig: Hinrichs.
Rabban, N.
1952   "לפני ה'", Tarbiẓ 23, 1-8.
Rad, G. von
1929   *Das Gottesvolk im Deuteronomium*, BWANT 3.11. Stuttgart: Kohlhammer.
1931   "Zelt und Lade", *NKZ* 42, 476-498.
1938   *Das formgeschichtliche Problem des Hexateuchs*, BWANT 78. Stuttgart:
        Kohlhammer.
1947   *Deuteronomium-Studien*, FRLANT 58. Göttingen: Vandenhoeck &
        Ruprecht.
²1952   *Der Heilige Krieg im Alten Israel*, ATANT 20. Göttingen: Vandenhoeck &
        Ruprecht.
1953a   *Das erste Buch Mose: Genesis Kapitel 25,19-50,26*, ATD 4. Göttingen:
        Vandenhoeck & Ruprecht.
1953b   *Studies in Deuteronomy*, SBT 9. London: SCM.
1958   *Theologie des Alten Testaments*, 1. München: Kaiser.
1959   "The Origin of the Concept of the Day of Yahweh", *JSS* 4, 97-108.
1964   *Das fünfte Buch Mose: Deuteronomium*, ATD 8. Göttingen: Vandenhoeck
        & Ruprecht.
Rehm, M.
1979   *Das erste Buch der Könige: Ein Kommentar*. Würzburg: Echter Verlag.
1982   *Das zweite Buch der Könige: Ein Kommentar*. Würzburg: Echter Verlag.
Reichert, V.E.
1958   *Job*, SBBS. London: Soncino.
Reider, J.
1937   *Deuteronomy*. Philadelphia: The Jewish Publication Society of America.
Reindl, J.
1970   *Das Angesicht Gottes im Sprachgebrauch des Alten Testaments*, ETS 25.
        Leipzig: St. Benno-Verlag.
Rennes, J.
1967   *Le Deutéronome*. Genève: Labor et Fides.
Ridderbos, J.
1984   *Deuteronomy*, Bible Student's Commentary. Grand Rapids: Zondervan.
Roberts, J.J.M.
1976   "Zion Tradition", *IDBSup*, 985-987.
Robinson, H.W.
n.d.   *Deuteronomy and Joshua*, CeB. Edinburgh: T.C. & E.C. Jack.
1937   *The Old Testament: Its Making and Meaning*. London: University of
        London Press.
Robinson, J.
1972   *The First Book of Kings*, CBC. Cambridge: Cambridge University Press.

Rofé, A.
1985   "The Laws of Warfare in the Book of Deuteronomy: Their Origins, Intent and Positivity", *JSOT* 32, 23-44.
Rose, M.
1975   *Der Ausschließlichkeitsanspruch Jahwes*, BWANT 106. Stuttgart: Kohlhammer.
Rost, L.
1938   *Die Vorstufen von Kirche und Synagoge im Alten Testament*, BWANT 76. Stuttgart: Kohlhammer.
1965   "Das kleine geschichtliche Credo", *Das kleine Credo und andere Studien zum Alten Testament*. Heidelberg: Quelle & Meyer, 11-25.
Roussel, L.
n.d.   *Le Livre de Josué*, 1: *L'Invasion (Chapitre 1-12)*. Nîmes: Barnier.
Rowley, H.H.
1970   *Job*, NCB. London: Nelson.
Rudolph, W.
1938   *Der "Elohist" von Exodus bis Josua*, BZAW 68. Berlin: Töpelmann.
Ruprecht, E.
1980   "Exodus 24, 9-11 als Beispiel lebendiger Erzähltradition aus der Zeit des babylonischen Exils", *Werden und Wirken des Alten Testaments* (Fs C. Westermann), eds. R. Albertz, H.-P. Müller, H.W. Wolff und W. Zimmerli. Göttingen: Vandenhoeck & Ruprecht, 138-173.
Rylaarsdam, J.C.
1952   The Book of Exodus, *IB* 1, 831-1099.
Ryle, H.E.
1907   *The Books of Ezra and Nehemiah*, CBSC. Cambridge: Cambridge University Press.
Šanda, A.
1911   *Die Bücher der Könige*, 1: *Das erste Buch der Könige*, EHAT 9.1. Münster: Aschendorff.
1912   *Die Bücher der Könige*, 2: *Das zweite Buch der Könige*, EHAT 9.2. Münster: Aschendorff.
Scharbert, J.
1989   *Exodus*, Die Neue Echter Bibel. Würzburg: Echter Verlag.
Schmidt, M.
1948   *Prophet und Tempel: Eine Studie zum Problem der Gottesnähe im Alten Testament*. Zollikon-Zürich: Evangelischer Verlag.
Schmitt, R.
1972   *Zelt und Lade als Thema alttestamentlicher Wissenschaft*. Gütersloh: Mohn.
Schneider, H.
1959   *Die Bücher Esra und Nehemia*, HSAT 4.2. Bonn: Hanstein.
Schnutenhaus, F.
1964   "Das Kommen und Erscheinen Gottes im Alten Testament", *ZAW* 76, 1-22.
Schreiner, J.
1963   *Sion-Jerusalem, Jahwes Königssitz: Theologie der Heiligen Stadt im Alten Testament*, SANT 7. München: Kösel-Verlag.
Schwally, F.
1901   *Semitische Kriegsaltertümer*, 1: *Der heilige Krieg im alten Israel*. Leipzig: Dieterich.

Seitz, G.
1971   *Redactionsgeschichtliche Studien zum Deuteronomium*, BWANT 93. Stuttgart: Kohlhammer.

Sellin, E.
1910   *Einleitung in das Alte Testament*, ETB 2. Leipzig: Quelle & Meyer.

Sheriffs, D.C.T.
1979   "The Phrases *ina IGI DN* and *lipĕnēy Yhwh* in Treaty and Covenant Contexts", *JNSL* 7, 55-68.

Simian-Yofre, H.
1989   "פָּנִים *pānîm*", *TWAT* 6, 629-659.

Skinner, J.
²1929   *The Book of the Prophet Isaiah: Chapters XL-LXVI*, CBSC. Cambridge: Cambridge University Press.
²1930   *A Critical and Exegetical Commentary on Genesis*, ICC. Edinburgh: T. & T Clark.

Slotki, I.W.
1950   *Kings*, SBBS. London: Soncino.
1957   *Isaiah*, SBBS. London: Soncino.

Smend, R.
1893   *Lehrbuch der alttestamentlichen Religionsgeschichte*. Freiburg: Mohr-Siebeck.
1912   *Die Erzählung des Hexateuch*. Berlin: Reimer.

Smend, R.
1978   *Die Entstehung des Alten Testaments*, Th Wiss 1. Stuttgart: Kohlhammer.

Smith, G.A.
1918   *The Book of Deuteronomy*, CBSC. Cambridge: Cambridge University Press.

Smith, H.P.
1899   *A Critical and Exegetical Commentary on the Books of Samuel*, ICC. Edinburgh: T. & T. Clark.

Snaith, N.H.
1967   *Leviticus and Numbers*, CeB (New Edition). London: Nelson.

Soggin, J.A.
1970   *Le Livre de Josué*, CAT 5a. Neuchâtel: Delachaux & Niestlé.

Sollamo, R.
1985   "Den bibliska formeln 'Inför Herren/Inför Gud'", *SEÅ* 50, 21-32.

Stade, B.
1888   *Geschichte des Volkes Israel*, 2. Berlin: Grote.
1905   *Biblische Theologie des Alten Testaments*, 1: *Die Religion Israels und die Entstehung des Judentums*, GThW 2.2. Tübingen: Mohr-Siebeck.

Stalker, D.M.G.
1968   *Ezekiel*, TBC. London: SCM.

Staton, C.P., Jr.
1988   "'And Yahweh Appeared...': A Study of the Motifs of 'Seeing God' and of 'God's Appearing' in Old Testament Narratives" (PhD. Diss.). Oxford.

Steuernagel, C.
1900   *Deuteronomium und Josua*, HKAT 1.3. Göttingen: Vandenhoeck & Ruprecht.
²1923   *Das Deuteronomium*, HKAT 1.3.1. Göttingen: Vandenhoeck & Ruprecht.

Stolz, F.
1972   *Jahwes und Israels Kriege*, ATANT 60. Zürich: Theologischer Verlag.
Strahan, J.
1913   *The Book of Job*. Edinburgh: T. & T. Clark.
Sturdy, J.
1976   *Numbers*, CBC. Cambridge: Cambridge University Press.
Taylor, J.B.
1969   *Ezekiel*, TOTC. London: Tyndale.
Terrien, S.
1954   The Book of Job, *IB* 3, 875-1198.
1970   "The Omphalos Myth and Hebrew Religion", *VT* 20, 315-338.
1978   *The Elusive Presence: Toward a New Biblical Theology*. San Francisco: Harper & Row.
Thompson, J.A.
1968   "The Cultic Credo and the Sinai Tradition", *RTR* 27, 53-64.
1974   *Deuteronomy*, TOTC. London: Inter-Varsity.
Tillesse, G.M. de
1962   "Sections 'tu' et sections 'vous' dans le Deutéronome", *VT* 12, 29-87.
Tournay, R.J.
1988   *Voir et entendre Dieu avec les Psaumes*, CRB 24. Paris: Gabalda.
Unnik, W.C. van
1959   "*Dominus vobiscum*: the background of a liturgical formula", *New Testament Essays* (Fs T.W. Manson), ed. A.J.B. Higgins. Manchester: Manchester University Press, 270-305.
Van Seters, J.
1988   "'Comparing Scripture with Scripture': Some Observations on the Sinai Pericope of Exodus 19-24", *Canon, Theology, and Old Testament Interpretation* (Fs B.S. Childs), eds. G.M. Tucker, D.L. Petersen and R.R. Wilson. Philadephia: Fortress, 111-130.
Vaulx, J. de
1972   *Les Nombres*, SB. Paris: Gabalda.
Vaux, R. de
1958   *Les Institutions de L'Ancien Testament*, 1. Paris: Cerf.
1960   *Les Institutions de L'Ancien Testament*, 2. Paris: Cerf.
1966   Review of R.E. Clements, *God and Temple*, *RB* 73, 447-449.
1967   "'Le lieu que Yahvé a choisi pour y établir son nom'", *Das ferne und nahe Wort* (Fs L. Rost), ed. F. Maass, BZAW 105. Berlin: Töpelmann, 219-228.
Vawter, B.
1977   *On Genesis: A New Reading*. London: Chapman.
Veijola, T.
1975   *Die ewige Dynastie*, STAT 193. Helsinki: Suomalainen Tiedeakatemia.
Vries, S.J. de
1985   *1 Kings*, WBC 12. Waco: Word.
Vriezen, Th.C.
1963   "The Credo In The Old Testament", *Studies on the Psalms*, ed. A.H. van Zyl. Potchefstroom: Pro Rege-Pers Beperk, 5-17.
[2]1970   *An outline of Old Testament theology*. Oxford: Blackwell.

Watts, J.D.W.
1970   Deuteronomy, *The Broadman Bible Commentary*, 2. Nashville: Broadman, 175-296.
1987   *Isaiah 34-66*, WBC 25. Waco: Word.
Webb, B.G.
1987   *The Book of the Judges: An Integrated Reading*, JSOTSup 46. Sheffield: JSOT.
Weinfeld, M.
1972a   *Deuteronomy and the Deuteronomic School*. Oxford: Oxford University Press.
1972b   "Presence, Divine", *EncJud* 13, 1015-1020.
1983   "Divine Intervention in War in Ancient Israel and in the Ancient Near East", *History, Historiography and Interpretation*, eds. H. Tadmor and M. Weinfeld. Jerusalem: Magnes, 121-147.
1991   *Deuteronomy 1-11*, AB 5. New York: Doubleday.
Weippert, H.
1980   "'Der Ort, den Jahwe erwählen wird, um dort seinen Namen wohnen zu lassen'. Die Geschichte einer alttestamentlichen Formel", *BZ* 24, 76-94.
Weiser, A.
1950   "Zur Frage nach den Beziehungen der Psalmen zum Kult: Die Darstellung der Theophanie in den Psalmen und im Festkult" (Fs A. Bertholet), eds. W. Baumgartner, O. Eißfeldt, K. Elliger und L. Rost. Tübingen: Mohr-Siebeck, 513-531.
⁶1966   *Einleitung in das Alte Testament*. Göttingen: Vandenhoeck & Ruprecht.
Welch, A.C.
1924   *The Code of Deuteronomy: A New Theory of its Origin*. London: James Clark.
1932   *Deuteronomy: The Framework to the Code*. London: Oxford University Press.
1939   *The Work of the Chronicler: Its Purpose and its Date*, SchL. London: Oxford University Press.
Wellhausen, J.
³1886   *Prologomena zur Geschichte Israels*. Berlin: Reimer.
Wenham, G.J.
1971   "Deuteronomy and the Central Sanctuary", *TynBul* 22, 103-118.
1979   *The Book of Leviticus*, NICOT. Grand Rapids: Eerdmans.
1981   *Numbers*, TOTC. Leicester: Inter-Varsity.
Westermann, C.
1960   "Die Begriffe für Fragen und Suchen im Alten Testament", *KD* 6, 2-30.
1966   *Das Buch Jesaia: Kapitel 40-66*, ATD 19. Göttingen: Vandenhoeck & Ruprecht.
1981   *Genesis 12-36*, BKAT 1.2. Neukirchen-Vluyn: Neukirchener Verlag.
Westphal, G.
1908   *Jahwes Wohnstätten nach den Anschauungen der alten Hebräer*, BZAW 15. Gießen: Töpelmann.
Wevers, J.W.
1969   *Ezekiel*, NCB. London: Nelson.

Whitelam, K.W.
1979 *The Just King: Monarchical Judicial Authority in Ancient Israel*, JSOTSup 12. Sheffield: JSOT.

Whybray, R.N.
1975 *Isaiah 40-66*, NCB. London: Oliphants.
1989 *Ecclesiastes*, NCB. London: Marshall, Morgan & Scott.

Williamson, H.G.M.
1982 *1 and 2 Chronicles*, NCB. London: Marshall, Morgan & Scott.
1985 *Ezra, Nehemiah*, WBC 16. Waco: Word.

Willis, J.T.
1980 *Isaiah*, LWC 12. Austin: Sweet.

Wolff, H.W.
1961 "Das Kerygma des deuteronomistischen Geschichtswerks", *ZAW* 73, 171-186.

Woude, A.S. van der
1976 "פָּנִים *pānîm* Angesicht", *THAT* 2, 432-460.
1977 "Gibt es eine Theologie des Jahwe-Namens im Deuteronomium?", *Übersetzung und Deutung: Studien zu dem Alten Testament und seiner Umwelt* (Fs A. R. Hulst), eds. H.A. Brongers et al. Nijkerk: Callenbach, 204-210.

Woudstra, M.H.
1981 *The Book of Joshua*, NICOT. Grand Rapids: Eerdmans.

Wright, G.E.
1944 "The Significance of the Temple in The Ancient Near East. Part III. The Temple in Palestine-Syria", *BA* 7, 65-77.
1953 The Book of Deuteronomy, *IB* 2, 309-537.
1960 "God Amidst His People: The Story of the Temple", *The Rule of God: Essays in Biblical Theology*. New York: Doubleday, 55-76.

Würthwein, E.
1977 *Die Bücher der Könige: Das erste Buch der Könige, Kapitel 1-16*, ATD 11.1. Göttingen: Vandenhoeck & Ruprecht.

Wüst, M.
1975 *Untersuchungen zu den siedlungsgeographischen Texten des Alten Testaments*, 1: *Ostjordanland*, BTAVO (Ser. B) 9. Wiesbaden: Reichert.

Young, E.J.
1972 *The Book of Isaiah*, 3: *Chapters 40 through 66*, NICOT. Grand Rapids: Eerdmans.

Zenger, E.
1968 "Die deuteronomistische Interpretation der Rehabilitierung Jojachins", *BZ* 12, 16-30.
1971 *Die Sinaitheophanie: Untersuchungen zum jahwistischen und elohistischen Geschichtswerk*, FB 3. Würzburg: Echter Verlag.
1978 *Das Buch Exodus*, Geistliche Schriftlesung 7. Düsseldorf: Patmos.

Zimmerli, W.
1956 "Das Wort des göttlichen Selbsterweis (Erweiswort); eine prophetische Gattung", *Mélanges Bibliques* (Fs A. Robert), TICP 4. Paris: Bloud & Gay, 154-164.
1969 *Ezekiel 25-48*, BKAT 13.2. Neukirchen-Vluyn: Neukirchener Verlag.

1982   "Visionary experience in Jeremiah", *Israel's Prophetic Tradition* (Fs. P.R. Ackroyd), eds. R.J. Coggins, A. Phillips and M.A. Knibb. Cambridge: Cambridge University Press, 95-118.

Zorell, F.
1947   *Lexicon Hebraicum et Aramaicum Veteris Testamenti.* Roma: Pontificio Instituto Biblico.

INDEX OF REFERENCES

INDEX OF AUTHORS